COOKING FROM SCRATCH

COOKING FROM SCRATCH

120 Recipes for Colorful, Seasonal Food
from PCC Community Markets

PCC
COMMUNITY
MARKETS

with Jill Lightner
Photographs by Charity Burggraaf

SASQUATCH BOOKS
SEATTLE

DEDICATED TO THE MEMORY OF Jackie DeCicco, who planted the seed for this cookbook many years ago. She was a beloved longtime member of the PCC family, a good friend to many, and an earnest lover of good food— from baguettes on the streets of Paris, to lunchtime leftovers at work, to celebratory hours-long multicourse feasts. She would have used this book all the time.

And to our co-op members and staff, the heart and soul of our community.

CONTENTS

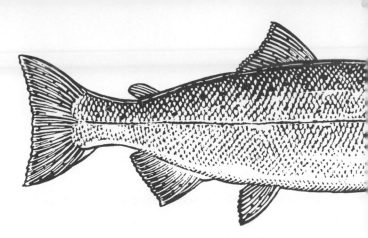

MAIN COURSES 91

SIDE DISHES 123

SNACKS & APPS 181

EASY WEEKNIGHT MEALS 147

DRINKS 213

DESSERTS 239

INTROD

A Short History of PCC Community Markets

OUR DEVOTION TO ORGANIC, NON-GMO, SUSTAINABLY SOURCED
foods dates back to 1971. That's when we shifted our focus to good, wholesome, health-oriented foods and made a commitment to cutting out unnatural,
chemical-stuffed food products and reducing ecological pollutants. Today, this
idea seems like a no-brainer, but in the early '70s, it was controversial. When
our co-op was founded by fifteen Seattle families who first gathered in a garage
belonging to one of the original founders, John Affolter, back in 1953, it was a
food-buying club with the simple goal of efficiently stretching pennies. Even
when we moved to member ownership in 1961, becoming Puget Consumers
Co-op (PCC), the emphasis was still on financial frugality, not healthy living.
Our revised thinking set us on a new path, leading us to become Seattle's first
real destination for what were then called "natural foods."

We became early advocates of the organic movement, carrying products
from Washington State farmers who were among the first to get organic
certification in the state, like Twin Springs Farm in Rice (organic certification
number 47 in 1988), Ralph's Greenhouse in Mount Vernon (organic certification
number 68 in 1989), and Rents Due Ranch in Stanwood (organic certification
number 138 in 1989). We still partner with each of these organic pioneers, who
provide us with everything from butternut squash to snap peas to strawberries;
in fact, it's just these sorts of local ingredients that supply much of the inspiration as our chefs develop new recipes. Over the ensuing decades, we embraced
transparency in the food-supply chain—whether that was a company's Fair
Trade certification, how animals were raised, whether food was genetically
modified, or what methods were used to catch all of the seafood we sold. As we
celebrate our sixty-fifth anniversary as a food co-op and look down the road to
our one hundredth, our dedication to responsibly sourced, environmentally
friendly, wholesome, well-seasoned food won't change.

Education is a fundamental part of being a co-op and it's one we take
seriously. Our nutrition and cooking education program, now known as PCC
Cooks, was founded in 1983. Today, we offer more than 1,600 classes a year by
sixty skilled instructors, covering topics ranging from basics like knife skills,

UCTION

to international cuisine such as Thai, Turkish, and Italian cooking, to food as medicine. We have also educated through two publications: *Sound Consumer*, a monthly food-policy newsletter we've published since 1961, and *Taste*, a seasonal magazine (2011 to 2017). You'll find favorite recipes from all three—PCC Cooks, *Sound Consumer*, and *Taste*—in this cookbook, as well as recipes from our deli and bakery. We hope you'll fall in love with a new-to-you ingredient, be inspired to cook more seasonally, and enjoy modern twists on classics, like our upside-down cake that replaces canned pineapple with a topping of sour cherries and balsamic vinegar (see page 241).

And to make sure you pick up flexible skills along with new recipes, each chapter includes a technique-driven section called Flavor in Five, inspired partly by our classes. These walk you through the five basic steps you need to bake up a seasonal fruit crisp or whisk together a homemade vinaigrette, so you understand the role each part of the process plays and how the ingredients fit together. You'll find a few suggested flavor combinations, plus a formal recipe to give you an idea for ingredient amounts and cooking times. It's easy to get the kids involved (try the Homemade Energy Bars, page 211) or keep it strictly for the grown-ups and make fantastic sangria out of almost anything (see page 237). We think that life is more satisfying if you know how to cook at least one thing without referring to a written recipe, and these are a great place to start.

Some things will never change as we grow. Each day, our bakers arrive before sunrise and fire up the ovens to bake dozens of fresh scones made with organic cream and butter plus a sprinkling of seasonal fruit. Our chefs start their mornings scrambling a batch of local eggs with cheddar cheese and salsa for a pan of Chilaquiles (page 22), and checking the seasoning on the day's batch of Tiger Mountain Turkey Chili (page 30). Perhaps more than anything else, we'll continue to believe in the power of good food—to bring people together, to create a sustainable food system, and to change the world. Because, as our co-op principles have taught us, good food is never about dividing up the pie so everyone gets a sliver. It's about making that pie as big as possible and sharing it among friends.

HOW TO USE

WHILE THE RECIPES STAND ON THEIR OWN, there are a few things to know before you start cooking.

ADAPTING RECIPES

These recipes were all tested thoroughly as written. That said, one of the most frequent questions we're asked about our recipes is how they can be adapted for those with allergies, dietary preferences, or nutritional needs, so we'll cover a few broad categories.

- Use vegan shortening or coconut oil to substitute for softened butter; any cooking oil you like can be substituted for melted butter. The flavor will vary depending on what you choose.
- Gluten-free flour mixes that can be substituted at a one-to-one ratio with all-purpose flour are suitable. The final texture may vary from our results.
- It's best to incorporate whole grain flours into a recipe by replacing no more than half the all-purpose flour. If that switch meets your approval, consider swapping a higher percentage next time. You may need to adjust cooking times, and the flavor will vary depending on the flour used.
- Almond milk is generally considered the most versatile milk alternative. To make a vegan buttermilk substitute, add two tablespoons lemon juice to one cup nondairy milk and let sit for ten minutes. This is not as thick as cultured buttermilk, and it may bake differently.
- It's fine to leave nuts out of recipes, even granola. In some baked goods, you might try substituting rolled oats to provide texture.
- When baking, the easiest way to reduce sugar is by decreasing the stated amount by 10 percent. If you substitute a different type of sweetener than what we used in the recipe, it can alter the flavor, browning, texture, and baking time.
- For any recipes that use mayonnaise, use whatever type you prefer, including vegan, which is what our deli uses.
- Wherever fresh produce is called for, you can always choose organic, just as the chefs in our deli use.

THIS BOOK

MAKE IT A MEAL

As this book makes clear, we're fans of fruits and vegetables and are always looking for ways to encourage people to eat more of them. Where appropriate, our Make It a Meal suggestions will balance out the flavor, textures, and nutritional aspects of one recipe with the right vegetable-forward side dish; in other spots, we'll add on protein suggestions to round off a salad.

PAIRINGS

Traditional wine pairings suggest very specific brands and years, which can be tough to chase down or leave you at a loss if the wine is out of your price range. Our pairings include wine, beer, cider, and spirits, depending on the dish, and offer recommendations only for appropriate varietals or styles so you can find something that suits. You'll spot a few that give preference to specific regions too, including our home state of Washington.

FREEZER STORAGE

Occasionally, we note dishes that freeze before they're baked or freeze particularly well as leftovers. In general, remembering to freeze extra portions is a great way to reduce household food waste. While stashing leftovers in the refrigerator will provide them with a few days of extra life, freezing can extend that extra life to six months or more. The list of what not to freeze is fairly short:

- Mashed potatoes
- Dairy-based or potato soups
- Cooked pasta
- Mayonnaise or other emulsions
- Raw vegetable salads
- Cooked egg whites
- Gelatin-based salads and desserts

NUTRITIONAL ANALYSIS GUIDELINES

As is our standard procedure for printed recipes, we have provided the nutritional facts for each recipe: calories, fat, saturated fat, cholesterol, sodium, carbohydrates, fiber, sugar, and protein. We've provided a few notes for clarity, so you can understand our process.

Dairy
When it is not specified by the recipe, we select a reduced-fat (but not skim) option for milk, cottage cheese, mozzarella cheese, yogurt, and other dairy products.

Marinades
If a recipe calls for a marinade that is used only to marinate the food but not actually in cooking, then we analyze the recipe based on half of the ingredients in the marinade, assuming that the other half of the marinade is tossed out.

Meats
If a recipe calls for ground beef, we use a 15 percent fat content; for ground pork or lamb, we use a 28 percent fat content. Our nutrition database does not provide data for grass-fed and pasture-raised meats, which are generally leaner and lower in saturated-fat content.

Optional Ingredients
We do not include any optional ingredients, such as sour cream or parsley, in the nutritional analysis. We also do not include any ingredients or dishes mentioned as serving suggestions.

Sodium
If a recipe states to "salt to taste" we add one dash of salt per serving.

Servings
If a recipe states four to six servings, we use a middle option of five servings in the analysis. If the recipe states that it makes a volume rather than a number of servings, here are the serving sizes we analyzed:
- Salad dressings/condiments: two tablespoons
- Dips/spreads: one-quarter cup
- Soups/stews: one cup

FIVE KITCHEN STAPLES

While basics like olive oil, garlic, salt, and pepper will never go out of style, and it's rare to run out of any of them, they're not enough to make a meal on their own. The ingredients here make numerous appearances throughout this book, and they help us mark the seasons, eat healthfully, and enjoy flavors from seriously sweet to deeply earthy.

Northwest-Grown Lentils: Yellow, red, green, brown, or black, lentils appear in almost as many recipes as olive oil in this book. There's a lot to love: great nutrition, fast and simple cooking, and a different texture and flavor for every color, so it seems like there's almost always a great one for the job, regardless of the time of year. Try them in Spiced Squash Salad with Lentils and Goat Cheese (page 58), Curried Lentil and Mango Wraps (page 100), or Lentil and White Bean Stew (page 38).

Plain Greek Yogurt: Running out of yogurt can feel like a household crisis. While it has interesting benefits as a cultured dairy product, it also seems like it's the perfect condiment for something at every meal, aside from regular use as a smoothie ingredient. Sure, different flavors are fun to taste, but the plain is the most versatile, so that's the one we try to have on hand. Stir it into Cornmeal Pancakes (page 14), serve it with Roasted Cumin Carrots (page 135), or use it in a Mango Lassi (page 218).

Fresh or Frozen Blueberries: What's not to love about a nutritional powerhouse that's also a sweet little flavor bomb? Peak-season blueberries are a summer classic, but they freeze so very well we have them on hand in one form or another year-round. You can dress up Heavenly Scones (page 7) with berries straight from the freezer, or take advantage of the fresh season by tossing together a Blueberry-Nectarine Caprese Salad (page 55). You can also brighten up an afternoon with Sparkling Blueberry Lemonade (page 217), whether the berries are fresh or frozen.

Winter Citrus: Sure, lemons and limes are in the kitchen year-round—they're a reliable fix for dishes that need a little something extra, since a squeeze of fresh acidity seems to solve so many problems. But from November to March, conveniently the same months when our local farms' offerings can get a bit monotonous, the flavors of citrus keep our cooking fresh, interesting, and more fruit-focused than it would otherwise be. Try Emmer Farro with Tangerines and Persimmons (page 139), Hibiscus Lemon Bars (page 248), or Broccoli, Lemon, and Parmesan Soup (page 41).

Pastured Eggs: Eggs have so much going for them that they're likely already a kitchen staple for you in one form or another, but it's worth experiencing just how wonderful they can be at their best—they're even seasonal, just like the green pastures and sunshine that ebb and flow over the course of a year. Eggs laid by hens who spend their days outdoors scratching in the soil have such beautiful color and richness that they're truly irresistible once you've tasted them (or baked with them). Eggs naturally have a long life in the refrigerator too, so they're a protein that's easy to keep on hand, and they can be cooked in less than two minutes. Let them shine in Stir-Fried Cabbage with Fried Eggs (page 2), or whip up Egg Korma (page 172) for a vegetarian dinner.

SUSTAINABILITY GLOSSARY

When you're grocery shopping, you may come across labels that are unfamiliar. Understanding what they mean is helpful. Here are a few we think you should know:

Bycatch: This refers to marine life caught unintentionally while commercial fishers are using equipment to haul in their intended catch. Bycatch may include sea turtles, sharks, seabirds, and juvenile fish.

Cage-Free: This simply indicates that hens can move around in a shared indoor space but have no access to the outdoors.

Local: When we use this word, we are referring to Washington State (our home), plus our Pacific Northwest neighbors of Oregon, Idaho, and southern British Columbia.

Non-GMO: This is the approved shorthand way to describe food that does not contain genetically modified organisms (GMOs) and was not produced through genetic engineering. Corn, soy, sugar (from sugar beets), canola, and Hawaiian papaya are the most common GMO foods. GMOs are prohibited in organic farming, ensuring all organic products are non-GMO.

Non-GMO Project Verified: As explained on its website, "The Non-GMO Project is a mission-driven nonprofit organization dedicated to building and protecting a non-GMO food supply." It is the first third-party certifier to establish best practices and testing throughout the supply chain to verify non-GMO claims in North America. Its standards, process, and verified product listings are available at NonGMOProject.org.

Organic: The USDA organic standards relate to soil quality, pest and weed control, and animal-raising practices that govern antibiotics, feed, and living conditions. Strict production, handling, and labeling practices are also required. Genetic engineering is prohibited, as are most synthetic pesticides and fertilizers, sewage, and irradiation.

Pastured: This applies to the living conditions where farm animals are raised, allowing sheep and cattle to graze on grass and ensuring that chickens eat an omnivorous diet and scratch in the dirt. Pastured animals are not necessarily 100 percent grass-fed, as they may be given supplemental grain.

rBGH: This stands for recombinant bovine growth hormone, a genetically engineered hormone given to some dairy cows to increase milk production. It's been shown to have an adverse effect on animal health. Look for dairy products produced without it; this is frequently stamped on the packaging. (It's not permitted in any certified organic dairy production.)

Seafood Watch: This is a program of the Monterey Bay Aquarium that helps consumers make ocean-friendly seafood choices. Seafood Watch scientists compile and review relevant data through government reports, articles, and white papers to develop sustainability standards: red (avoid), yellow (good), or green (best choice). The recommendations are available via the Seafood Watch app and SeafoodWatch.org.

BREAKFAST

MORE THAN ANY OTHER MEAL, breakfast shows us up as creatures of habit. Eggs, scrambled. Bread, toasted. Coffee, lots. But if you're willing to think a bit outside the cereal box, it's not difficult to tweak those go-to morning dishes by adding flavors and ingredients you love to explore at dinnertime. Start with eggs (you'll find the brightest yolks are from local, pastured hens) and turn them into a breakfast stir-fry with a Southeast Asian influence (Stir-Fried Cabbage with Fried Eggs, page 2), or perch them on top of spicy sweet potato hash in all their runny-yolked glory (Sweet Potato Hash, page 26).

Whole grains are another morning ingredient that gets us, dare we admit it, excited. The options are so far beyond porridge these days, and they're a real help in staving off breakfast boredom. Whether you're layering your favorite granola with the newest seasonal yogurt flavor or trying our method for overnight oatmeal (Berry Cobbler Overnight Oatmeal, page 11—it sounds odd, but it's a winner), oats are only the starting point. If you haven't yet added chia, flax, or sunflower seeds to your morning mix, we promise you're in for a treat.

And of course, there are those prized (and all-too-rare) lazy week-ends. Brunching with friends or stirring up something special for the kids can make mornings at home an absolute pleasure—and maybe even inspire a new tradition. From Seattle's homegrown classic Baked Dutch Baby Pancakes (page 13) to our modern Carrot Cake Waffles (page 21), we've looked for ways for these special-occasion breakfasts to offer balanced nutrition along with crave-worthy flavors. Vegetables can be a meaningful part of weekend breakfasts, and we're not just talking about hash browns.

THESE FLAVORS TOTALLY RESET THE idea of a basic egg breakfast. The cabbage has a light sweetness and sturdy crunch that make it the perfect foil to a creamy fried egg, particularly with the rich, nutty flavor of toasted sesame oil in the background. If you shred the cabbage the night before (or even a few days in advance), this is a breakfast you can stir up almost as quickly as you can brew a pot of tea to go with it.

STIR-FRIED CABBAGE WITH FRIED EGGS

Makes 2 servings

In a large skillet or wok over medium-high heat, heat 1 tablespoon of the high-heat oil and 1 teaspoon of toasted sesame oil. Add the garlic and ginger and stir-fry for 30 seconds or until light golden. Add the cabbage and stir-fry until it turns bright green and translucent, about 2 minutes. Turn off the heat and season with the rice vinegar and tamari.

In a small sauté pan over medium heat, heat the remaining 1 tablespoon high-heat oil plus the remaining 1 teaspoon toasted sesame oil. Crack the eggs into the pan and cook to desired doneness: about 2 minutes for runny yolks, 2½ minutes for soft set, or 3 minutes for firm.

Divide the cabbage between two plates. Top with the fried eggs and serve immediately with the hot sauce.

2 tablespoons high-heat oil, such as sunflower or refined peanut oil, divided
2 teaspoons toasted sesame oil, divided
2 cloves garlic, minced
1 tablespoon minced peeled fresh ginger
1 small head Napa cabbage (about 2 pounds), sliced into ribbons
2 teaspoons rice vinegar
2 teaspoons tamari, or to taste
4 large eggs
Hot sauce, for serving (optional)

½ RECIPE: 330 CAL., 28G FAT (5G SAT.), 370MG CHOL., 490MG SODIUM, 5G CARB., 1G FIBER, 2G SUGAR, 14G PROTEIN

KNOW YOUR VINEGARS

Of all the vinegars, rice vinegar is the mildest one—it's only slightly tangy, with some obvious sweetness to the flavor. Its label might read "rice wine vinegar," too, making it a little too easy to mix up with your bottle of rice wine, or mirin, which is lightly sweet but not tangy at all.

If you don't have rice vinegar, don't simply choose a different white vinegar from your pantry; it will almost certainly be too acidic and strongly flavored for these purposes. Instead, replace it with either 1 teaspoon cider vinegar or 1 teaspoon cider vinegar plus 1 teaspoon mirin. Seasoned rice vinegar is also a fine substitute.

GRANOLA IS REALLY MORE OF a technique than a precise recipe; this version is loaded with three different types of seeds, which gives every bite a slightly different flavor. Don't skip stirring it as it bakes, as this will make sure all the oats toast evenly. If an occasional dessert-for-breakfast treat sounds appealing, this granola is delicious with Roasted Rhubarb and Strawberries (page 253) and Greek yogurt.

WHOLE GRAINS, NUTS, AND SEEDS GRANOLA

Makes about 1 quart (8 [½-cup] servings)

Preheat the oven to 375 degrees F. Line a baking sheet with parchment paper.

In a large bowl, combine the oats, coconut, flaxseeds, nuts, sesame seeds, sunflower seeds, salt, oil, honey, and vanilla. Spread the mixture on the prepared baking sheet. Bake for 20 to 25 minutes, stirring three times during the baking process. The granola should be a toasted golden brown.

Cool the granola completely before stirring in the dried fruit. Store in an airtight container in the refrigerator for up to 2 months.

½ CUP: 540 CAL., 23G FAT (5G SAT.), 0MG CHOL., 280MG SODIUM, 78G CARB., 7G FIBER, 38G SUGAR, 11G PROTEIN

3½ cups rolled oats (not quick-cooking)

½ cup unsweetened coconut flakes

¼ cup flaxseeds

½ cup raw nuts (your favorite variety)

¼ cup white sesame seeds

¼ cup sunflower seeds

1 teaspoon kosher salt

¼ cup high-heat oil, such as sunflower or refined peanut oil

½ cup honey

1 teaspoon vanilla extract

2 cups dried fruit, chopped into bite-size pieces

GRANOLA FLAVOR SUGGESTIONS

Granola can be a great way to simply use up the odds and ends in your pantry, but if you want to make a special batch, here are some favorite dried fruit and nut combinations. With larger dried fruits like figs and mango slices, it's best to cut them into bite-size pieces before adding them to the granola.

- Hazelnuts and dried cranberries
- Pecans and dried peaches
- Pistachios and dried cherries
- Walnuts and dried apples
- Sliced almonds and dried mangoes
- Whole almonds and dried figs
- Macadamia nuts and dried apricots

RHUBARB IS A VEGETABLE THAT is typically used as a fruit, and that's only one of the ways it refuses to fall into stereotypes. It's a relative of buckwheat; the plants will grow enormous flowers that look like cock's combs; and the stalks can be pink, green, or spotted pink and green. Its leaves are famously toxic, but those pretty stalks are packed with calcium and vitamin K. When vegetables are this determined to be odd, all we can do is enjoy them in their weirdness. These warm, mildly spiced muffins with punchy bits of tart rhubarb are deeply enjoyable, and they tame every bit of that weirdness into a cozy little breakfast treat.

RHUBARB-CARDAMOM MUFFINS

Makes 9 muffins

Preheat the oven to 400 degrees F. Grease nine muffin cups or line them with paper liners.

In a small bowl, combine the rhubarb, sugar, and ¼ teaspoon of the cardamom. Let stand until the rhubarb releases some of its juice, about 15 minutes. Drain off the juice.

In a small bowl, beat together the butter and brown sugar until fluffy, about 2 minutes with an electric mixer or 4 minutes by hand. Add the eggs, one at a time, and beat until combined, and the mixture is completely smooth.

In a large bowl, whisk together the flour, baking powder, salt, and remaining ¼ teaspoon cardamom. Alternate adding the butter mixture and the half-and-half, mixing until just moistened. Gently fold in the rhubarb. Divide the batter among the prepared muffin cups.

Bake until the muffins are dry and springy to the touch, 20 to 25 minutes. Cool in the pan for 5 minutes before removing. Serve warm.

Unsalted butter or shortening, for the muffin cups
1½ cups chopped rhubarb (from 2 large stalks)
¼ cup granulated sugar
½ teaspoon ground cardamom, divided
6 tablespoons (¾ stick) unsalted butter, softened
¼ cup packed light brown sugar
2 large eggs
2 cups all-purpose flour
1 tablespoon baking powder
½ teaspoon kosher salt
1 cup half-and-half

1 MUFFIN: 260 CAL., 11G FAT (6G SAT.), 65MG CHOL., 140MG SODIUM, 36G CARB., 1G FIBER, 13G SUGAR, 6G PROTEIN

A BIT LESS SWEET THAN the usual American scone and every bit as rich as the English version, these beloved drop-style scones are baked every day in each of our stores. As they bake, their tops develop crunchy ridges and more tender valleys that add up to blissfully rustic shortcake fixings. They freeze well if you want to bake them ahead of time by a week (or even a few days)—just pop them into an airtight container once they're cool. To reheat, wrap them loosely in aluminum foil while they're still frozen and warm them in a 300-degree-F oven for about twenty minutes.

HEAVENLY SCONES PCC Bakery Favorite

Makes 8 large scones

Preheat the oven to 375 degrees F. Line a baking sheet with parchment paper.

In a medium bowl, whisk together the flour, sugar, baking powder, and salt. Using your fingers or a pastry cutter, add the cold butter pieces and mix until the butter is very small and the mixture is like damp sand or coarse crumbs.

In a small bowl, whisk the half-and-half and egg. Make a well in the dry ingredients and pour in the wet ingredients. Mix with a spatula until the wet ingredients are incorporated, then gently knead by hand five or six times to bring the dough together. It will be fairly stiff.

Using a ⅓-cup measuring scoop, drop 8 round balls of dough on the prepared baking sheet, 2 inches apart. Bake for about 25 minutes, until their bottoms have browned and their tops are cracked and golden brown.

3 cups all-purpose flour
⅓ cup granulated sugar
1 tablespoon baking powder
½ teaspoon kosher salt
½ cup (1 stick) cold unsalted butter, cut into small pieces
¾ cup half-and-half
1 large egg

1 SCONE: 340 CAL., 14G FAT (8G SAT.), 55MG CHOL., 140MG SODIUM, 46G CARB., 2G FIBER, 9G SUGAR, 8G PROTEIN

HOW TO DRESS UP A SCONE

You can add all kinds of fruit to this recipe and, properly prepared, their addition won't affect the baking time. Frozen berries work perfectly. Don't thaw them out—stir 1 cup of frozen berries into the dry ingredients right before adding the wet ingredients. In general, frozen apples or stone fruit are too large—make sure to partially thaw them and chop into small pieces, or use diced fresh fruit. As with berries, you want about 1 cup total fruit.

ARRANGED ON A BIG PLATTER, these baskets offer the prettiest way possible to serve simple hash browns and eggs to brunch guests. They're particularly suited to springtime, when pastured hens kick their productivity into high gear and eggs with gorgeously bright yolks are in abundance. Be sure to grease the pan thoroughly on the bottom and sides so you can easily slip the baskets out of the muffin cups.

POTATO AND EGG BASKETS

Makes 12 baskets

Preheat the oven to 425 degrees F. Lightly grease a twelve-cup muffin tin.

Spread out a piece of cheesecloth or a clean kitchen towel and place the grated potatoes in the center. Gently squeeze out the excess liquid.

In a medium bowl, combine the potatoes, butter, ¼ cup of the cheese, and salt and pepper to taste. Divide the potato mixture evenly among the prepared muffin cups and gently press with your fingers to form a thin layer on the bottom and sides of each cup.

Bake until just golden brown, 15 to 18 minutes. Remove from the oven and reduce the temperature to 350 degrees F.

Carefully crack 1 egg into each potato basket; you don't want to break the yolks. Sprinkle each egg evenly with the prosciutto, chives, and parsley, and top with the remaining ¼ cup cheese.

Return to the oven and bake until the eggs are set to preferred degree of doneness, 10 to 13 minutes. Sprinkle with the cayenne to taste just before serving.

1 BASKET: 170 CAL., 9G FAT (4G SAT.), 200MG CHOL., 460MG SODIUM, 10G CARB., 0G FIBER, 0G SUGAR, 12G PROTEIN

Unsalted butter or extra-virgin olive oil, for the muffin tin
1½ pounds Yukon gold potatoes (4 medium or 8 small potatoes), peeled and grated
2 tablespoons unsalted butter, melted
1¾ ounces (½ cup) shredded Parmesan cheese, divided
Kosher salt and freshly ground black pepper
12 large eggs
3 slices prosciutto, chopped
2 tablespoons chopped chives
1 tablespoon chopped fresh Italian parsley
Cayenne pepper, for garnish

MAKE IT A MEAL: For a nonfussy but elegant brunch, set off the combination of crispy potatoes and salty Parmesan and prosciutto with sweet Spring Pea Soup (page 33), which you can prepare before you bake the egg baskets.

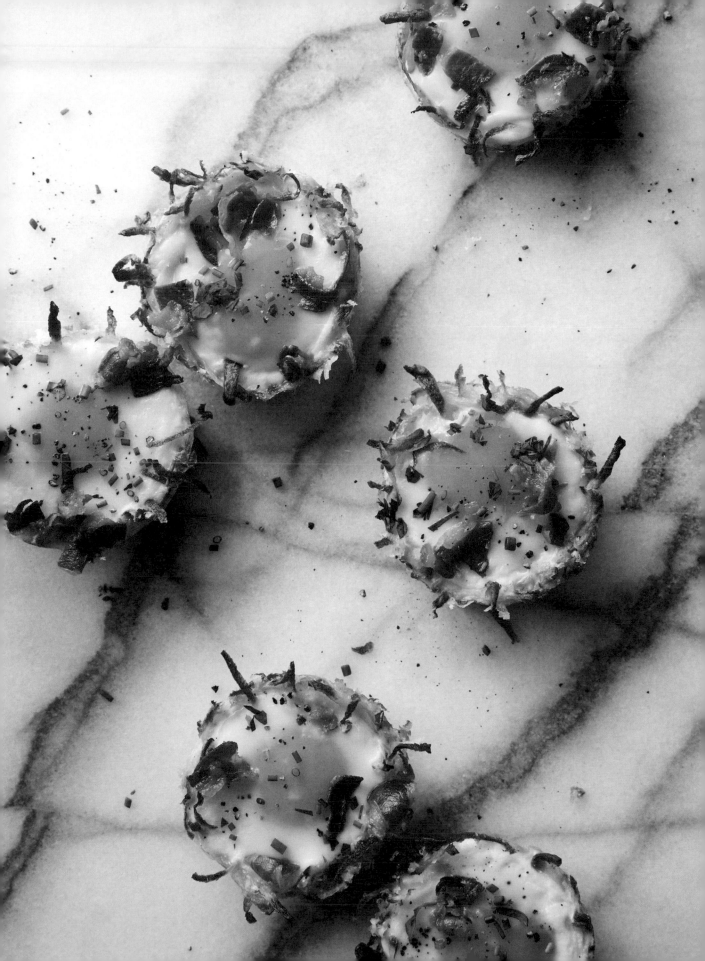

THIS METHOD OF "COOKING" OATMEAL combines minimal effort with the ultimate flexibility. It works just as well if you double or triple it, and you can use whatever type of milk you desire—the goal is a thick, custard-like base to top with your favorite morning fruits. Just make sure to use regular or thick-cut rolled oats; steel cut are too thick, and both quick-cooking and instant oats are much too thin to hold up to the overnight soak. Either recommended type offers a welcome serving of fiber and good, highly portable nutrition.

BERRY COBBLER OVERNIGHT OATMEAL

Makes 1 serving

In a small bowl or 8-ounce mason jar, combine the oats, yogurt, milk, and chia seeds. Put in the refrigerator overnight.

In the morning, top the oatmeal with the berries and granola.

NOTE: You may add the mix-ins the night before if you like, but keep in mind that whatever you incorporate will be very soft by morning. It can work well to add the fruit at night, but reserve the granola until morning.

⅓ cup rolled oats (not quick-cooking)
⅓ cup plain yogurt
⅓ cup milk (any dairy or dairy alternative)
1 tablespoon chia seeds (optional)
¼ cup fresh blueberries
¼ cup fresh raspberries
Handful of granola

8 OUNCES: 440 CAL., 13G FAT (4G SAT.), 10MG CHOL., 200MG SODIUM, 68G CARB., 7G FIBER, 29G SUGAR, 15G PROTEIN

FOLLOW THE FIBER

The more processed a food is, the lower its fiber content will be. A whole apple provides about 4 grams of fiber, while a peeled apple provides 2 grams and apple juice contains no fiber at all. Peeling fruits and vegetables lowers their fiber content, but chopping, cooking, or blending foods will not affect this.

Most Americans consume less than half of the recommended fiber we should be consuming each day, so there is plenty of room for improvement. That said, it's smart to go slowly when increasing your fiber intake to allow your body to adapt—cramping or gas may occur if you transition too quickly, although the human body can handle much more than the 38 grams per day recommended by the USDA.

Increasing your fiber intake will help stabilize your blood sugar and help keep you full in between meals.

SEATTLE LIKES TO TAKE CREDIT for the Dutch baby, a baked pancake with crisp edges and a delicate, puffy center, thanks to its first appearance at Manca's Café in the early years of the twentieth century. More truthfully, the name is what began in the Puget Sound area, not the recipe—the egg-leavened German pancake *pfannkuchen* is identical.

Our basic recipe can be served with either sweet or savory accompaniments, from maple syrup to smoked salmon. If you like, swing the pancake toward sweet by adding one teaspoon vanilla extract to the milk, or shift to savory by stirring in one-quarter cup shredded Gruyère or cheddar cheese right after you add the last of the milk to the batter.

BAKED DUTCH BABY PANCAKES

Makes 4 servings

Preheat the oven to 425 degrees F. Lightly oil a 9- or 10-inch ovenproof skillet (cast iron works great) and put it in the oven until very hot, about 15 minutes.

Meanwhile, in a small bowl, whisk the eggs until light and frothy. Stir in the milk and butter.

In a medium bowl, combine the flour, sugar, lemon zest, and salt. Whisk one-third of the milk mixture into the flour mixture, until no lumps remain. Slowly whisk in the remaining milk mixture.

Carefully remove the skillet from the oven and pour the batter into the skillet.

Bake until the pancake is crisp and golden, about 20 minutes. Transfer from the skillet to a wire rack and let cool 10 minutes. Cut into wedges and serve warm.

High-heat oil, for the pan
2 large eggs
½ cup whole milk, at
  room temperature
1 tablespoon unsalted
  butter, melted
½ cup all-purpose flour
1 teaspoon granulated sugar
1 teaspoon freshly grated
  lemon zest
½ teaspoon kosher salt

¼ RECIPE: 150 CAL., 8G FAT (3.5G SAT.), 105MG CHOL., 290MG SODIUM, 15G CARB., 0G FIBER, 1G SUGAR, 6G PROTEIN

WHILE CORNMEAL PANCAKES DATE BACK to at least the mid-1700s in North America, this is a modern version with two leaveners for an airy texture, yogurt for richness, and a combination of flours to provide the right balance of tenderness and crunch. A cast-iron skillet will give them a fantastic crispy crust, and they're particularly good with berry syrup or jam. Cornmeal pancakes can also serve as a base in a pancake sandwich with fried eggs and cheese; if you're going this route, a sprinkle of chopped chives or green onions is a welcome addition. If you want to make them gluten-free, substitute your favorite flour mix for the all-purpose flour. Using all cornmeal will lead to a heavy pancake that's more grainy than is pleasant to eat.

CORNMEAL PANCAKES

Makes about 6 (5-inch) pancakes

In a medium bowl, whisk together the flour, cornmeal, sugar, baking soda, baking powder, and salt. In a small bowl, combine the milk, yogurt, egg, and melted butter; whisk until smooth. Add the wet ingredients to the dry ingredients and stir with a spatula until they're just combined and no streaks of the cornmeal remain.

Heat a large skillet over medium heat and grease the pan well with cooking spray. Working in batches, pour about ⅓ cup of batter per pancake into the pan, leaving plenty of room between them so you can flip them easily (remember that the batter will spread as they cook). Cook the pancakes until golden brown on the bottom and matte on top with small bubbles, 4 to 6 minutes. Flip the pancakes and cook another 3 minutes, until golden brown. Repeat with the remaining batter, adding more cooking spray as needed. Serve hot with the syrup.

¾ cup all-purpose flour
½ cup medium cornmeal
1 tablespoon granulated sugar
½ teaspoon baking soda
¼ teaspoon baking powder
¼ teaspoon kosher salt
⅔ cup milk (not nonfat)
½ cup plain yogurt
1 egg
1 tablespoon unsalted butter, melted and cooled
Cooking spray, for the pan
Quick Mixed Berry Syrup (recipe follows), for serving

1 PANCAKE: 160 CAL., 4G FAT (2G SAT.), 40MG CHOL., 230MG SODIUM, 25G CARB., 1G FIBER, 5G SUGAR, 6G PROTEIN

THIS SYRUP IS QUICK ENOUGH to pull together that you can even make it while the pancakes are cooking. Use whatever berries you have on hand; just know that it will be slightly different each time you make it, as berries will have varying amounts of juice. If you are using strawberries, be sure to hull and halve them before proceeding; all other berries can be used whole. If you want a completely thin syrup, strain the fruit pulp out with a fine-mesh sieve before serving; this method will make about half as much syrup.

Quick Mixed Berry Syrup

Makes about 1¼ cups syrup

In a small saucepan over medium heat, combine the berries (including the juice if using frozen berries that you've thawed) and water. Mash the berries with a wooden spoon or potato masher. Stir in ¼ cup of the sugar and cook, stirring frequently, for 4 to 6 minutes, until berries are soft and have released their juices. Reduce the heat to low and add the lemon zest.

Taste a small amount and add up to ¼ cup more sugar to taste, stirring to dissolve it in the juice. Serve warm.

Leftovers may be refrigerated for up to 1 week.

1 cup fresh or frozen berries (if using frozen, thaw them and keep the juice)
1 tablespoon water
¼ cup granulated sugar, plus up to ¼ cup more as needed
½ teaspoon freshly grated lemon zest

1 TABLESPOON: 25 CAL., 0G FAT (0G SAT.), 0MG CHOL., 0MG SODIUM, 6G CARB., 0G FIBER, 6G SUGAR, 0G PROTEIN

EGG BOATS HAVE MUCH IN common with quiche, but they're infinitely more casual and much easier to prepare, using a hollowed-out baguette instead of a pie crust. These egg boats' flavors of cheddar cheese and roasted peppers are truly just a suggestion. Swiss or Gouda are fine substitutes for cheddar; stir in a scoop of leftover braised greens or a handful of sautéed mushrooms instead of the peppers, and you have a meal that turns leftovers into something new. Slices of the finished egg boat are great when portable finger foods are needed, whether that's on the way to school or in front of the TV while you're cheering for your favorite team.

CHEESY EGG BOATS

Makes 4 to 6 servings

Preheat the oven to 350 degrees F. Line a baking sheet with parchment paper.

Make a V-shaped cut along the length of the baguette, being careful to leave the ends intact. Remove the wedge from the baguette and set aside for another use. Gently hollow out the baguette, being careful to not cut through the bottom or sides, so you have a long, skinny bread boat to fill with the egg mixture. Place the baguette on the prepared baking sheet.

In a medium bowl, beat the eggs and add the milk, beating until completely combined. Stir in the cheese, peppers, chives, cayenne, and salt and pepper to taste. Slowly pour the egg mixture into the prepared baguette, using a spoon as needed to spread the cheese and peppers evenly along the length of the bread.

Bake for 25 to 35 minutes, until the filling is completely set and the cheese is light brown in places. Let cool for 3 to 5 minutes, then slice into 1-inch segments and serve.

1 baguette

3 large eggs

2 tablespoons whole milk

5 ounces (1¼ cups) shredded cheddar cheese

2½ tablespoons drained and finely chopped pickled or roasted peppers

1 tablespoon chopped chives

1 to 3 pinches of cayenne pepper (optional)

Kosher salt and freshly ground black pepper

MAKE IT A MEAL: Turn these crisp, cheesy slices into a brunch entrée by serving them alongside Hearty Greens Caesar (page 72).

⅕ **RECIPE: 280 CAL., 14G FAT (6G SAT.), 140MG CHOL., 660MG SODIUM, 24G CARB., 0G FIBER, 1G SUGAR, 14G PROTEIN**

NOTHING BRIGHTENS A COLD, GRAY morning like a juicy grapefruit. Modern varieties have lost much of their old-school bitterness, so the flavor is now tart-sweet, not tart-acerbic. To complement the tartness and subtler sweetness of the fruit, use a honey with a lot of deep, spicy flavor, like fireweed, alfalfa, or buckwheat. For a weekday breakfast, you can prep the fruit the evening before and stash the segments in the refrigerator, but this is also a grown-up accompaniment to weekend brunch alongside Greek yogurt and French toast.

WARM GRAPEFRUIT WITH HONEY AND GINGER

Makes 2 to 3 servings as a side

Trim a thin slice off the blossom end and stem end of the grapefruit and stand it upright on a cutting surface. With a very sharp paring knife, remove the entire peel from the grapefruit in strips, maintaining the curved shape of the fruit. Holding the grapefruit in one hand, cut out the juicy segments between the membranes, being sure to remove all the tough bits from the center along with the seeds (this is called "supreming"). You should have about 1½ cups of grapefruit.

In a small sauté pan over medium heat, warm the honey and add the ginger. Bring to a simmer, so the honey bubbles gently around the edges of the pan. Remove from the heat. Using a slotted spoon, add the grapefruit segments to the warm honey while leaving the extra juice behind. Gently toss them to coat with the spiced honey and serve warm.

1 medium grapefruit
1 tablespoon honey
1 teaspoon grated or minced peeled fresh ginger

½ RECIPE: 80 CAL., 0G FAT (0G SAT.), 0MG CHOL., 0MG SODIUM, 21G CARB., 1G FIBER, 8G SUGAR, 1G PROTEIN

RETHINK GRAPEFRUIT

Red grapefruits have become the automatic choice for the best flavor, but newer cultivars like Melogold and Oroblanco are worth a second look. They're crosses between white grapefruit and the pomelo, with sweet flesh and a tart finish. Pink and red types have vitamin A and lycopene, while all offer soluble fiber, potassium, and vitamin C.

STIRRING IN A BIT OF whole grain spelt flour isn't absolutely necessary (you can make up the difference with more all-purpose flour if you like), but it's a fine way to experiment with a less common flour. The whole grain boosts the fiber and protein content of the final product, and spelt is a bit lower in gluten than wheat, so the waffles stay appealingly delicate. These fragrant waffles are delicious plain or dressed up.

CARROT CAKE WAFFLES

Makes about 6 (10-inch) waffles

Preheat a waffle iron, and preheat the oven to 200 degrees F. Put a baking sheet in the oven to preheat as well.

In a medium bowl, whisk together the flours, baking powder, sugar, cinnamon, and salt.

In a small bowl, whisk together the eggs and buttermilk. Blend this mixture into the dry ingredients with a broad spatula or wooden spoon, stirring just until no streaks of flour remain. Stir in the melted butter, being careful not to overmix. Gently fold in the carrots, coconut, and raisins.

Cook the waffles according to the waffle-iron manufacturer's instructions (usually about ½ cup batter and a 5-minute cooking time). Keep the waffles warm by placing them on the baking sheet in the oven while cooking the remaining batter; to keep them crisp, don't cover them. Serve with mascarpone, syrup, and pecans.

To freeze cooked waffles, cool them to room temperature and wrap well. They'll keep for up to 1 month. To reheat, pop into the toaster or toaster oven until crisp.

1 cup all-purpose flour

¾ cup whole spelt flour

1 tablespoon plus 1 teaspoon baking powder

1 tablespoon granulated sugar

1½ teaspoons ground cinnamon

½ teaspoon kosher salt

3 large eggs

2 cups cultured buttermilk

½ cup (1 stick) unsalted butter, melted

1½ cups peeled and finely shredded carrots (from about 3½ medium carrots)

⅓ cup shredded unsweetened coconut

¼ cup raisins (optional)

Mascarpone, for garnish (optional)

Maple syrup, for garnish (optional)

Toasted pecans, for garnish (optional)

1 WAFFLE: 390 CAL., 22G FAT (14G SAT.), 135MG CHOL., 370MG SODIUM, 37G CARB., 4G FIBER, 8G SUGAR, 11G PROTEIN

CHILAQUILES CAN BE AS SIMPLE as fried eggs and salsa on top of tortilla chips or as elaborate as a layered dish with a base of homemade chili sauce topped with poached eggs. Ours is a quick casserole of spiced scrambled eggs enriched with a salsa–sour cream blend; it needs just fifteen minutes to bake. If you like, pass your favorite guacamole around the table as a garnish.

CHILAQUILES PCC Deli Favorite

Makes 4 servings

Preheat the oven to 375 degrees F.

In a medium bowl, beat together the eggs, salt, cumin, and chili powder; set aside.

In a large skillet over medium heat, melt the butter until bubbling hot. Cook the tortilla pieces until tender, 1 to 2 minutes, flipping as needed if any spots seem to be over-browning. Reduce the heat to low and add the egg mixture; fold to mix with the tortillas until the eggs are clumpy but still moist. Remove from the heat and transfer to a 9-by-13-inch baking dish.

Add half the salsa and sour cream in dollops. Create a marbled effect by folding the mixture gently, without actually stirring it. Top with dollops of the remaining salsa and sour cream. Sprinkle the cheese on top.

Bake, uncovered, for 15 minutes, until the cheese is melted and the salsa is hot. Serve hot.

6 large eggs
1 teaspoon kosher salt
½ teaspoon ground cumin
¼ teaspoon chili powder
1 tablespoon unsalted butter
5 (6-inch) corn tortillas, cut into 1½-inch pieces
½ cup salsa
¼ cup sour cream
4 ounces (1 cup) shredded cheddar cheese

¼ RECIPE: 350 CAL., 22G FAT (11G SAT.), 320MG CHOL., 890MG SODIUM, 18G CARB., 0G FIBER, 1G SUGAR, 18G PROTEIN

HASH

Hash has a long history of being a popular way to combine a few leftovers with inexpensive ingredients to get an entire second meal out of whatever might be in the larder. From the mid-1800s to the early twenty-first century, it remained essentially the same: finely chopped bits of cooked meat, an onion and any other available vegetable scraps, plus fried potatoes and soft-yolked eggs for a plate full of crispy textures and earthy flavors. When high-end chefs started playing around with it (and the *New York Times* officially anointed its version in 2011), the diner dish got fancy, with all sorts of roasted vegetables plus prime rib, duck confit, lobster meat, or smoked trout. However you fry it up, it can help you reduce food waste by giving new life to leftovers (including leftover prime rib), and it's infinitely adaptable to your dietary preferences and budget.

1   CHOOSE YOUR MEAT (OPTIONAL)

Don't get us wrong: veggie hash is delicious. If you intend on skipping the meat, by all means proceed straight to the next step. But if you're including meat, choose one that has some fat. Think pork—sausage, bacon, chorizo—or corned beef. That way, you can cook your potatoes in the rendered fat that develops from cooking the meat, which the potatoes in turn absorb for extra flavor.

2   CUBE THE ROOTS

To ensure crisp potatoes, choose Yukon golds or russets; red potatoes are too waxy for hash. Feel free to use sweet potatoes, parsnips, beets, or peeled winter squash as alternatives for some or all of the potatoes. Cut your potatoes into ½-inch cubes and fry them in oil or rendered fat until golden brown, seasoning them with salt and freshly ground black pepper once or twice along the way. For extra crispness, and if you've got the time: before you start frying them, parboil your root vegetables in water with a splash of white wine vinegar just until they're fork-tender.

3 USE UP SCRAPS

This is where you can get creative and make something great out of what you have on hand. Use up that half onion, the leftover kale, that last broccoli crown, the fennel bulb that seemed like a good idea at the store, or the half can of black beans you thriftily saved in the freezer. Keep the veggies in uniform pieces so they cook evenly, and don't forget to season them with plenty of salt and freshly ground black pepper. Smoked paprika, fresh thyme, red pepper flakes, and a splash of balsamic vinegar are great multipurpose seasonings for hash.

4 ADD SOME EGGS

You can fry or poach them separately, or keep it simple and cook them directly in the hash. If opting for the latter, make a few wells in the hash and crack an egg into each one. Cover and cook over medium-low heat until the whites are set, between 8 and 10 minutes.

5 DRESS IT UP

Before digging in, top your hash with fresh parsley, cilantro, green onions, chunks of avocado, or your favorite hot sauce.

FLAVOR COMBINATIONS TO TRY

- Chorizo, sweet potatoes, black beans, avocado, fresh cilantro
- Bacon, Yukon gold potatoes, fennel, asparagus, fresh Italian parsley; add goat cheese once it's off the heat
- Turkey and apple sausage, parboiled turnips, spinach, fresh sage, apple wedges
- Butternut squash, chanterelles, smoked paprika, Lacinato kale, hot sauce
- Russet potatoes, yellow onion, smoked salmon, chard, green onions; add sour cream once it's off the heat

PART OF THE BEAUTY OF hash is what a complete, substantial meal it is all on its own. There's no real need for anything other than coffee on the side, although hot sauce might be appreciated. Use your favorite pork, turkey, chicken, or vegetarian sausage for this recipe; it works equally well with Italian sausage, Mexican chorizo, or breakfast sausage with or without bits of apple.

SWEET POTATO HASH

Makes 4 to 6 servings

In a medium cast-iron skillet over medium-high heat, warm 1 tablespoon of the oil. Add the sausage; crumble and cook it while stirring until it is no longer pink, about 3 minutes. Add the onion, garlic, thyme, and fennel; cook until the onions are soft, 5 to 7 minutes. Remove the mixture from the pan.

In the same skillet, heat the remaining 1 tablespoon oil and add the sweet potatoes. Cook until they are golden and tender, stirring occasionally, about 20 minutes. Return the sausage mixture to the skillet. Stir in the kale and cook until tender, 5 to 7 minutes. Season to taste with salt and pepper. Using a spoon, make four shallow indentations in the hash and crack 1 egg into each indentation. Reduce the heat to medium-low, cover, and cook until the whites are set, 8 to 10 minutes. Serve immediately.

⅙ RECIPE: 620 CAL., 42G FAT (14G SAT.), 215MG CHOL., 1160MG SODIUM, 36G CARB., 6G FIBER, 7G SUGAR, 22G PROTEIN

2 tablespoons high-heat oil, such as sunflower or refined peanut oil, divided
1 pound fresh sausage
½ cup thinly sliced yellow onion (from about ½ medium onion)
3 cloves garlic, minced
1 teaspoon chopped fresh thyme
½ teaspoon fennel seeds
1½ pounds Red Garnet or Jewel sweet potatoes (about 4 medium), scrubbed and cut into ½-inch cubes
1 bunch Lacinato kale, tough stems removed and leaves chopped
Kosher salt and freshly ground black pepper
4 large eggs

MAKING SENSE OF SWEET POTATOES

Sweet potatoes aren't potatoes and they aren't yams. These tubers include dark-orange Red Garnets and Jewels; Hannah, a pale, creamy variety that has a milder, less sweet flavor and somewhat drier texture; and the Filipino sweet potato known as *ube*, which has a brilliantly purple interior.

Like potatoes, they offer potassium, vitamin B6, and fiber. Orange sweet potatoes are particularly high in vitamin A, while purple sweet potatoes offer the antioxidant known as anthocyanin, a promoter of heart health and brain function. It's the same pigment that gives blueberries, red cabbage, and red grapes their vibrant color.

SOUPS & STEWS

WE'RE ROOTED IN THE PACIFIC NORTHWEST, a region that sometimes experiences six straight months of cool, overcast weather, when it pays to be good friends with your soup pot. Wherever you spend the chilly part of the year, a classic simmering stew is a symbol of all the good parts of the season, where everyone's warm and cozy, the house smells great, and a hearty meal is just a little while away.

These days, roasting and other quick, hot methods of cooking vegetables reign supreme. There are plenty of good reasons for this, but it's become something of a rarity to taste vegetables without rich caramelization. Soup is a means of rediscovering the simple, pure flavor of gently cooked seasonal ingredients, a way of sipping the season rather than crunching your way through it.

Soup isn't particularly thought of as a special-occasion food, but when you consider that chili and chowder are absolutely make-a-giant-pot-and-invite-everyone meals, you'll notice how much socializing happens around bowls of soup. Something that's slowly catching on as a January twist on the holiday cookie exchange is the soup swap. Make a few quarts of your favorite, invite your friends to do the same, and get together to sample and swap. Everyone goes home with a few containers of new varieties to stock their freezer with (and recipe cards, if they're really lucky), and everyone's had a cozy evening around, yes, soup.

THIS IS A HEARTY, KID-FRIENDLY soup that is lean and infinitely adaptable. You can substitute chipotle Field Roast for the turkey to spice the chili up and make it vegetarian. Or add a bit of Mexican chorizo when you brown the turkey. Serve it with cornbread and cheese, or nothing but a big green salad. Spike it with cayenne if everyone loves spicy heat, or pass the hot sauce at the table. The dish also takes well to being frozen and cooks almost as quickly if you make a double batch. Our store chefs make it so often, they may well be able to recite the recipe in their sleep.

TIGER MOUNTAIN TURKEY CHILI PCC Deli Favorite

Makes about 8 servings

Spray a large, heavy-bottomed soup pot with cooking spray and put over medium heat. Add the turkey and cook, stirring occasionally to prevent sticking and to break up the meat into smaller pieces, about 5 minutes. Once the turkey is no longer pink, drain off and discard all the liquids.

Stir in the onion, bell peppers, garlic, chili powder, black pepper, chipotle, cumin, thyme, and salt. Cook, stirring occasionally, for 3 minutes, until the onions are translucent and the spices are deeply colored and fragrant. Add the tomatoes and tomato sauce, then stir in the water. Bring to a simmer, cover, and cook for 20 to 30 minutes, until the vegetables have slightly softened and flavors have melded. Stir in the beans and sugar, heat through, and serve.

> **BEER PAIRING:** A Washington State pilsner would be a great choice to sip alongside this not-too-spicy chili. Go with balanced malt and hops that are subtle and piney, making a light, crisp beer.

Cooking spray, for the pot
1½ pounds ground turkey
½ medium yellow onion, diced
½ medium green bell
   pepper, diced
½ medium red bell
   pepper, diced
2 cloves garlic, minced
1½ teaspoons chili powder
1 teaspoon freshly ground
   black pepper
½ teaspoon ground chipotle
½ teaspoon ground cumin
½ teaspoon dried thyme
1 teaspoon kosher salt
1 (15-ounce) can crushed
   tomatoes, drained
1 (15-ounce) can tomato sauce
1½ cups water
1 (15-ounce) can kidney
   beans, drained
1 tablespoon packed light
   brown sugar

1 CUP: 240 CAL., 11G FAT (3G SAT.), 65MG CHOL., 560MG SODIUM, 16G CARB., 4G FIBER, 5G SUGAR, 19G PROTEIN

THINK THAT PEA SOUP MEANS nothing more than dried split peas and a ham hock? Think again. Basil, parsley, and tarragon all highlight the sweetness of fresh peas (it's OK to use frozen peas if you want to skip the shelling), while the tiny croutons add a welcome bit of crunch. This is quick to pull together, and each component is actually quite simple; instead of relegating this to dinner parties, serve alongside a rotisserie chicken, have the family pull on sweaters, and sit outside on the first nonrainy evening of the season.

SPRING PEA SOUP

Makes 6 to 8 small servings

To make the croutons, preheat the oven to 425 degrees F. In a medium bowl, combine the butter and basil. Use tongs to toss the bread cubes in this mixture until they are well coated. Sprinkle with a pinch of salt, spread in a single layer on a rimmed baking sheet, and toast in the oven for 2 to 4 minutes, until golden brown and crispy.

To make the herb oil, in a blender or food processor, combine the basil, parsley, garlic, salt, and oil and blend until smooth.

To make the soup, in a medium soup pot over medium heat, melt the butter and add the shallots. Cook for 5 to 6 minutes, or until tender but not yet browned. Stir in the tarragon and basil and cook for 30 seconds, until the herbs are wilted. Add the peas and broth.

Increase the heat to medium-high and bring the broth to a low boil. Cook until the peas are just tender, about 8 minutes for fresh or 5 minutes for frozen peas. Reduce the heat to low and stir in the cream. Season to taste with salt and pepper.

Carefully puree the warm soup using a blender, food processor, or immersion blender, or pass through a food mill until completely smooth. Divide among small bowls and garnish each with a drizzle of basil oil and a few croutons.

---

1 CUP: 370 CAL., 30G FAT (10G SAT.), 40MG CHOL., 480MG SODIUM, 21G CARB., 5G FIBER, 6G SUGAR, 6G PROTEIN

FOR THE CROUTONS:

¼ cup unsalted butter, melted

2 tablespoons chopped fresh basil

2 cups fresh ½-inch ciabatta or sourdough bread cubes

Pinch of kosher salt

FOR THE HERB OIL:

¼ cup chopped fresh basil

¼ cup chopped fresh Italian parsley

2 cloves garlic

¾ teaspoon kosher salt

½ cup extra-virgin olive oil

FOR THE SOUP:

2 tablespoons unsalted butter

¼ cup sliced shallots

1 teaspoon chopped fresh tarragon

1 teaspoon chopped fresh basil

4 cups shelled English peas (4¼ pounds unshelled pea pods, or 15 ounces frozen peas)

2 cups vegetable broth or water

¼ cup heavy cream

Kosher salt and freshly ground black pepper

THIS PRETTY BRIGHT-ORANGE SOUP IS a cozy bowl of fall's finest produce. With rich coconut milk, vegetable broth, and apple juice as the liquid components, this creamy soup freezes well, unlike dairy-based soups. If you're not vegan, swirling a little crème fraîche through the soup just before eating provides a tart contrast to the smooth sweetness. When choosing an apple variety, try a Granny Smith, Jazz, Braeburn, or Cripps Pink, as their tangy flavors will balance the flavors of the butternut squash.

BUTTERNUT SQUASH– APPLE SOUP

Makes 4 to 6 servings

In a large, heavy-bottomed soup pot over medium heat, heat the oil just until it shimmers. Sauté the squash, apple, and onion in the oil for about 8 minutes, until some deeper color develops on their edges and the onion is translucent. Add the ginger and garlic, and stir for 1 minute.

Slowly pour in the apple juice, the coconut milk, and 1½ cups of the broth and stir until well blended with the squash mixture. Add the salt, increase the heat to medium-high, and bring the mixture to a boil. Promptly reduce the heat to low, cover the pot, and simmer until the squash is completely soft, about 30 minutes, stirring twice as it cooks and adding up to 1½ cups of the remaining vegetable broth if it seems too thick.

Carefully puree the warm soup using a blender, food processor, or immersion blender, or pass through a food mill until completely smooth. Season to taste with black pepper. Serve hot.

> **CIDER PAIRING:** Look for a dry, spicy, ginger-infused craft cider to play up the ginger in the soup and to provide a strong counterpoint to the rich coconut milk. There are almost two dozen Northwest-made ginger ciders and each has its die-hard fans, but in truth it's hard to go wrong.

1 CUP: 370 CAL., 23G FAT (16G SAT.), 0MG CHOL., 870MG SODIUM, 43G CARB., 5G FIBER, 18G SUGAR, 4G PROTEIN

2 tablespoons extra-virgin olive oil
1 medium butternut squash (about 2 pounds), peeled and cut into 1-inch cubes
1 large tart apple, peeled, cored, and diced
1 medium white onion, diced
2-inch knob fresh ginger, peeled and finely chopped
4 cloves garlic, chopped
2 cups unsweetened apple juice
1 (15-ounce) can coconut milk
3 cups vegetable broth, divided
2 teaspoons kosher salt
Freshly ground black pepper

UNLIKE BROWN, BLACK, OR GREEN lentils, red lentils cook down into a thick pulp, making this a fantastic soup alongside rustic sourdough bread and a crisp salad. The soup freezes beautifully, and stirring up a double batch makes almost no difference to the cooking time. Adding the salt, lemon, and cilantro right before serving creates a perfect kick of flavor; if you plan on making it ahead and freezing it, it's fine to add the salt before freezing, but reserve the lemon and cilantro until you've reheated the soup and are ready to eat. That way, you'll get the biggest pop of bright flavor.

EGYPTIAN RED LENTIL SOUP PCC Deli Favorite

Makes about 4 servings

In a large, heavy-bottomed soup pot over medium heat, heat the oil just until it shimmers. Add the onion, garlic, red pepper flakes, cumin, and coriander and sauté until the onions are very soft and the spices are deeply fragrant, about 7 minutes.

Add the lentils, tomatoes, and broth to the pot. Increase the heat to medium-high and bring the pot to a boil, stirring frequently. Once it's vigorously boiling, reduce the heat to low, cover the pot, and simmer for about 25 minutes, until the lentils are completely tender, stirring once or twice to break up any clumps.

Just before serving, stir in the lemon juice, salt, and cilantro. Season to taste with more red pepper flakes.

> **MAKE IT A MEAL:** With plenty of crunch and bright, tangy flavor, Apple, Bok Choy, and Carrot Slaw (page 52) is a cheerful alternative to a green salad to serve alongside this soup.

2 tablespoons extra-virgin olive oil

1 medium yellow onion, diced

2 cloves garlic, minced

½ teaspoon red pepper flakes, plus more as needed

2 teaspoons ground cumin

1 teaspoon ground coriander

1¼ cups red lentils, rinsed

1 (15-ounce) can diced tomatoes, drained

4½ cups vegetable broth

1 tablespoon freshly squeezed lemon juice

1¼ teaspoons kosher salt

¼ cup chopped fresh cilantro or Italian parsley

1 CUP: 220 CAL., 6G FAT (.5G SAT.), 0MG CHOL., 640MG SODIUM, 31G CARB., 7G FIBER, 5G SUGAR, 12G PROTEIN

CANNED CHIPOTLE PEPPERS IN ADOBO sauce are one of those magical ingredients that create layers of flavor with minimal effort. Here, their heat balances the sweet potatoes and corn, while enriching the beer–chicken broth base.

Kept warm in a slow cooker, this hearty stew makes a fantastic lunch for midday football games and will go perfectly with the same lager you use in cooking. Leftover stew can also be frozen nicely for up to two months.

SPICY PORK AND SWEET POTATO STEW

Makes about 6 servings

In a large, heavy-bottomed soup pot over medium-high heat, heat the oil just until it shimmers. Add the pork in batches (don't overcrowd the pot) and brown the pieces on all sides, 1 to 2 minutes per side. Using a slotted spoon or tongs, remove them from the pot and set aside in a bowl.

Reduce the heat to low and add the onion and garlic. Cook, scraping the browned bits from the bottom of the pot, until the onions are deep golden, about 10 minutes. Add the browned pork, cumin, coriander, chipotle peppers, adobo sauce, and salt and pepper to taste; stir to combine.

Increase the heat to medium, pour in the lager and chicken broth, and bring to a boil. Reduce the heat to low, cover the pot, and simmer for 1 hour, stirring occasionally. Add the sweet potatoes and corn. Cover and simmer until the pork is tender and the sweet potatoes are cooked through, 30 to 45 additional minutes. Ladle into bowls and top with cilantro and sour cream.

NOTE: If you would prefer to skip the beer, just add an extra 1½ cups chicken broth in its place.

> **CIDER PAIRING:** Bold apple flavor is a classic choice for pork, particularly with a spicier recipe such as this. Both off-dry and semisweet blends can balance the heat from the adobo sauce.

1 CUP: 350 CAL., 16G FAT (5G SAT.), 70MG CHOL., 370MG SODIUM, 26G CARB., 3G FIBER, 6G SUGAR, 21G PROTEIN

1 tablespoon high-heat oil, such as sunflower or refined peanut oil

1½ pounds boneless pork shoulder, cut into 1-inch cubes

1 medium yellow onion, diced

3 cloves garlic, minced

2 teaspoons ground cumin

1 teaspoon ground coriander

2 chipotle peppers in adobo sauce, minced, plus 2 tablespoons adobo sauce (from the can)

Kosher salt and freshly ground black pepper

1 (12-ounce) bottle lager or pale ale (see note)

3 cups chicken broth

2 large Red Garnet or Jewel sweet potatoes (about 1 pound), peeled and cut into ¾-inch cubes

1 cup corn kernels (fresh, frozen, or canned)

Fresh cilantro leaves, for garnish

Sour cream, for garnish

USUALLY LENTIL SOUP AND BEAN soup are two separate kinds of soup, but combining them is both a nutritional powerhouse and absolutely delicious—so much for tradition. Brown lentils are fine to substitute for the green recommended here, but red will fall apart and black are so small some of the textural pleasure will be lost. The goal is choosing a firm lentil to offer an appealing textural contrast with soft, creamy white beans. The leftovers will freeze well, but you may need to add more vegetable broth upon reheating, to thin the stew out a bit. Add another splash of balsamic after it's hot too, as the brightness it adds dissipates quickly.

LENTIL AND WHITE BEAN STEW

Makes 6 servings

In a large, heavy-bottomed soup pot over medium heat, heat the oil. Add the onion, carrots, celery, and garlic and cook, stirring occasionally, until the vegetables are soft, about 10 minutes. Stir in the thyme, then add the lentils, salt, pepper, and vegetable broth; bring to a boil, stirring several times to prevent the lentils from clumping. Reduce the heat to low, cover the pot, and simmer until the lentils are cooked, 25 to 30 minutes. The lentils will keep their shape but should be tender all the way through.

Add the beans, kale, and vinegar. Simmer until the beans are heated through and the kale is tender, about 8 minutes. Remove the thyme and season to taste with more salt, pepper, and perhaps another splash of vinegar. Serve hot.

BEER PAIRING: A pale ale is the right choice. The extra body and mild hops hold up to the earthy lentil-kale combination.

1 CUP: 200 CAL., 3G FAT (0G SAT.), 0MG CHOL., 460MG SODIUM, 31G CARB., 7G FIBER, 5G SUGAR, 11G PROTEIN

1 tablespoon extra-virgin olive oil

½ medium white onion, finely chopped

3 medium carrots, peeled and finely chopped

3 ribs celery, finely chopped

2 cloves garlic, minced

6 sprigs fresh thyme

1 cup French green lentils, rinsed

1 teaspoon kosher salt, plus more as needed

½ teaspoon freshly ground black pepper, plus more as needed

3 cups vegetable broth

1 (15-ounce) can cannellini beans, rinsed and drained

1 bunch Lacinato kale, tough stems removed and leaves shredded

Splash of balsamic vinegar, plus more as needed

BROCCOLI CHEDDAR IS A COZY, familiar soup, so familiar that it's worth playing around with the tradition. Our updates are simple but definitely worthwhile. Shifting to Parmesan adds complexity, while lemon lightens the whole eating experience and brightens up winter evenings.

If you'd like to make this ahead of time and freeze it, it's best to stop before you add the Parmesan, as cheese (and other forms of dairy) tends to change its texture when frozen. Reheat the soup and finish it off with the Parmesan, lemon, and seasonings.

BROCCOLI, LEMON, AND PARMESAN SOUP

Makes 4 to 6 servings

In a large, heavy-bottomed soup pot over medium heat, melt the butter. Add the onion and garlic and cook until soft, translucent, and pale gold, 5 to 7 minutes. Stir in the thyme and broccoli; cook until the broccoli begins to soften, about 10 minutes. Add enough broth to cover the vegetables and bring to a boil. Reduce the heat to low, cover the pot, and simmer until the broccoli is completely tender, 10 to 20 minutes.

Let the soup cool slightly with the lid off. Carefully puree using a blender, food processor, or immersion blender, or pass through a food mill until completely smooth. Stir in the Parmesan and lemon zest and juice. Season to taste with salt and pepper and serve garnished with more Parmesan.

NOTE: For a chunkier texture, puree only half the soup.

2 tablespoons unsalted butter

½ medium yellow onion, chopped

2 cloves garlic, minced

½ teaspoon chopped fresh thyme

2 pounds broccoli florets (from about 4 medium heads)

4 to 6 cups vegetable broth

1¾ ounces (½ cup) shredded Parmesan cheese, plus more for garnish

½ medium lemon, freshly zested and juiced

Kosher salt and freshly ground black pepper

⅕ RECIPE: 150 CAL., 8G FAT (4G SAT.), 20MG CHOL., 490MG SODIUM, 16G CARB., 5G FIBER, 5G SUGAR, 8G PROTEIN

CRUCIFERS

The family of brassicas, or cole crops, includes broccoli, cabbage, cauliflower, collards, kale, and all their kin—extending even to mustard greens and some roots. What unites this nutritious family botanically is its similarly patterned flowers—four petals in the form of a cross, hence crucifer, a crossbearer. As a general rule, crucifers are a very good source of dietary fiber and contain vitamins K, C, and E; folate; minerals such as potassium and calcium; and several carotenoids.

SERVED HOT OR COLD, A classic vichyssoise will be thick and smooth, and it will always have potatoes, leeks, and cream. The asparagus here is the bonus of early spring, and it gives both its beautiful color and its fresh, grassy flavor to this simple soup.

If you'd like to serve the vichyssoise cold, it will be just right if it's slightly warmer than straight out of the refrigerator, but not so warm as room temperature: take it out of the refrigerator about twenty minutes before you want to serve it. Because of the potatoes and cream, the texture can become grainy if frozen, but the soup may be made up to four days ahead and kept refrigerated with no loss of quality.

ASPARAGUS VICHYSSOISE

Makes 6 to 8 servings

In a large, heavy-bottomed soup pot over medium heat, heat the oil and add the leeks, garlic, and thyme. Sauté for 6 to 8 minutes, or until the leeks are soft.

Add the vegetable broth and potatoes and simmer for about 20 minutes, until they fall apart. Add the asparagus and simmer for about 6 minutes, until the asparagus is soft and tender.

Let the soup cool slightly with the lid off. Carefully puree using a blender, food processor, or immersion blender, or pass through a food mill until completely smooth. Season to taste with salt and pepper, and add the nutmeg. Stir in the cream and heat through on low. The soup may be served hot or at room temperature.

1 CUP: 130 CAL., 4G FAT (500MG SAT.), 0MG CHOL., 240MG SODIUM, 21G CARB., 0G FIBER, 2G SUGAR, 3G PROTEIN

2 tablespoons extra-virgin olive oil

¾ cup sliced leeks (white and pale-green parts only), washed thoroughly

3 cloves garlic, minced

1 teaspoon fresh thyme leaves

4 cups vegetable broth

3 medium russet potatoes (about 1½ pounds), peeled and finely chopped

1 (1-pound) bunch asparagus spears, tough ends removed and stems coarsely chopped

Kosher salt and freshly ground black pepper

⅛ teaspoon freshly grated nutmeg

¼ cup heavy cream

TRADITIONAL WHITE CAULIFLOWER WILL GET the job done just fine, but the bright-orange variant offers extra nutrition in the form of beta-carotene, although its color will disappear behind the yellow cheddar. When it comes to choosing that cheddar, steer clear of very aged varieties, as they don't melt as smoothly. A medium cheddar, or a blend of sharp and medium, will make for a creamier soup. Soups with this much dairy don't freeze well, but leftovers will last in the refrigerator for three days.

CAULIFLOWER-CHEDDAR SOUP

Makes 6 servings

In a large, heavy-bottomed soup pot over medium heat, melt the butter. Add the onion and cook until it is soft and translucent with golden-brown edges, about 8 minutes. Stir in the garlic and cauliflower. Cook, stirring occasionally, until the cauliflower just begins to soften, about 10 minutes.

Pour in the broth and milk and bring to a boil. Reduce the heat to low, cover the pot, and simmer until the cauliflower is very tender, about 30 minutes.

Let the soup cool slightly with the lid off, and then carefully puree using a blender, food processor, or immersion blender, or pass through a food mill until completely smooth. Return the pureed soup to the stove, increase the heat to medium-low, and sprinkle in the cheese. Stir until the cheese is melted and smooth, 1 to 2 minutes (or a bit longer if the cheese is very cold or very coarsely shredded). Season to taste with salt and pepper and serve.

> **MAKE IT A MEAL:** Providing a perfect contrast to the creamy richness of this soup, Citrus-Beet Slaw (page 67) is a quick slaw of grated beets and fresh orange.

2 tablespoons unsalted butter

½ medium yellow onion, chopped

2 cloves garlic, minced

1 medium head cauliflower (about 2 pounds), trimmed and cut into 1-inch pieces

4 to 5 cups low-sodium vegetable broth

1 cup whole milk

4 ounces (1 cup) shredded cheddar cheese

Kosher salt and freshly ground black pepper

1 CUP: 180 CAL., 12G FAT (7G SAT.), 35MG CHOL., 430MG SODIUM, 11G CARB., 2G FIBER, 6G SUGAR, 8G PROTEIN

CHOWDER

Of all the soup families—chicken, minestrone, bean, or bisque—it's chowder that takes some understanding to bring out its best. It needs a distinct, umami-rich base layer upon which the simple combination of broth, milk, and potatoes is added for relatively slow cooking. Go about this process quickly and the chowder can be too salty, or even gluey. Go about it properly and you have some of the finest soup available at a great value for your food budget.

1   BUILD YOUR BASE

Start by slowly cooking several slices of bacon; when the bacon is halfway done, begin sautéing diced aromatic ingredients—onions, celery, carrots—in the fat. If you're going vegetarian, stick with olive oil, perhaps with a small piece of kombu, a type of seaweed, added for its umami-building abilities. Either way, sautéing the aromatics will boost flavor in the final soup, and it is best if the vegetables aren't cooked until completely soft.

2   ADD BROTH

Slowly stir in clam juice, seafood broth, or a light-tasting vegetable broth. You can combine any two of these or lighten one with water to reduce the overall saltiness and adapt the flavor to your preference. Chicken broth is fine in vegetable chowders but a little rich for clam or fish chowders.

3   ADD MILK AND POTATOES

Add peeled and cubed russet potatoes (waxy potatoes don't thicken the soup as well), or sweet potatoes if you're going nontraditional, along with milk (whole milk has the best texture). Add cooked clams or small pieces of uncooked fish, or additional vegetables like kale or corn. Simmer rather than boil until the potatoes are cooked. If you are making a creamy vegan chowder, choose the least-sweet milk alternative you have; oat milk or a blend of hemp and cashew milks can work well. If you want to reduce the carbs, try adding finely chopped cauliflower in place of potatoes; the cooking time will be shorter.

4 BLEND

For the best texture, pour the soup through a fine-mesh sieve, reserving all liquid. Carefully whirl up the reserved liquids in a blender on low speed until smooth, then return it to the pot with the strained ingredients. You can also return the liquid to the pot and use an immersion blender before adding the strained ingredients. Finish with cream and a final taste to adjust seasoning—remember that the barest splash of balsamic vinegar or brine from a jar of capers can brighten up the flavor of a rich, salty soup.

Time-saving tip: if you're making a tomato-based Manhattan-style clam chowder, you can skip the blending step; these chowders are meant to have a thinner base.

5 EAT IT ALL UP

Chowder is best when eaten within 2 days—and the potatoes tend to dissolve into mush if the soup is frozen, so it's not a great choice for a double batch for the freezer. Some believe that chowder, like chili, is always better the second day; the potatoes continue to break down and take on flavor.

FLAVOR COMBINATIONS TO TRY

- Russet potatoes, bacon, mussels
- Yukon gold potatoes, caramelized leeks, sliced kale
- Sweet potatoes, wild salmon, sliced chard
- Cauliflower, pancetta, clams

SWEET CORN AND FRESH TARRAGON turn chowder into a meal that's perfectly suited to the very end of summer. Simmering the cobs to make a quick corn broth provides a remarkable amount of sweet-corn essence to the final soup.

Chowder, with both dairy and cubed potatoes, does not freeze well. You can refrigerate leftovers for two days; some believe that chowder is at its finest the day after it's made.

TARRAGON CORN CHOWDER

Makes 4 servings

Shuck the corn, removing as much silk as possible. With a sharp knife, slice the kernels off the cobs and collect them in a broad, shallow bowl with as much liquid as possible; set aside. Trim off the stems and break or cut the cobs in half.

In a large, heavy-bottomed soup pot over medium heat, melt the butter. Add the onion and celery; cook until the onions are soft and translucent, 5 to 7 minutes. Stir in the garlic, bay leaves, tarragon sprigs, and cobs; cook for 2 minutes, until the garlic is soft. Pour in the wine and reduce by half, about 2 minutes. Add the water and milk and bring just to a boil. Promptly reduce the heat to low and gently simmer for 20 minutes. Using tongs or a slotted spoon, carefully remove the bay leaves, tarragon sprigs, and corn cobs.

Add the potatoes, salt, and pepper. Return to a simmer and cook for 10 minutes, until the potatoes are beginning to soften. Stir in the corn kernels and continue to cook until the potatoes are tender, about 5 minutes more. Season to taste with more salt and pepper.

If you want a thinner soup, carefully puree one-third of the soup using a blender until smooth and then return to the pot (or briefly use an immersion blender). Heat through and serve garnished with chopped tarragon.

5 medium ears white or
yellow corn

3 tablespoons unsalted butter

1 medium yellow
onion, chopped

2 ribs celery, finely chopped

3 cloves garlic, minced

2 bay leaves

3 sprigs fresh tarragon, plus
chopped leaves, for garnish

¼ cup dry white wine

2 cups water

2 cups whole milk

1 pound Yukon gold potatoes,
cubed (about 3 cups)

½ teaspoon kosher salt, plus
more as needed

½ teaspoon freshly ground
black pepper, plus more
as needed

1 CUP: 390 CAL., 16G FAT (8G SAT.), 40MG CHOL., 330MG SODIUM,
54G CARB., 3G FIBER, 14G SUGAR, 13G PROTEIN

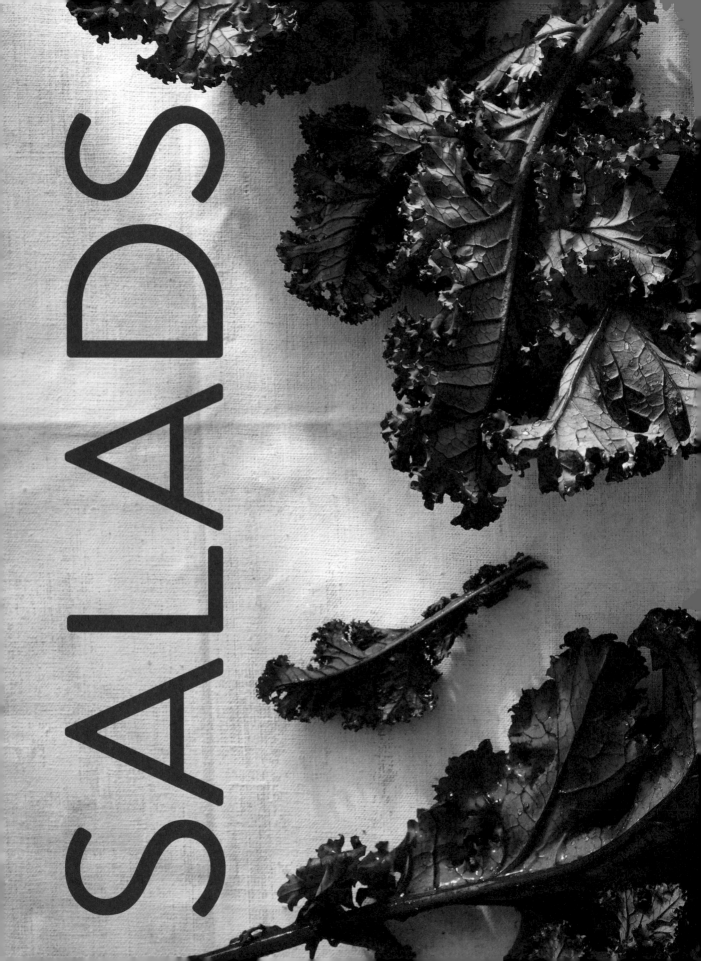

SALADS

IF WE HAD TO DEFINE WHAT WE MEAN BY "SALAD," we'd start by calling it our favorite course. A good salad is seasonal, yes, but can be cold or warm, light or hearty, a meal by itself or a dainty accessory for a five-course spread. It can have fruit, grains, meats, or cheese in addition to vegetables, but vegetables are a definite component. Some ingredients might need cooking, but a handful of them will be raw. Lastly, there will be dressing, perhaps as simple as olive oil, lemon juice, and salt, but enough to be noticed.

The salad course is when certain habits of picky eaters can be witnessed at their most prominent, but it is also a time to discover that formerly distasteful ingredients are your new favorites. Think lentils taste like dirt? Taste Spiced Squash Salad with Lentils and Goat Cheese (page 58) and think again. Certain that endive is inedible? One bite of Endive Salad with Bacon, Blue Cheese, and Pears (page 63) may convince you otherwise. Do the kids act like salad is a crime against humanity? Try them on Blueberry-Nectarine Caprese Salad (page 55) or Apple, Bok Choy, and Carrot Slaw (page 52) and see them grudgingly reconsider.

One of the most helpful things about salads is how well they take to adaptation. Nuts, seeds, and other assorted garnishes can be easily swapped without complicated recipe revisions. A few cups of one whole grain can be traded for your family's favorite. If a recipe mentions that a dish can be served warm or at room temperature, it might still have plenty of appeal served cold.

This is also the chapter where you'll find some of the biggest hits from our deli. Dishes like Emerald City Salad (page 61), California Potato Salad (page 53), and Perfect Protein Salad (page 76) are Seattle classics, and they have topped our list of most requested recipes over the years. Now you can make them whenever the mood strikes.

CORN SALAD IS ONE OF the highlights of summer—its natural sweetness only improves on the grill, and tossing it together with sweet-tart peak-season tomatoes and creamy goat cheese provides just the right balance. Serve it as a side to grilled salmon, steaks, or burgers, or turn it into a Meatless Monday main dish alongside a heap of your favorite dark leafy greens, with wedges of fresh watermelon for dessert. If you want the onion to have a milder flavor, soak it in ice water for fifteen minutes after chopping it; it'll crisp up but taste sweeter.

GRILLED CORN SALAD

with Goat Cheese

Makes 4 to 6 servings

Peel all but the innermost layers of husk from each ear of corn. Remove as much of the silk as possible and gently tuck the remaining thin husk in place around as many of the kernels as possible.

Preheat the grill to high (425 degrees F). Grill the corn until it is charred on all sides and tender, using tongs to turn it every few minutes, for a total cooking time of 12 to 15 minutes. Cool the ears until you can handle them comfortably and remove the husks. With a sharp knife, slice the kernels off the cobs and collect them in a large bowl. Add the tomatoes and onion, and toss gently with tongs to combine.

In a small bowl, whisk together the lime juice, mustard, and garlic. Slowly whisk in the oil until the dressing is emulsified, and season to taste with salt and pepper. Drizzle the dressing over the salad, tossing to combine. Garnish with the cheese, basil, and a little additional pepper. Serve warm or at room temperature.

4 medium ears corn

1 pint grape or cherry
tomatoes, halved

¼ medium red onion,
finely chopped

¼ cup freshly squeezed lime
juice (from 2 large limes)

1 tablespoon Dijon mustard

1 clove garlic, minced

3 tablespoons extra-virgin
olive oil

Kosher salt and freshly ground
black pepper

6 ounces (about ¾ cup) soft
fresh goat cheese

¼ cup chopped fresh basil

⅙ **RECIPE: 270 CAL., 19G FAT (7G SAT.), 45MG CHOL., 360MG SODIUM, 22G CARB., 3G FIBER, 7G SUGAR, 10G PROTEIN**

51

THIS QUICK SLAW CAN SERVE several purposes, whether your goal is picnic fare or a year-round kid-friendly salad. Its crunch and clean flavor make it suited to being served as a topping for grilled chicken or shrimp, while its simplicity (especially if you have a food processor to grate the apple and carrot) makes it easy to toss together as a modern update to the carrot-raisin classic. The baby bok choy might even be acceptable to kids who reject other greens—it's so mild and so very crunchy that it's easy to appreciate.

APPLE, BOK CHOY, AND CARROT SLAW

Makes 4 servings

Cut the baby bok choy in half lengthwise, removing the core and any bruised leafy tops. Rinse each half thoroughly, checking for grit between the layers, then slice it crosswise into thin strips. Rinse in a colander and shake out the water.

In a medium bowl, whisk together the lemon juice, oil, and ginger. Using tongs, gently add the apple, carrot, and bok choy and toss to coat in the dressing. Add the salt and sprinkle lightly with pepper. Toss once more and refrigerate for at least 15 minutes before serving.

¼ RECIPE: 45 CAL., 2G FAT (0G SAT.), 0MG CHOL., 500MG SODIUM, 7G CARB., 1G FIBER, 5G SUGAR, 0G PROTEIN

3 medium heads baby bok choy (about 1 pound)

1½ tablespoons freshly squeezed lemon juice

1½ teaspoons mild-tasting oil, such as sunflower

½-inch knob fresh ginger, peeled and grated

1 medium apple, peeled, cored, and coarsely grated

1 medium carrot, peeled and coarsely grated

1 teaspoon kosher salt

Freshly ground black pepper

THIS POTATO SALAD IS SEVERAL steps more savory than the classic American version because it uses dill pickle relish rather than sweet and Dijon mustard instead of yellow, and gets finished with a sprinkle of briny black olives rather than a sugary dressing with hard-boiled eggs. It's close enough to tradition to satisfy while offering the West Coast preference for salt over sweetness in side dishes. For the final seasoning, you might find yourself adding anywhere from a quarter teaspoon to a full teaspoon of extra salt—the potatoes definitely need it, but the mustard and olives do contribute some.

CALIFORNIA POTATO SALAD PCC Deli Favorite

Makes 8 servings

In a large, deep saucepan over high heat, combine the potatoes with enough water to completely cover them. Bring to a boil and cook until just tender when pierced with a fork, 15 to 20 minutes. Drain and cool to room temperature in a colander or medium bowl.

In a small bowl, whisk together the mayonnaise, mustard, and relish to make the dressing. Season to taste with salt and pepper.

When the potatoes have cooled to room temperature, toss them with the dressing and mash lightly with a wooden spoon or potato masher to combine, retaining as many chunks as you like. Sprinkle on the parsley, onion, celery, and olives, and toss with a wooden spoon to combine. Season to taste with salt and pepper. Keep refrigerated until ready to serve.

2 pounds red potatoes, quartered

¾ cup mayonnaise

1½ teaspoons Dijon mustard

⅓ cup dill pickle relish

Kosher salt and freshly ground black pepper

2 tablespoons coarsely chopped fresh Italian parsley

1 green onion, thinly sliced (both green and white parts)

3 ribs celery, finely chopped

½ cup sliced black olives

⅛ RECIPE: 260 CAL., 18G FAT (1G SAT.), 5MG CHOL., 570MG SODIUM, 21G CARB., 0G FIBER, 0G SUGAR, 3G PROTEIN

PERFECT FOR HOT AUGUST DAYS, this salad takes full advantage of two of Washington State's most beloved midsummer crops: stone fruit and fat, preposterously sweet blueberries. With the fresh, sweet simplicity of the fruit and the creamy, ever-so-slightly salty cheese, it feels like fruit salad should always be like this. It's fine to substitute peaches for the nectarines, although the texture is best if the peaches are peeled.

Fresh mozzarella comes in several sizes. If you can't find *ciliegine*, use the larger *bocconcini* (bite-size) cut in half or *ovoline* (egg-size) diced into one-inch pieces.

BLUEBERRY-NECTARINE CAPRESE SALAD PCC Deli Favorite

Makes 4 servings

In a medium bowl, combine the mozzarella, blueberries, and nectarines. Sprinkle on the basil and lemon zest, and toss gently to combine. Drizzle with the oil and sprinkle with salt, then toss gently a few more times. Season to taste with more salt. Chill in the refrigerator for at least 1 hour before serving.

¼ RECIPE: 300 CAL., 17G FAT (9G SAT.), 55MG CHOL., 650MG SODIUM, 15G CARB., 2G FIBER, 10G SUGAR, 22G PROTEIN

12 ounces *ciliegine* (cherry-size) fresh mozzarella cheese, drained

1 cup fresh blueberries

2 medium nectarines, pitted and thinly sliced

⅓ cup fresh basil, sliced into ribbons

¼ teaspoon freshly grated lemon zest

1 tablespoon extra-virgin olive oil

¼ teaspoon kosher salt, plus more as needed

FORGING ORGANIC PARTNERSHIPS, ONE ACRE AT A TIME

One farm we've worked with for decades is in Zillah, Washington, a small town in the Yakima Valley, on the sunnier side of the state. We began purchasing organic nectarines and cherries from LaPierre Farms in 1989, and it added blueberry bushes to the property in 2009. In 2010, the LaPierre family (Mark, Marni, Garrett, and Lauren) handpicked the entire blueberry harvest and packed it into the back of a rented refrigerated truck to drive over the Cascade Mountains to us. We bought the whole crop that first year and are still doing so; these days, it's big enough that about half the annual harvest is frozen immediately, so your homemade smoothies (and the blueberry muffins we bake year-round) can taste just like peak season for a full 12 months.

SPICY SPANISH CHORIZO AND SWEET, deep-red roasted cherries—it's a match made in salad heaven. The flavor of dark-red cherries such as Lapins or Bings is better suited to this dish than that of mild Rainier cherries, which can be overwhelmed by the chorizo. One of the practical benefits of this salad is how good it is served either warm or cool. When fresh Pacific Northwest cherries are being harvested, the local weather can shift from sunshine to gloom at a moment's notice, and the salad's flexibility is appreciated by anyone in a region subject to June storms.

ROASTED CHERRY, CHORIZO, AND ORZO SALAD

Makes 6 servings

Bring a large pot of salted water to a boil and cook the orzo according to the package directions, until al dente (typically 7 to 9 minutes). Drain, set aside, and let cool to room temperature.

Preheat the oven to 375 degrees F. On a rimmed baking sheet, toss the cherries with about 1 tablespoon of the oil and season to taste with salt and pepper. Roast for 15 to 20 minutes, until tender and slightly charred. Set aside.

In a medium skillet over medium heat, add about 1 tablespoon of the oil, just enough to barely coat the bottom of the pan. Stirring regularly to prevent burning, fry the chorizo for about 4 minutes, until crisp. Drain on paper towels and set aside.

In a small bowl, whisk to combine the vinegar, mustard, and garlic. Slowly whisk in the remaining 6 tablespoons oil and season to taste with salt and pepper.

In a serving bowl or on a platter, combine the orzo, roasted cherries, chorizo, and arugula, and gently toss together with the dressing. Top with the Manchego and pine nuts. Serve at room temperature or refrigerate for several hours and serve chilled.

Kosher salt

1 pound orzo pasta

8 ounces fresh sweet cherries, pitted

7 to 8 tablespoons extra-virgin olive oil

Freshly ground black pepper

6 ounces cured Spanish chorizo or salami, thinly sliced

¼ cup sherry vinegar

2 tablespoons Dijon mustard

1 clove garlic, minced

5 cups baby arugula (about 5 ounces)

¾ ounce (about ¼ cup) shaved Manchego cheese

3 tablespoons toasted pine nuts (optional)

⅙ RECIPE: 500 CAL., 18G FAT (4G SAT.), 15MG CHOL., 590MG SODIUM, 65G CARB., 1G FIBER, 9G SUGAR, 16G PROTEIN

USING FROZEN SQUASH CUBES MINIMIZES the prep time for this salad without changing the time in the oven—and conveniently, the squash and lentils need almost exactly the same amount of time to cook. This salad makes a beautiful, colorful side alongside roast chicken, but it's hearty enough to serve as a great vegetarian entrée too. Because it's served at room temperature, it's also a convenient dish to bring to friends or family for part of a holiday menu that features ham or smoked turkey.

SPICED SQUASH SALAD

with Lentils and Goat Cheese

Makes 4 servings

Preheat the oven to 400 degrees F. Put a rimmed baking sheet in the oven to preheat as well.

In a medium bowl, toss the squash cubes with 2 tablespoons of the oil, the cumin, paprika, and salt. Carefully arrange them in a single layer on the preheated baking sheet and roast for 25 minutes; they will still be fairly wet, but the side sitting on the pan will have a darker color. Flip the pieces so the light sides are on the bottom and roast for an additional 10 to 15 minutes, until soft with caramelized edges. Cool to room temperature.

Meanwhile, in a small bowl, cover the lentils with cold water and soak for 10 minutes, then drain. In a medium saucepan over medium-high heat, cook the soaked lentils in plenty of boiling salted water until tender but firm, 25 to 30 minutes. Rinse in cold water, drain, and cool to room temperature.

Combine the lentils, arugula, mint, and half the cheese in a large bowl. Drizzle on the remaining 1 tablespoon oil and the vinegar and toss gently to distribute the dressing evenly. Sprinkle the squash and remaining cheese on top, seasoning with salt, pepper, and additional vinegar to taste. Serve at room temperature.

5 cups peeled, seeded, and cubed butternut squash (or 2 [10-ounce] bags frozen butternut squash cubes)

3 tablespoons extra-virgin olive oil, divided

1 teaspoon ground cumin

1 teaspoon sweet Spanish paprika

¾ teaspoon kosher salt, plus more as needed

¾ cup green lentils, rinsed

4 cups baby arugula (about 4 ounces)

2 tablespoons thinly sliced fresh mint

5 ounces (about ⅔ cup) soft fresh goat cheese, divided

1 tablespoon white wine vinegar, plus more as needed

Freshly ground black pepper

¼ RECIPE: 380 CAL., 19G FAT (7G SAT.), 15MG CHOL., 700 SODIUM, 42G CARB., 9G FIBER, 5G SUGAR, 16G PROTEIN

OUR DELI'S MOST ICONIC SALAD is so beloved it was even mentioned as part of an exhibit on Seattle's food history at the Museum of History and Industry in 2016. It's colorful and highly nutritious thanks to its wide range of leafy greens, bell peppers, fresh herbs, and wild rice. It can be served year-round and has big pops of lemony flavor and plenty of crunch; you can even make this salad up to four days ahead and refrigerate it until ready to serve.

This recipe can be easily modified if you prefer to use one whole bell pepper of a single color or stick with only chard or kale rather than combining the two.

EMERALD CITY SALAD PCC Deli Favorite

Makes 8 servings

In a medium saucepan over high heat, bring the water to a boil. Season generously with salt and stir in the rice. Stirring occasionally, return the water to a boil, cover, and reduce the heat to low. Simmer for 60 to 65 minutes, until the water is absorbed and the rice is cooked. Remove from the heat, take off the lid, and cool to room temperature.

In a small bowl, whisk together the oil, lemon juice, and garlic, and season to taste with salt and pepper.

Transfer the cooled rice to a large serving bowl and toss with the dressing.

Remove the tough stems from the kale and chard and cut the leaves into thin ribbons. Collect the ribbons into a pile and cut across them, so you have very small pieces of the leaves, about ½-inch squares. In a medium bowl, combine the greens with the peppers, fennel, onions, and parsley. (If you're making the dish in advance, you can pack this mixture into a sealed airtight container).

Just before serving, combine the dressed wild rice with the vegetables. Use tongs to mix well. Serve chilled or at room temperature.

3 cups water

Kosher salt

1 cup wild rice

½ cup extra-virgin olive oil

½ cup freshly squeezed lemon juice (from 1½ medium lemons)

1 clove garlic, minced

Freshly ground black pepper

½ bunch Lacinato kale

½ bunch chard

½ medium red bell pepper, diced

½ medium yellow bell pepper, diced

½ medium fennel bulb, cored and thinly sliced

1 bunch green onions, thinly sliced (both green and white parts)

½ cup chopped fresh Italian parsley

⅛ RECIPE: 220 CAL., 14G FAT (2G SAT.), 0MG CHOL., 190MG SODIUM, 21G CARB., 3G FIBER, 2G SUGAR, 4G PROTEIN

THIS MORE FORMAL SALAD IS just right for a winter dinner party thanks to its swanky accessories, but if you prefer, you can serve it family style in one big bowl rather than dividing it among individual plates. A red-skinned pear will add appealing color to the blend of pistachios, blue cheese, and bacon, while the pleasantly bitter greens offer just the right flavor contrast.

While Roquefort is a classic cheese pairing with pears, it's also one of the strongest blue cheeses around. If you prefer something milder, look for Gorgonzola dolce or Bleu d'Auvergne.

ENDIVE SALAD WITH BACON, BLUE CHEESE, AND PEARS

Makes 6 servings

In a large bowl, combine the vinegar, mustard, honey, shallots, and garlic. Let sit for 15 minutes to soften the shallots and garlic and to infuse their flavor into the vinegar. Slowly whisk in the oil until the dressing is emulsified. Season to taste with salt and pepper.

Add the endive and arugula to the dressing and toss gently with tongs to coat. Divide the salad among six plates and sprinkle each with bacon, blue cheese, pistachios, and pears.

⅙ RECIPE: 230 CAL., 16G FAT (3.5G SAT.), 15MG CHOL., 490MG SODIUM, 17G CARB., 7G FIBER, 7G SUGAR, 9G PROTEIN

3 tablespoons sherry or apple cider vinegar

2 tablespoons Dijon mustard

1 tablespoon honey

1 tablespoon minced shallots

1 clove garlic, minced

3 tablespoons extra-virgin olive oil

Kosher salt and freshly ground black pepper

2 medium heads Belgian endive, cored and thinly sliced

5 cups baby arugula (about 5 ounces)

3 strips cooked bacon, crumbled

2 ounces (¼ cup) crumbled blue cheese

¼ cup shelled pistachios

1 medium pear, halved, cored, and thinly sliced

PICK THE PERFECT PEAR

While pears are often lumped in with apples because they come into season in the fall, it's better to think of them as something more like winter peaches. The best pears are fairly soft and can bruise easily, and some varieties are so juicy it might be easiest to push up your sleeves and eat them over the sink. All pears are very high in fiber and offer numerous antioxidants, particularly flavonols.

Anjou: Available in both red- and green-skinned varieties, Anjou are a great choice for salads or for eating out of hand. Even at their ripest, their fruit maintains a little firmness that makes them easy to slice, and while they're juicy, it won't run all over the plate. The red-skinned variety are particularly pretty arranged on a salad or cheese plate.

Asian: While there are a large number of cultivars that are Asian pears, only one is commonly found across the United States, the 20th Century, which is one of the green pear group, rather than the russet pear group. This pear is meant to be crisp, firm, and juicy—as juicy as a European pear, with a snappy-light texture that's half apple and half watermelon—and it is best eaten fresh or in salads. If you're ever lucky enough to spot

a russet Asian pear, its thick brown skin is a dull disguise for dense, creamy fruit with sometimes surprisingly buttery caramel-rum flavors.

Bartlett: Sweet, soft, and a little grainy, Bartletts are the most common variety and the one that's available canned as well as fresh. When perfectly ripe, they are so juicy that they're better to eat out of hand than use in a salad.

Bosc: With a firmness that makes them well suited to cooking, Boscs have a thick olive-brown skin and distinctively narrow neck. They keep their shape well in desserts, whether they're peeled and poached whole or diced and used in pie or crisp. Their less sweet, almost musky flavor is appealing in salads, but they're a little more pleasant to eat peeled, which makes for an extra step.

Comice: An almost round, fat pear with red and green stripes, the Comice is the most peach-like of all thanks to its buttery texture and sweet juice. Because of its popularity in gift baskets and availability around the holidays, it's sometimes called the "Christmas pear." While it is as juicy as a Bartlett, its texture keeps it well suited for salads, as well as eating out of hand or as part of a cheese plate.

IF YOU THINK RAW BEETS in a salad sound odd, this combination may well surprise you—the citrus brightens up that strong earthy flavor of beets in a light and appealing way. You can also choose to use either Chioggia or golden beets for a sweet, mild crunch. Try serving this alongside roasted or grilled chicken, like Spicy Chicken Thighs (page 117), or before the rich Fennel and Basil Lasagne (page 94).

CITRUS-BEET SLAW

Makes 4 servings

SALADS

Using a fine grater, grate 1 teaspoon zest from one of the oranges. Juice two of them. Peel, seed, and dice the remaining orange.

In a small bowl, combine the orange juice and zest, oil, and lemon juice and zest. Whisk in the salt and set aside.

In a salad bowl, combine the diced oranges with the shredded beets. Drizzle with the dressing, cover, and refrigerate for 30 minutes, tossing at least twice as it chills. Season to taste with more salt. Sprinkle with the parsley and serve.

3 medium oranges

2 teaspoons extra-virgin olive oil

2 tablespoons freshly squeezed lemon juice

½ teaspoon freshly grated lemon zest

¼ teaspoon kosher salt, plus more as needed

4 medium beets (about 1 pound), peeled and shredded

Fresh Italian parsley, chopped, for garnish (optional)

¼ RECIPE: 120 CAL., 2.5G FAT (0G SAT.), 0MG CHOL., 180MG SODIUM, 23G CARB., 5G FIBER, 16G SUGAR, 2G PROTEIN

MEET THE BEETS

Related to spinach, chard, and (more surprisingly) quinoa, beets can be found in young bunches with their edible tops still attached, or purchased in a form more like rutabagas, when they're larger than a fist and have had their tops cut off. Red beets are the most common, but beets are also available in a milder-tasting golden-orange color as well as a pink-and-white-striped variety.

In all varieties, betalains are found—these are the nitrogen-packed, water-soluble pigments that give beets their rich color. The betalains that give beets their deep-red or purple color are called betacyanins; they are also found in bright-red to pink foods like amaranth, prickly pear fruits, rhubarb, and red chard. Yellow beets (and yellow chard) have a closely related set of betalains called betaxanthins. Both groups of betalains have antioxidant and anti-inflammatory properties that are seemingly quite different from carotenoid antioxidants.

WITH A DEEP, EARTHY FLAVOR from both beets and walnuts, this salad is a natural companion to beef steaks and rib roasts. It also holds its own alongside equally earthy pulses, like those in Lentil and White Bean Stew (page 38). You can substitute extra-virgin olive oil for the walnut oil here if you like, although the nutty flavor will be much milder. As it is, this salad is vegan friendly; if that isn't a concern for your household or guests, a sprinkle of soft goat cheese is a tasty addition.

WALNUT-BEET SALAD PCC Deli Favorite

Makes 6 to 8 servings

In a large saucepan over high heat, put the beets and cover them generously with cold water. Bring to a boil, and boil the beets until they can be easily pierced with a fork, 25 to 45 minutes depending on the size of the beets. Drain. When the beets are just cool enough to handle but still warm, cut off the root and stem ends and slip off the skins under cool running water. Chill the peeled beets in the refrigerator for several hours or overnight.

Preheat the oven to 350 degrees F. Spread the walnuts in a single layer on a baking sheet and toast for 4 to 5 minutes, until fragrant. Cool the toasted walnuts to room temperature, then roughly chop them.

In a small bowl, whisk together the vinegar, mustard, salt, pepper, and oil until the mixture is smooth.

Cut the cooled peeled beets into 1-inch wedges and put them in a serving bowl. Use tongs to toss them with the dressing. Garnish with the green and red onions and toasted walnuts, then toss gently to combine.

3 pounds beets

½ cup raw walnuts

¼ cup balsamic vinegar

2 teaspoons Dijon mustard

½ teaspoon kosher salt

½ teaspoon freshly ground black pepper

¼ cup walnut oil

¾ bunch green onions, thinly sliced (green and light-green parts only)

¼ small red onion, thinly sliced

⅛ RECIPE: 220 CAL., 14G FAT (1.5G SAT.), 0MG CHOL., 310MG SODIUM, 22G CARB., 6G FIBER, 15G SUGAR, 5G PROTEIN

THIS STURDY SALAD HOLDS UP wonderfully as part of a buffet or cookout because unlike more tender greens or pasta, the kale and quinoa won't continue to absorb the dressing and become soggy. Swap out the sunflower seeds if you like—pine nuts, pumpkin seeds, or sliced almonds work just as well to supply a bit of crunch. If the salad won't be sitting at room temperature for very long, a little sprinkle of feta is a nice touch too. The tahini in the dressing makes the dish a good choice alongside lamb burgers, gyros, or souvlaki.

KALE AND QUINOA SALAD

with Lemon-Garlic Dressing

Makes 6 servings

In a medium saucepan over high heat, combine the quinoa, broth, and a pinch of salt. Bring to a boil, cover, and reduce the heat to low. Simmer, without stirring, until all the liquid is absorbed, about 15 minutes. Remove from the heat and let sit, covered, for 10 additional minutes, until the grains are tender. Fluff the grains with a fork.

In a large bowl, whisk together the tahini, oil, vinegar, sugar, hot sauce, garlic, lemon zest and juice, and salt and pepper to taste. Stir in the kale; gently mix with a wooden spoon or massage with your hands for 1 to 2 minutes so that the kale breaks down and softens slightly. Add the onion, sunflower seeds, parsley, and quinoa; mix to combine.

⅙ RECIPE: 340 CAL., 20G FAT (2.5G SAT.), 0MG CHOL., 260MG SODIUM, 33G CARB., 5G FIBER, 4G SUGAR, 10G PROTEIN

1 cup quinoa, rinsed and drained

2 cups vegetable broth

Pinch of kosher salt, plus more as needed

¼ cup tahini

3 tablespoons extra-virgin olive oil

2 tablespoons apple cider vinegar

1 teaspoon granulated sugar

1 teaspoon hot sauce (optional)

2 cloves garlic, minced

2 medium lemons, freshly zested and juiced

Freshly ground black pepper

1 bunch Lacinato kale, tough stems removed and leaves sliced into ribbons

½ small red onion, finely chopped

½ cup sunflower seeds

¼ cup chopped fresh Italian parsley

ASIDE FROM THE POTENTIAL HEALTH benefits of using nutrient-dense greens like kale and chard rather than the Caesar's classic romaine lettuce, there's a decided benefit when it comes to food waste: kale and chard stay fresh for a noticeably longer time both before and after you make this salad. This is a salad you can make a full day ahead and have it seem like it was prepared just before it hit the table.

HEARTY GREENS CAESAR PCC Deli Favorite

Makes 4 servings

In a large salad bowl, combine the chard and kale.

Toss the greens with the dressing and half the cheese. Sprinkle the remaining cheese over the top to garnish.

½ bunch chard, stemmed and cut into 1-inch pieces

½ bunch Lacinato kale, tough stems removed, cut into 1-inch pieces

2 tablespoons Caesar Dressing (recipe follows)

¾ ounce (about ¼ cup) shredded Parmesan cheese

¼ RECIPE: 90 CAL., 6G FAT (1G SAT.), 5MG CHOL., 240MG SODIUM, 5G CARB., 2G FIBER, 1G SUGAR, 4G PROTEIN

BECAUSE THE MAYONNAISE AND WORCESTERSHIRE sauce both have salt, and the salad is dressed with additional Parmesan, there's no need to add salt to the dressing. The extra dressing can be refrigerated for up to two weeks. Whisk or shake to reemulsify it as needed once it's been in the refrigerator; the pepper might sink to the bottom even if the dressing retains its emulsion. Aside from using it as part of a Caesar salad, try tossing it with grilled asparagus, substituting it as the dressing for Roasted Brussels Sprouts Caesar (page 131), or smearing it on cold cuts in a sandwich.

Caesar Dressing

Makes about ¾ cup

In a blender or the bowl of a food processor, combine the mayonnaise, lemon juice, Worcestershire, garlic, vinegar, mustard, and pepper. Blend briefly on medium speed or pulse several times to combine.

With the motor running on low, slowly add the oil and blend until the dressing is emulsified.

- ½ cup mayonnaise
- 2 tablespoons freshly squeezed lemon juice
- 1 tablespoon Worcestershire sauce
- 2 cloves garlic, minced
- 1½ teaspoons sherry vinegar
- ¾ teaspoon Dijon mustard
- ¾ teaspoon freshly ground black pepper
- ¼ cup extra-virgin olive oil

2 TABLESPOONS: 220 CAL., 24G FAT (2G SAT.), 5MG CHOL., 160MG SODIUM, 1G CARB., 0G FIBER, 0G SUGAR, 0G PROTEIN

THE GREATEST GREENS

Dark-green vegetables like kale and chard are "nutrient-dense" foods—low in calories but full of vitamins, minerals, and other phytonutrients. Experts estimate that a single serving of greens provides more than 100 phytochemicals. The USDA recommends eating at least 2 cups a week.

Kale, collards, broccoli, bok choy, and turnip and mustard greens are wonderful nondairy sources of calcium and are absorbed well by the body. One serving contains between 75 and 250 milligrams of calcium. Other greens, such as spinach, chard, and beet greens, are less effective sources of calcium when eaten raw. While their calcium content is high, they also contain higher amounts of oxalic acid, which interferes with our absorption of calcium. Cooking them will greatly reduce the oxalic acid.

Carotenoids are better absorbed by the presence of fat. So, either use a dressing made from a healthy fat such as olive oil, or add some avocado or nuts, which have their own built-in sources of healthy fats.

IT TAKES JUST THIRTY MINUTES (and most of that time is sitting with your feet up) to turn onions into a quick pickle. In this case, the pickling liquid even does double duty as the dressing for this cool, summery grain salad. If you prefer, substitute a different cooked and cooled grain for the brown rice—quinoa, spelt berries, and barley all have a light texture that suits the juicy peaches well. Whichever grain you choose, this salad pairs perfectly with refreshing Sangria Blanca (page 237).

PEACH AND PICKLED ONION SALAD

with Brown Rice

Makes 4 to 6 servings

In a small bowl, combine the onion and garlic and set aside.

In a small saucepan over medium-high heat, combine the salt, vinegar, and sugar. Bring to a boil, stirring to dissolve the sugar. Pour the pickling liquid over the onion and garlic and let stand for 30 minutes. Drain, reserving the liquid.

In a large bowl, combine the pickled onion, peaches, feta, oil, tarragon, and 3 tablespoons of the pickling liquid. Season to taste with salt and pepper. Fold in the brown rice and arugula. Drizzle with additional pickling liquid to taste.

⅕ RECIPE: 330 CAL., 16G FAT (4G SAT.), 10MG CHOL., 830MG SODIUM, 40G CARB., 4G FIBER, 9G SUGAR, 9G PROTEIN

½ medium red onion, thinly sliced

1 clove garlic

1 teaspoon kosher salt, plus more as needed

¾ cup champagne vinegar

1 tablespoon packed light brown sugar, or to taste

2 medium peaches, pitted and sliced

4 ounces (¾ cup) feta cheese, crumbled

¼ cup extra-virgin olive oil

1 tablespoon chopped fresh tarragon

Freshly ground black pepper

3 cups cooked brown rice

5 cups baby arugula or watercress, or a combination (about 5 ounces)

FREEZING COOKED RICE AND OTHER GRAINS

Freezing portions of cooked wild rice, quinoa, brown or white rice, barley, emmer farro, or spelt is a substantial time-saver. Cook them to your preferred degree of doneness and with any basic seasonings you typically include, like salt, broth, butter, or olive oil. Cool and use a 1- or 2-cup measure to divide the grains between freezer tubs. To use, don't thaw them overnight in the refrigerator—this can create overly soft, mushy grains. Either thaw them on the counter as you prepare the rest of the meal or pop them briefly into the microwave.

THE NAME FOR THIS SALAD comes from the combination of a whole grain (spelt) and a bean (chickpeas) that creates a perfect blend of all nine essential amino acids. It's been a PCC Deli classic for well over a decade, and it seems like each one of its fans has a slightly different way of serving it. Because of its robust protein content, it takes very little to turn it into a complete meal—a few Roasted Cherry Tomatoes (page 187) are a sweet companion, or serve it with Avocado Toast with Goat Cheese and Radishes (page 195). If you can, soaking the spelt berries overnight before you cook them will speed up the cooking time the next day, but it's not an absolute requirement. Even two hours of soaking can noticeably reduce their cooking time.

PERFECT PROTEIN SALAD PCC Deli Favorite

Makes 8 servings

In a medium saucepan over high heat, bring the water to a rolling boil. Add the spelt, stir, cover, and reduce the heat to low. Simmer for about 1 hour, until the grains are pleasantly chewy; if the grains were soaked overnight, they will cook in 40 to 45 minutes. Drain any excess water from the spelt, rinse, and cool to room temperature.

While the spelt is cooling, make the dressing. In a small bowl, whisk together the mayonnaise, lemon juice, vinegar, dill, salt, basil, and garlic. Cover and keep it chilled until you are ready to dress the salad.

In a large salad bowl, mix together the spelt, chickpeas, cucumber, bell pepper, celery, carrot, red onion, green onion, and parsley.

Pour the dressing over the salad and toss well with a wooden spoon or broad spatula. Cover and chill in the refrigerator for at least 2 hours before serving. Serve chilled.

⅛ RECIPE: 260 CAL., 9G FAT (0G SAT.), 5MG CHOL., 340MG SODIUM, 36G CARB., 7G FIBER, 3G SUGAR, 9G PROTEIN

3 cups water

1 cup spelt berries

⅓ cup mayonnaise

2 tablespoons freshly squeezed lemon juice

2 tablespoons apple cider vinegar

1 teaspoon dried dill

1 teaspoon kosher salt

1 teaspoon dried basil

1 clove garlic, minced

2 (15-ounce) cans chickpeas, drained

1 small English cucumber, peeled, seeded, and diced

1 medium green bell pepper, diced

3 ribs celery, diced

1 medium carrot, peeled and diced

¼ medium red onion, diced

½ bunch green onions, thinly sliced (both green and white parts)

⅓ bunch fresh Italian parsley, chopped

WHAT'S SO PERFECT ABOUT PROTEIN?

The United Nations declared 2016 the "International Year of Pulses" to recognize the role of beans and peas in sustainable agriculture and healthy diets. Pulses—which include lentils, chickpeas, split peas, and a wide assortment of beans—are all excellent sources of protein.

Each day, we all should get eight grams of protein per 20 pounds of body weight; so if you weigh 160 pounds, you need about 64 grams of protein each day. Our protein requirement goes up the more we exercise, and it's helpful to consume some protein right after a workout to prevent the breakdown of muscle. Older adults need to consume even more protein each day to prevent normal, age-related muscle loss. When you consume more protein than your body requires, it is converted into either glucose or fat for energy or storage.

We once thought we needed to combine beans with grains at each meal to create a perfect protein, but now we know we need only to get these over the course of the day, not necessarily together in a meal.

It's actually best to get a little bit of protein at each meal, including snacks, rather than try to eat your total daily grams in one meal. Protein helps keep you feeling full and helps keep blood sugar levels balanced, but it's needed throughout the day to support the body's requirement for amino acids.

THIS SALAD OFFERS IMPOSSIBLY BIG flavor from pulling together a few simple components. The preserved lemon is a pure hit of citrus intensity that sets off the briny beauty of white anchovies and meaty Castelvetrano olives. The fennel and Bibb lettuce soften things with their sweetness, and red onion adds a whiff of gentle heat. The result is the sort of salad that impresses your most challenging gastronome friends while not being remotely difficult to prepare. Try making your own Quick Pickled Lemons (page 80) or pick up a jar of preserved lemons.

PRESERVED LEMON AND ANCHOVIES

with Fennel

Makes 4 servings

In a small bowl, whisk together half the preserved lemon, the vinegar, the mustard, and the garlic. Drizzle in the oil, whisking constantly until the dressing is emulsified. Season to taste with salt and pepper.

Arrange the lettuce on a large serving platter. Scatter with the fennel, onion, anchovies, remaining preserved lemon, and olives. Drizzle with a small amount of dressing and sprinkle with Parmesan; serve the remaining dressing on the side.

¼ RECIPE: 280 CAL., 25G FAT (4G SAT.), 20MG CHOL., 1050MG SODIUM, 7G CARB., 2G FIBER, 3G SUGAR, 9G PROTEIN

¼ cup Quick Pickled Lemons (recipe follows), or ½ preserved lemon, finely chopped, divided

2 tablespoons white wine vinegar

1 tablespoon Dijon mustard

1 clove garlic, minced

6 tablespoons extra-virgin olive oil

Kosher salt and freshly ground black pepper

5 ounces Bibb or romaine lettuce, chopped

½ large fennel bulb, cored and thinly sliced

½ small red onion, thinly sliced

3 ounces white anchovy fillets

¼ cup pitted Castelvetrano olives, sliced

¾ ounce (¼ cup) shaved Parmesan cheese

THIS QUICK PICKLE IS DIFFERENT FROM MOST: the lemon pieces are pickled in their own highly acidic juice, with just a little salt and sugar to help out the process. Aside from using them in Preserved Lemon and Anchovies with Fennel (page 79), this strongly flavored condiment is wonderful on grilled lamb or lamb burgers, and is welcome alongside simple green salads or Slow-Roasted Salmon (page 97).

Quick Pickled Lemons

Makes 6 servings

In a small bowl, mix together the sugar, salt, and saffron threads. Using a sturdy spoon and a firm hand, add the diced lemons and their juices to the bowl, and macerate until the sugar mixture is evenly distributed. Transfer to a sterilized jar (see note) and let sit for 4 hours at room temperature.

Put the jar in the refrigerator to let rest overnight. The lemons will be ready to use the following day and will keep for up to 2 weeks in the refrigerator.

NOTE: To sterilize your jar, wash the jar, band, and lid in hot, soapy water. Place the jar in a large pot and completely cover with water. Bring to a boil over high heat, and then boil for 10 minutes. Turn off the heat and leave in the hot water for up to 1 hour before filling.

1 tablespoon granulated sugar
½ teaspoon kosher salt
2 to 3 threads saffron
1 large lemon, diced, including peel and retaining juice

⅙ RECIPE: 10 CAL., 0G FAT (0G SAT.), 0MG CHOL., 190MG SODIUM, 3G CARB., 0G FIBER, 2G SUGAR, 0G PROTEIN

LEARN TO LOVE ANCHOVIES

Canned seafood is a nutritious protein choice to stock in your pantry. In addition to being a good value, it has a long shelf life and waits patiently to be cracked open when you're short on time. All varieties are packed with protein and nutrients, including omega-3s and calcium. Anchovies, sardines, wild salmon, albacore, and herring have the highest amounts of healthy fats.

If you're new to anchovies and are skeptical of the flavor based on your dislike of them on pizza, go slow. Start with half of a fillet in the dressing of the Hearty Greens Caesar (page 72) or mixed into an olive tapenade to spread on a sandwich. Once you've come to appreciate their flavor, try a whole fillet in your favorite tomato pasta sauce. Used thoughtfully, almost everyone can learn to love them.

A BRIEF MARINADE SOFTENS THE bell peppers while the briny olives, feta, and artichoke hearts create a distinctly Mediterranean profile in this salad, even though its greens are the cold-hardy, sturdy Lacinato kale and red chard. With such strong flavors, it will make simple grilled halibut or chicken skewers more interesting; add pita or a lemony rice pilaf and a bottle of Vinho Verde, and you've got a meal that's worthy of Santorini.

ARTICHOKE AND GREENS SALAD PCC Deli Favorite

Makes 4 servings

In a large bowl, whisk together the vinegar, garlic, black pepper, and oil until smooth. Toss the artichokes, olives, and bell peppers with the dressing. Cover and marinate this mixture for at least 1 hour before adding other ingredients; it can marinate for as long as overnight.

Just before serving, use tongs to toss in the onion, kale, and chard. Mix well and garnish with the parsley and feta.

¼ RECIPE: 210 CAL., 15G FAT (5G SAT.), 25MG CHOL., 680MG SODIUM, 13G CARB., 3G FIBER, 5G SUGAR, 7G PROTEIN

2 tablespoons white wine vinegar

1 clove garlic, minced

1 teaspoon freshly ground black pepper

2 tablespoons extra-virgin olive oil

1 cup marinated artichoke hearts, drained and chopped

⅓ cup pitted kalamata olives, rinsed

1 medium red bell pepper, diced

½ medium green bell pepper, diced

¼ medium red onion, diced

4 leaves Lacinato kale, tough stems removed, chopped into 1-inch pieces

4 leaves chard, stemmed and chopped into 1-inch pieces

2 tablespoons chopped fresh Italian parsley, for garnish

4 ounces (¾ cup) feta cheese, crumbled, for garnish

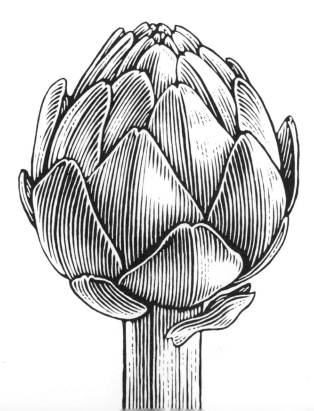

THOUGH A PAPAYA'S EXTERIOR MAY be green when it's either ripe or unripe, the name "green papaya" specifically refers to an unripe papaya. It is the same fruit as the creamy, deep-orange, very low-acid papaya that's a popular part of tropical breakfasts. Picked before they've ripened, green papaya are crisp and mild, the perfect backdrop for an intense dressing that mixes lime juice, fish sauce, and chilies. When green papaya is not available, substitute shredded jicama, green cabbage, or small, firm zucchini.

SHREDDED SEASONAL VEGETABLES

with Lime-Peanut Dressing (Som Tum)

Makes 4 servings

Using a mortar and pestle or a blender on low speed, crush the garlic, chili, sugar, and 1 tablespoon of the peanuts together until a paste forms. Stir in the fish sauce and lime juice, using a circular motion with a mortar or low speed with a blender, until it becomes a smooth dressing.

In a salad bowl, combine the remaining 3 tablespoons peanuts, tomatoes, beans, papaya, and chopped lime. Pour the dressing over the salad and gently mix them together, using tongs or by hand, until the salad is well coated with the dressing. Serve immediately.

¼ RECIPE: 150 CAL., 4.5G FAT (.5G SAT.), 0MG CHOL., 720MG SODIUM, 26G CARB., 3G FIBER, 14G SUGAR, 4G PROTEIN

3 cloves garlic, peeled

1 small serrano chili, or 3 small Thai chilies

1½ to 2 tablespoons packed light brown sugar

4 tablespoons dry-roasted salted peanuts, divided

2 tablespoons fish sauce

3 tablespoons freshly squeezed lime juice

5 medium cherry tomatoes, halved

½ cup green beans, trimmed and cut into 1-inch pieces

2 cups shredded green papaya (see headnote) or seasonal vegetables

1 tablespoon finely chopped lime, seeded, with zest

FLAVOR IN FIVE

VINAIGRETTE

Making your own vinaigrette is fast, requires minimal kitchen equipment, and allows for all sorts of creativity in coming up with your own flavor combinations. It can cost a lot less than buying prepared salad dressings, particularly if you rely on oils, vinegars, and aromatics that you have on hand. If your pantry or refrigerator is packed with an array of vinegars and oils, making your own vinaigrettes will help you use them up (you don't want any of those delicious and pricey nut oils going bad)!

Once you have a vinaigrette, don't limit its use to dressing a basic mix of salad greens. Drizzle it on steamed potatoes for a warm potato salad, or toss it with pasta and grilled seasonal vegetables for a quick meal. Swirl some into the pan at the last minute the next time you cook a fish fillet, or brush it on bread instead of plain olive oil. This last suggestion works wonders when you make crostini too.

1 DO THE MATH TO MAKE THE RIGHT SIZE BATCH

The basic ratio is three parts oil (fat) to one part vinegar (acid). If you prefer a tangier dressing, add more vinegar. If you're seeking creamier, add more oil. By following the ratio, you can use teaspoons to make a small amount of dressing for a single salad or a big bottle for a crowd—and ideally, cut down on food waste.

2 SEASON

A dab of stone-ground mustard or Dijon are classics in French vinaigrettes and will help to make a creamy, stable emulsion. Minced shallots, garlic, green onions, or chives are equally versatile. Chopped fresh herbs can be plucked from the garden, or use whatever you have on hand in the refrigerator. Poppy or sesame seeds give mild flavor and great crunch, while a dollop of honey or sprinkle of brown sugar is great for salads with lots of fruit. Dried herbs and spices can be combined to mimic your favorite prepared dressing and don't impact the shelf life of your vinaigrette the same way that fresh herbs do.

3   WHISK AWAY

Add your chosen vinegar to the aromatics and whisk to blend. Make sure to season generously with kosher salt and freshly ground black pepper at this stage; a little salt does absolute wonders for leafy green salads of all kinds.

4   MAKE AN EMULSION

Add the oil in a slow, steady stream, whisking until the mixture is emulsified and thick. Alternatively, you can add all your ingredients to a jar with a tight-fitting lid and simply shake your vinaigrette into creation. If you have a small empty olive-oil bottle around, it is a great size for dressing, and the plastic insert will help when it comes time to drizzle your dressing on a salad.

5   WRAP IT UP

Vinaigrette will keep in the refrigerator for up to a week, longer if it doesn't have fresh herbs. The vinegar and oil will separate after a few minutes; shake or whisk to recombine. If the oil has solidified (or gotten thick enough to be cloudy), bring the dressing to room temperature before shaking.

FLAVOR COMBINATIONS TO TRY

- Garlic, Dijon mustard, red wine vinegar, olive oil
- Shallots, fresh tarragon, Dijon mustard, white wine vinegar, olive oil
- Ground ginger, tamari, toasted sesame oil, rice vinegar, peanut oil
- Maple syrup, stone-ground mustard, cider vinegar, hazelnut oil
- Muddled raspberries, honey, champagne vinegar, avocado oil, poppy seeds

THIS SALAD SHOWS YOU JUST how seasonal specific citrus fruits can be. These two special oranges are available from right around New Year's to the end of January. If you can find one but not the other, try substituting other special varieties like clementines or tangelos. Cara Caras are the hardest to find a perfect substitute for, as they have a surprising and quite noticeable flavor of raspberries. Nonetheless, the sweet chili–sesame will be enjoyable on any two sweet orange varieties you can find.

CARA CARA AND BLOOD ORANGE SALAD

with Sweet Chili–Sesame Vinaigrette

Makes 4 servings

In a small bowl, whisk together the vinegar, honey, ginger, chili sauce, sesame seeds, salt, and pepper. Slowly pour the oil into the vinegar mixture in a thin stream, whisking continuously, until the dressing is emulsified. Cover the bowl and set aside at room temperature.

Cut a small slice off each end of the 4 oranges and stand them upright on a cutting surface. With a paring knife, remove all of the peel in strips, maintaining the curved shape of the fruit. Cut each orange into four to six slices, crosswise, removing any seeds as needed. Cut the avocado in half lengthwise. Remove the pit and cut each half in half again lengthwise. With a sharp paring knife, peel the skin from each quarter. Cut each quarter into three to four slices.

Divide the orange slices among four plates. In a medium bowl, toss the greens with a little of the vinaigrette and mound the dressed greens on top of the orange slices. Top each with a quarter of the avocado, and drizzle with more vinaigrette to taste (you may have a little dressing left). Garnish with the sprigs of cilantro and serve immediately.

2 tablespoons red wine vinegar

1½ teaspoons honey

½-inch knob fresh ginger, peeled and minced

1½ teaspoons sweet chili sauce

1½ teaspoons toasted white sesame seeds

¼ teaspoon kosher salt

5 grinds of fresh black pepper

¼ cup extra-virgin olive oil

2 medium Cara Cara oranges

2 medium blood oranges

1 medium avocado

2 cups mixed baby greens or baby spinach (about 2 ounces)

Fresh cilantro sprigs, for garnish (optional)

¼ RECIPE: 300 CAL., 22G FAT (3G SAT.), 0MG CHOL., 150MG SODIUM, 27G CARB., 7G FIBER, 16G SUGAR, 3G PROTEIN

SWEETER THAN SUNSHINE

Is there a better antidote to winter doldrums than a sweet, tangy orange? It can brighten a cold, gray morning like sunshine itself. Loaded with nutrients, a single orange provides nearly 100 percent of the daily value for vitamin C. Plus, it boasts more than 170 different phytonutrients and more than sixty flavonoids, and offers good sources of fiber, potassium, folate, and thiamine.

When selecting citrus, don't worry about surface scratches or dings on those sturdy rinds. Instead, look for fruit that is heavy for its size—the more it weighs, the more juice you'll find inside. Oranges will keep longer in the refrigerator, but bring the fruit to room temperature before cooking with it, as it's easier to extract the juice. The zest, on the other hand, can be stripped in advance, frozen, and used as needed.

Thanks to genome typing, we now know that sweet oranges are long-ago natural hybrids of pomelos and mandarins. Because modern citrus continues to hybridize very easily, there are many variations on the extended family of sweet oranges, mandarins, and tangerines.

Satsuma mandarin: This is a mildly sweet and juicy variety of tangerine with few if any seeds. Owari satsumas are an old Japanese variety grown on a small ranch in California; they're extraordinarily easy to peel and an absolute standout for sweetness and flavor.

Clementine: Sometimes called a "Christmas orange" (it's in season from November through January), this small tangerine usually is seedless. It may not be as easy to peel as other tangerine varieties, such as satsuma, but it makes up for it with a full, sweet flavor.

Kishu: This tiny orange once ruled the mandarin world but eventually was overlooked for larger varieties. It's worth your attention. Though it's really small, it's packed with complex, intensely sweet flavor.

Blood orange (a.k.a. Moro orange): This tart orange has brilliant crimson flesh indicating that it's high in anthocyanin, a powerful antioxidant. Toss slices into salads, chop pieces up in salsas and chutneys, use the juice in a vinaigrette, or make colorful mimosas or sangria.

Cara Cara orange: Reddish-pink flesh distinguishes this cross between the familiar Washington variety of navel orange and the Brazilian Bahia navel. It has lower acidity than a Washington navel and a sweet flavor with clear overtones of raspberries and strawberries.

SuperNova Tangerine: A newcomer to the citrus world, this sweet baby is a cross between Lee and Nova mandarins. Incredibly juicy and easy to peel, it makes a sublime brunch cocktail—a Champagne Supernova!

89

MAIN COURSES

CALL THEM ENTRÉES, CALL THEM MAINS, call them protein, call them anything except late for dinner. These dishes are front and center during big holiday feasts, but they also go a long way in keeping weeknight meals from getting dull and too repetitive. Whether you're going seasonal with halibut, getting swanky with a leg of lamb, or simply rolling up a pan of enchiladas to feed the family, the goals remain pretty similar: the main course needs to taste good, and it needs to be worth the effort.

For omnivores, one of the most important pieces of cooking a great main course is knowing the source of your meat. These days, whether fish is fresh or frozen matters much less than whether it's farmed or wild; the same is true when it comes to terms like pastured, grass-fed, and grain finished for choosing lamb, pork, or beef. How the animals spent their lives makes an enormous difference in the amount of fat they'll have, as well as the flavor of their meat, and in some cases these differences change recommended cooking times or temperatures. If you're springing for a special cut and could use a bit of assistance with the prep work, or want an expert opinion on flavor differences between species of salmon, it's well worth your time to chat with the butcher. Good ones are a bit like personal shoppers in a high-end department store—they won't waste your time on suggestions that won't suit your goals, and you'll walk away with new confidence.

Whether it's grilled chicken thighs or spiced and baked tofu, some entrées lend themselves wonderfully to family adaptations. Use these recipes as a starting point for the meal, then consider what the schedule brings for a given week or what your family's dining preferences are. You might decide that plating the dish with sides won't work, but chop the protein into bite-size pieces and use it in a wrap for your next picnic, or shred it and top a packaged salad with it for a halfway-homemade meal. We might suggest udon noodles to go along with it but your kids are fans of *pancit* noodles or brown rice, or you're on a salad kick and need to skip the carbs. That's the great thing about the best main courses—they can adapt to the weather or your whim with equal ease.

TO BE SERVED AT ITS VERY BEST, today's mild-tasting, lean pork needs to be cooked to 145 degrees F, rather than the formerly suggested temperature of 160 degrees F—a guarantee for a very dry pork chop. A dry spice rub is the simplest solution to imbed flavor. The bit of sugar in this rub helps the meat caramelize on the grill and brings the spices together into a cohesive whole. The flavor combination works well with roasted sweet potatoes or black beans and rice.

SPICE-RUBBED GRILLED PORK CHOPS

Makes 4 servings

Combine the chili powder, sugar, mustard, coriander, garlic powder, and pepper in a small bowl.

Pat the chops dry with paper towels. Coat the chops evenly with the spice mixture and put them in a baking dish, and cover. Refrigerate for at least 1 hour and up to overnight.

Preheat the grill to medium (350 degrees F). Lightly oil the grates. Remove the chops from the refrigerator while the grill is heating and allow them to come to room temperature, about 20 minutes.

Sprinkle the salt evenly on both sides of the chops, adding more to taste. Grill, turning once, until the internal temperature reads 145 degrees F, 6 to 7 minutes per side. Let rest for 5 minutes before serving.

1 CHOP: 330 CAL., 21G FAT (6G SAT.), 95MG CHOL., 600MG SODIUM, 3G CARB., 1G FIBER, 2G SUGAR, 29G PROTEIN

1½ teaspoons chili powder

1½ teaspoons packed dark brown sugar

1½ teaspoons dry mustard

1½ teaspoons ground coriander

¾ teaspoon garlic powder

¾ teaspoon freshly ground black pepper

4 bone-in pork rib or loin chops (¾ to 1½ inches thick)

High-heat oil, for grilling

1 teaspoon kosher salt, plus more for seasoning

CIDER PAIRING: A single-varietal cider with a bit of spice and acidity can shine here. Look for Kingston Black for complexity or crab apple for a tart counterpoint.

THIS VEGETARIAN LASAGNE SKIPS THE red sauce in favor of fresh herbs, plenty of cheese, and little touches like lemon zest and freshly grated nutmeg. It's a comforting combination that brings some of summer's freshest flavors to a recipe that's perfect for a cool spring or fall evening. A bowl of Roasted Cherry Tomatoes (page 187) starts the meal off beautifully, and it doesn't matter if the tomatoes are less than peak-season perfection—the roasting process will cure whatever ails their flavor.

FENNEL AND BASIL LASAGNE

Makes 8 servings

Preheat the oven to 350 degrees F.

Bring a large pot of generously salted water to a boil and cook the noodles according to the package directions (usually 8 to 10 minutes); drain and set aside.

In a medium bowl, combine the ricotta, fontina, egg, lemon zest, nutmeg, and salt and pepper to taste; set aside.

In a medium skillet over medium heat, heat the oil, then add the leek and fennel, stirring regularly until they are soft and translucent, 8 to 10 minutes. Stir in the garlic and cook for 2 minutes, until fragrant. Add the spinach and wine, cover, and steam until the spinach is completely wilted, about 3 minutes. Remove the lid and season lightly with salt and pepper.

Using a pastry brush or spatula, spread one-third of the pesto in a thin layer over the bottom of a 9-by-13-inch baking dish; top the pesto with 3 noodles. Spoon half the vegetable mixture over the noodles and top with one-third of the ricotta mixture. Place half of the basil leaves over the cheese mixture. Top with 3 noodles, one-third of the pesto, and the remaining half of the vegetable mixture. Spread one-third of the ricotta mixture and all the remaining basil leaves on top. Finish with the remaining 3 noodles, the remaining one-third pesto, and the remaining one-third ricotta mixture. Sprinkle with the Parmesan and cover the pan with aluminum foil.

Kosher salt

9 lasagne noodles

16 ounces ricotta cheese

4 ounces (1 cup) shredded fontina cheese

1 large egg

2 teaspoons freshly grated lemon zest

⅛ teaspoon freshly grated nutmeg

Freshly ground black pepper

1 tablespoon high-heat oil, such as sunflower or refined peanut oil

1 large leek, washed thoroughly and thinly sliced (white and light-green parts only)

2 medium fennel bulbs (about 1 pound), cored and thinly sliced

2 cloves garlic, minced

2½ cups chopped baby spinach (about 5 ounces)

¼ cup dry white wine

⅓ cup basil pesto

1 cup fresh basil leaves, divided

4 ounces (1 cup) shredded Parmesan cheese

Bake, covered, for 30 minutes, then carefully remove the foil and bake, uncovered, for 10 to 15 minutes, until the filling is bubbly and the cheese has lightly browned. Let cool for about 10 minutes before serving.

WINE PAIRING: A full-bodied white wine like vermentino or Côtes du Rhône blanc will add a lovely perfume and soft, muted citrus notes that complement the anise flavors in the fennel and basil.

⅛ RECIPE: 440 CAL., 20G FAT (8G SAT.), 70MG CHOL., 670MG SODIUM, 43G CARB., 3G FIBER, 10G SUGAR, 23G PROTEIN

IF YOU'VE NEVER USED THIS method, the vivid color of the cooked fish will surprise you. The top of the fish might appear underdone, so rely on its texture and temperature to determine doneness. This salmon is delicious as is or served with simple accompaniments like melted butter or a sprinkle of chopped fresh tarragon. Chinook, sockeye, coho, or pink all work beautifully with this method of cooking, so just use your favorite species of wild salmon.

SLOW-ROASTED SALMON

Makes 4 servings

Line a rimmed baking sheet with parchment paper, and set aside.

Place the salmon skin side down on a flat surface. By lightly running your fingers along the fish, check the salmon carefully for any stray pin bones; gently remove with small needle-nose pliers or large tweezers. If using fillets, cut them into 4 wide slices of equal size. Gently rub the fish with the oil, lightly coating on all sides. Evenly space the fillets skin side down on the prepared baking sheet and cover loosely with more parchment paper or plastic wrap.

Preheat the oven to 275 degrees F. While the oven is heating, let the salmon come to room temperature.

Remove the parchment paper or plastic wrap. Sprinkle the salmon lightly and evenly with salt. Bake for about 20 minutes, until an instant-read thermometer inserted into the thickest part of the salmon reads 120 degrees F. Or place a knife tip (or your finger) in the thickest part of the salmon to check for doneness: When gently pressed, it should softly separate into flakes and pull slightly away from the skin. If it holds firmly together, cook for another 5 minutes. Serve immediately.

1½ pounds skin-on wild salmon fillets or steaks
3 tablespoons extra-virgin olive oil
Kosher salt

WINE PAIRING: Chinook Wines in the Yakima Valley has blended two specific wines for our markets (one white, one red) to pair with salmon. The crisp Yakima Valley White and fruity, balanced Yakima Valley Red both benefit Long Live the Kings, a nonprofit working to restore and protect habitat for wild steelhead and salmon.

¼ RECIPE: 290 CAL., 17G FAT (3G SAT.), 80MG CHOL., 240MG SODIUM, 0G CARB., 0G FIBER, 0G SUGAR, 34G PROTEIN

WITH ITS CONCENTRATED, BRIGHTLY FRUITY flavor, pomegranate molasses is practically an instant marinade, but a little garlic, paprika, and black pepper round things off with a spicy base note. If you have it on hand, the smoky Pimentón de la Vera in place of more standard forms of paprika will add complexity.

Typically, boneless and skinless chicken thighs are already well trimmed of fat, but check them over before placing them in the marinade and remove any easily accessed pieces of fat. These have a way of causing flares on the grill that can char the chicken to a less-than-perfect degree.

POMEGRANATE MOLASSES GRILLED CHICKEN

Makes 4 servings

In a small bowl, combine the pomegranate molasses, oil, garlic, pepper, paprika, red pepper flakes, salt, and cinnamon. Set aside half the marinade for serving. Place the remaining marinade and the chicken in a baking dish, and cover. Let rest in the refrigerator for 30 minutes to 1 hour.

Preheat the grill to medium (350 degrees F). Lightly oil the grates. Remove the chicken thighs from their marinade and grill until they are cooked through (the internal temperature taken with an instant-read thermometer should be 165 degrees F), 7 to 10 minutes per side, depending on the thickness of the chicken. It should be firm to the touch and juices should run clear. Serve with reserved sauce on the side.

> **BEER PAIRING:** A deep, mellow Scotch ale or brown ale will provide rich malt that rests below the tangy pomegranate molasses. If you prefer lighter beer, go with a classic lager—anything too hoppy will conflict with the sauce.

⅓ cup pomegranate molasses

2 tablespoons extra-virgin olive oil, plus more for grilling

4 cloves garlic, minced

1 teaspoon freshly ground black pepper

1 teaspoon sweet paprika

½ teaspoon red pepper flakes, or to taste

½ teaspoon kosher salt, plus more as needed

¼ teaspoon ground cinnamon

4 boneless, skinless chicken thighs (about 1½ pounds)

¼ RECIPE: 300 CAL., 13G FAT (2.5G SAT.), 140MG CHOL., 380MG SODIUM, 14G CARB., 1G FIBER, 9G SUGAR, 30G PROTEIN

POMEGRANATE MOLASSES IS HALF WRONG

Pomegranate molasses has nothing to do with molasses and everything to do with pomegranates. It's a thick, minimally sweetened syrup made from pomegranate juice that offers a huge pop of pure tangy flavor. In addition to making a pleasing ingredient in marinades for all sorts of poultry, pomegranate molasses can be added to salad dressings, brushed on toast to replace the more usual jam, swirled into Greek yogurt or berry smoothies, and used to sweeten green tea or plain seltzer water. It also goes well with lamb stew or *kofta* kebabs.

While it's much more common in grocery stores than it was even a few years ago, you can make your own if you have trouble finding it. Some recipes start with making caramel and then adding pomegranate juice, but there's an easier way—and here's where a bit of molasses is involved after all. In a heavy-bottomed saucepan, combine 4 cups of unsweetened pomegranate juice with 1 tablespoon of dark brown sugar (it's brown thanks to molasses) and 1 tablespoon of freshly squeezed lemon juice. Bring to a boil, stirring regularly, then reduce the heat to keep it at a very low boil or strong simmer and reduce for 50 to 60 minutes, until you have only about 1 cup of thick fuchsia-red syrup. Let it cool to room temperature and store in a glass jar in the refrigerator for up to 6 months.

EARTHY LENTILS SUIT CURRY SPICES to a *T*, particularly when brightened up with an extra dash of lemony coriander. Adding fresh mango and cucumber? That takes a good idea and makes it a great one—picture an Indian riff on a Vietnamese fresh roll. Use rice-paper wrappers to make smaller wraps; go gluten-free with coconut wraps or lettuce leaves. If you prefer, use frozen diced mango instead of the fresh. Just thaw out one cup and chop the pieces a little finer, so the chunks aren't too big. If you have leftover filling, it will keep for two days in the refrigerator; serve over steamed rice for an easy lunch.

CURRIED LENTIL AND MANGO WRAPS

Makes 6 servings

In a medium, heavy-bottomed saucepan over medium heat, heat the oil just until it shimmers and add 1 cup of the onion. Cook, stirring occasionally, for 5 to 7 minutes, until they are soft and translucent. Stir in the garlic, garam masala, and coriander, and cook until the spices coat the onions and are quite fragrant, 1 to 2 minutes.

Mix in the lentils and broth and bring to a gentle boil, stirring occasionally to make sure the lentils don't clump together. Reduce the heat to low and simmer until the liquid is absorbed and the lentils are completely tender, 20 to 30 minutes. Remove from the heat and fold in the mango, cucumber, cilantro, and remaining 2 tablespoons onion. Season to taste generously with salt and pepper.

Fill the warmed tortillas with the curried lentils, roll, and serve warm.

> **WINE PAIRING:** A bold rosé with tropical or stone-fruit flavors from Spain or Portugal will work wonders with both the lightly spiced lentils and the sweeter pieces of mango tucked into these wraps.

2 teaspoons high-heat oil, such as sunflower or refined peanut oil

1 cup plus 2 tablespoons finely minced red onion, divided

2 cloves garlic, chopped

2 teaspoons garam masala or curry powder

1 teaspoon ground coriander

1 cup red lentils, rinsed

2½ cups vegetable broth

1 small mango, peeled, pitted, and diced

¼ medium English cucumber, diced

3 tablespoons chopped fresh cilantro

Kosher salt and freshly ground black pepper

6 whole wheat tortillas, warmed

⅙ RECIPE: 300 CAL., 3.5G FAT (0G SAT.), 0MG CHOL., 350MG SODIUM, 54G CARB., 7G FIBER, 11G SUGAR, 14G PROTEIN

ORIGINALLY, WE ADDED THE CHEF'S name to any recipe they developed in our kitchens—back in the days when each store had its own repertoire of recipes, rather than just its own kitchen—and the name of this recipe is part of that old tradition. Some of what makes this dish successful is its cooking method. Baking tofu in its flavorful marinade gives it a firm texture and richly toasted crust that turns it into an ingredient you'll want to use in many different ways. Shred some lettuce and combine it with the tofu, then tuck them into a ciabatta roll for fresh vegan sandwiches, or toss it with soba noodles (to serve cold) or steamed rice (to serve hot). You can also add a few pieces to Mango and Avocado Fresh Rolls (page 198) instead of the plain sliced tofu.

STEPH'S TOFU PCC Deli Favorite

Makes 4 servings

Preheat the oven to 350 degrees F. Grease a 9-by-13-inch baking dish with 1½ teaspoons of the high-heat oil and set aside.

In a medium bowl, whisk together the remaining 1½ teaspoons high-heat oil, orange juice, mirin, tamari, sesame oil, rice vinegar, garlic, and ginger.

Put the tofu in the prepared baking dish and add all of the marinade. Marinate at room temperature for 30 minutes, gently stirring a few times with a wooden spoon or broad spatula (you can also use your fingers to flip the cubes). Use caution to avoid damaging the tofu.

Bake the tofu for 55 to 65 minutes, stirring every 15 minutes, until the edges of the tofu cubes have formed a rich crust and deep color has developed. Most of the sauce will be absorbed into the tofu while it is baking. Serve hot, cold, or at room temperature.

3 teaspoons high-heat oil, such as sunflower or refined peanut oil, divided

¼ cup orange juice

¼ cup mirin

2 tablespoons tamari

2 tablespoons toasted sesame oil

1 tablespoon rice vinegar

2 cloves garlic, minced

2-inch knob fresh ginger, peeled and minced

1 pound extra-firm tofu, cut into 1-inch cubes

WINE PAIRING: A refreshing *ginjo* sake will have a pleasant complexity to balance the contrasting components of the marinade, or grab the nearest grüner veltliner and see how well a full-bodied white goes with tofu.

¼ RECIPE: 260 CAL., 18G FAT (2.5G SAT.), 0MG CHOL., 520MG SODIUM, 10G CARB., 0G FIBER, 7G SUGAR, 14G PROTEIN

TODAY'S PASTURED LAMB TENDS TO be mild in flavor, and lean, boneless legs can win over even those who think all lamb is gamy. The garlic-and-herb paste that fills this roast isn't meant to be a smooth pesto; roughly chopping everything so it's thick and chunky is quick work, and it stays right where you want it during the roasting process.

If you have leftovers, all you need is pita or rice, feta crumbles, Greek yogurt, and a sprinkle of smoked paprika—it becomes a whole new meal.

ROASTED LEG OF LAMB

Stuffed with Herbs and Garlic

Makes 6 to 8 servings

Place an oven rack in the middle position and preheat the oven to 350 degrees F.

In the work bowl of a food processor, combine the parsley, basil, garlic, chives, oil, salt, and pepper and pulse until all ingredients are coarsely chopped. (You may easily do this step by hand. They needn't be finely minced, just chopped and well blended.)

Spread the leg of lamb out flat on a work surface, fat side down, and spread the herb mixture evenly over the interior surface. Roll the lamb back into its original shape and tie the roast with cooking twine at about 1-inch intervals. Squeeze the juice from the lemon halves over the lamb. Drizzle with a little oil and sprinkle with additional salt and pepper.

Roast the lamb until an instant-read thermometer inserted about 2 inches into the roast averages 130 to 135 degrees F for medium rare, about 20 minutes per pound. (Different parts of the leg cook at different speeds, so insert your thermometer in several places.) Or use your index finger and press firmly on several sections of the lamb. If the meat gives easily but still seems firm, it is likely medium rare. The firmer the texture, the more well done it will be.

Let rest for about 15 minutes. Remove the twine, slice, and serve.

½ cup fresh Italian
   parsley leaves
½ cup fresh basil leaves
5 cloves garlic
1 tablespoon coarsely chopped
   fresh chives
¼ cup extra-virgin olive oil, plus
   more for drizzling
1 teaspoon kosher salt, plus
   more as needed
¾ teaspoon freshly ground
   black pepper, plus more
   as needed
1 (2½-pound) boneless leg
   of lamb
1 medium lemon, halved

WINE PAIRING: It's hard to go wrong with a Rioja. Well-structured wines with bold but balanced fruit are a great choice with rich, garlicky lamb.

⅛ RECIPE: 370 CAL., 24G FAT (8G SAT.), 125MG CHOL., 400MG SODIUM, 3G CARB., 1G FIBER, 0G SUGAR, 36G PROTEIN

THE USUAL RULE OF THUMB when choosing how many ribs for your roast is to plan on one bone-in rib serving two people. This amount will provide generous portions for adults, so if several kids are on the guest list, or you want to end up with fewer leftovers, it can be fine to decide that one bone-in rib will actually serve three people. The lower-temperature roasting method gives very succulent results, but the higher-temperature method is more practical if you'll be cooking sides in the oven at the same time.

Roasting the bones with the meat provides noticeable additional flavor and richness compared to boneless roasts. To make carving easier, you can have the butcher cut the roast off the bones but then return them to the center of the roast and wrap it. Proceed with the recipe as is, and simply slide the bones out before slicing and serving.

GRASS-FED PRIME RIB

with Fresh Herbs

Makes 6 to 8 servings

In a small bowl, combine the parsley, rosemary, thyme, garlic, and oil to make a paste. Spread the herb paste over the top and sides of the roast and refrigerate, uncovered, for 8 to 12 hours.

Remove the roast from the refrigerator 1 hour before cooking to bring it to room temperature. Place the oven rack in the lower third of the oven. Sprinkle salt and pepper generously over roast. Place the roast on a V-rack in a roasting pan, with the fat cap facing up.

To slow roast the prime rib: Preheat the oven to 200 degrees F. Put the roast in the oven and cook until the internal temperature taken with an instant-read thermometer reaches 120 degrees F (medium rare), about 4 hours (the roast will continue to cook once removed from the oven). Remove from the oven, tent with aluminum foil, and let rest for at least 30 minutes and up to 1 hour. Meanwhile, increase the oven temperature to 500 degrees F.

To roast the prime rib: Preheat the oven to 325 degrees F. Put the roast in the oven and cook until the internal temperature taken with an instant-read thermometer $\longrightarrow$

¼ cup chopped fresh Italian parsley

1 tablespoon chopped fresh rosemary

1 tablespoon chopped fresh thyme

4 cloves garlic, finely minced

3 tablespoons extra-virgin olive oil

1 (3- or 4-rib) grass-fed prime rib roast (6 to 8 pounds)

Kosher salt and freshly ground black pepper

reaches 120 degrees F (medium rare), about 2 hours (the roast will continue to cook once removed from the oven). Remove from the oven, tent with foil, and let rest for at least 30 minutes and up to 1 hour. Meanwhile, increase the oven temperature to 500 degrees F.

Ten minutes before serving, remove the foil and put the roast back in the oven. Cook until the exterior is well-browned and crisp, 5 to 10 minutes. Remove from the oven, carve, and serve immediately.

> **WINE PAIRING:** Big red wines pair with beef roasts for very good reasons. Look for a Bordeaux, a Bordeaux blend, or a peppery syrah if you like firm, notable wines with plenty of structure. Merlot is a softer choice, but with spicy aromas and dark fruit, it can be wonderful.

STANDARD 10-OUNCE PORTION: 970 CAL., 83G FAT (33G SAT.), 200MG CHOL., 300MG SODIUM, 1G CARB., 0G FIBER, 0G SUGAR, 52G PROTEIN

HEALTHIER 3.5-OUNCE PORTION: 390 CAL., 33G FAT (13G SAT.), 80MG CHOL., 120MG SODIUM, 0G CARB., 0G FIBER, 0G SUGAR, 21G PROTEIN

GRASS-FED BEEF

For beef with a rounded, nuanced flavor, grass-fed can't be beat. A diet rich in forage enables grass-fed cattle to develop higher levels of many health-promoting nutrients, including conjugated linoleic acid, vitamin E, and beta-carotene, than grain-fed beef. Grass-fed beef also offers two to four times higher levels of omega-3s.

Raising cattle on pastures better manages a number of important environmental concerns for ranchers. While there has been little study comparing greenhouse-gas emission between grain-fed and grass-fed steers, moving cattle across pasturelands helps reduce erosion and water pollution, conserve soil while preserving biodiversity, and increase carbon sequestration. These are important improvements in the sustainability of ranching.

In 2016, the USDA announced it would no longer verify a producer's claim to a uniform standard of "grass fed" and revoked its former definition. The USDA continues to verify that meat-label claims are what a vendor says it means to them, but there is no longer assured consistency across different brands or labels. You can look for certified claims from third-party agencies or contact your preferred brand of grass-fed beef and ask them directly.

If you eat grass-fed beef you're consuming the heme form of iron, which enhances your absorption of non-heme iron, or iron from plant sources—so adding a small amount of beef to a bean, spinach, and rice casserole will significantly increase the absorption of iron from all of the ingredients. Supplements provide non-heme iron as well—so taking your supplement with a piece of beef jerky will boost the bioavailability of your supplement.

The number-one tip for using grass-fed beef in the kitchen: don't overcook! Grass-fed beef is visibly leaner than grain-fed, making it easier to dry out if it's cooked too long or at too high of a temperature. Grass-fed beef takes about 30 percent less time to cook than grain-fed beef, and it's best served medium rare.

These are approximate grilling times for medium-rare steak pulled from the grill with an internal temperature of 120 degrees F. As grills vary greatly, use these grilling times as guidelines. The key is to get a deep sear on the outside while keeping the inside juicy.

- Grass-fed New York strip steak, ¾ inch thick: 8 to 9 minutes
- Grass-fed flank steak, ¾ inch thick: 10 to 12 minutes
- Grass-fed top sirloin, 1 inch thick: 13 to 15 minutes
- Grass-fed Spencer steak, 1¼ inches thick: 22 to 25 minutes
- Grass-fed tenderloin (filet mignon), 1¾ inches thick: 17 to 19 minutes

FOR MOST HOUSEHOLDS, TURKEY IS both a beloved once-a-year roast and a slightly nerve-racking centerpiece for the biggest feast of the year. While turkeys are not as pricey as a beef roast, they're by no means inexpensive, and of course you want them to be both succulent and crispy-skinned. Magazines and cooking shows seem to reinvent the wheel each year when it comes to roasting a turkey, but it really doesn't have to be difficult. The most important tool you can have (aside from a pan big enough to hold the bird) is an instant-read thermometer. Because dark and light meat cook differently, and breasts and thighs can be of varying thicknesses even in birds of the same size, without one it's very difficult to determine when a turkey is cooked.

For this dish, choose a turkey that hasn't been injected with salt water (you can check the label or ask the butcher); fresh or frozen and thawed turkeys are equally acceptable. This method is a knockout when you're roasting an heirloom breed, which tend to have thicker skins and leaner meat than their modern counterparts. You can scale this up for larger turkeys. Use one tablespoon of salt and one-quarter teaspoon of pepper for every five pounds of turkey.

DRY-BRINED ROAST TURKEY

Makes 8 servings (with plenty of leftovers)

In a shallow dish, mix the salt and pepper.

Don't rinse the bird, but do pat it dry with paper towels and use tweezers to remove any stray pinfeathers you might find. Use your hands to loosen the skin over the breast and thighs, gently breaking the thin membrane that connects the skin to the meat. Rub half the salt mixture under the loosened skin, then sprinkle the remaining half in the cavity and on top of the skin. Tuck the wings under the breast and place the turkey in a roasting pan. Refrigerate, uncovered, for 1 to 3 days. When you're ready to cook it, there's no need to rinse it or pat it dry; it's ready to roast as is.

Preheat the oven to 500 degrees F. Place a rack in a large, heavy roasting pan. Place the turkey breast side up on the rack. Tuck the wing tips under the bird to prevent them from burning. Pour 3 cups of water into the roasting pan.

Put the turkey in the oven and immediately reduce the oven temperature to 350 degrees F. Baste the turkey with pan juices every 30 minutes, until the internal

2 tablespoons kosher salt
½ teaspoon freshly ground black pepper
1 (10-pound) turkey
Melted unsalted butter or extra-virgin olive oil, for basting (optional)

temperature taken with an instant-read thermometer inserted into the thickest part of the thigh without touching the bone reaches 160 degrees F, about 2½ hours. Baste with butter during the last 30 minutes to crisp the skin. If the skin becomes too dark while roasting, tent the turkey with aluminum foil.

To finish cooking to the final temperature of 165 degrees F, remove the turkey from the oven, tent loosely with foil, and let rest for 30 minutes before carving.

STANDARD 10-OUNCE PORTION: 380 CAL., 15G FAT (4G SAT.), 195MG CHOL., 780MG SODIUM, 0G CARB., 0G FIBER, 0G SUGAR, 58G PROTEIN

HEALTHIER 3.5-OUNCE PORTION: 140 CAL., 6G FAT (1.5G SAT.), 70MG CHOL., 290MG SODIUM, 0G CARB, 0G FIBER, 0G SUGAR, 21G PROTEIN

CIDER PAIRING: Cider was the drink of choice for Pilgrims and Puritans, and serving it at Thanksgiving harkens back to that tradition. A sturdy farmhouse style will have an apple-scented yeasty richness that offers a robust, old-fashioned taste.

BEER PAIRING: A nutty brown ale will have aromas and flavors that are similar to a hearty loaf of peasant bread—making it a great choice to accompany turkey, stuffing, and all the trimmings.

A BETTER WAY TO BRINE

Brining turkeys has been popular for years now—it's a reliable way to add both flavor and moisture. Dry brining is a similar method that still flies a little under the radar, but it's worth exploring for several reasons. First, not everyone has space to keep a big container of salt water cold for several days as the turkey brines. Second, it takes several gallons of water to submerge a turkey, and the water can't be reused, so it's not a great use of an important resource.

The science behind dry brining is interesting and fairly simple. It works as a three-step process:

1   The coating of salt pulls juice from the meat through osmosis.
2   The salt slowly dissolves into those juices it has extracted, creating a very salty liquid brine without any additional water.
3   This concentrated brine solution is reabsorbed by the meat, where it begins to soften and break down some of the proteins.

Those softened proteins don't lose nearly as much moisture during the cooking process as the proteins in turkeys that have not been brined, and this gives you a much more comfortable margin of error when it comes to roasting a big, special, once-a-year bird. The final result is tender, juicy, well-seasoned meat that cooks much more evenly than meat that has not been brined. For some, the skin is the best reason to switch to this method: because the turkey sits uncovered in the refrigerator rather than submerged in water, its skin dries out in exactly the way you want for it be extremely crispy and beautifully brown once it's been roasted. The larger the bird, the longer the process takes to finish, but most turkeys need two days or less.

SOMETIMES, IT FEELS LIKE SALMON gets all the love in the Pacific Northwest, and that's simply not fair to the other spectacular wild fish from Alaska and the Washington coast. Halibut is an impressively well-managed fishery, making it a fine choice when it comes to sustainability ratings. It's also a fine choice when it comes to flavor and texture: it's firm but still tender—not as dry as cod or as oily as black cod.

While the precise date varies by the year, the halibut season begins shortly before the year's crop of rhubarb makes its appearance. The combination makes a pretty plate, with pink rhubarb and red peppers creating a colorful sauce to dress the starkly white fillets.

HALIBUT WITH GINGER-RHUBARB SAUCE

Makes 4 servings

Preheat the oven to 425 degrees F. Line a baking sheet with parchment paper.

Place the halibut fillets skin side down in the prepared dish. Brush with 2 tablespoons of the tamari and sprinkle with the sesame seeds. Roast for 12 to 15 minutes, depending on the thickness of the fillets, until the halibut is just opaque throughout and flakes easily when checked with a fork.

While the halibut is roasting, in a small bowl, stir together the rhubarb and granulated sugar. In a large sauté pan or wok over medium-high heat, heat the oil just until it shimmers. Add the garlic and ginger and cook, stirring constantly, for 20 to 30 seconds, until light golden. Add the rhubarb and stir-fry for 30 seconds, then add the onions, bell pepper, and chili and stir-fry for 1 minute more, until the vegetables' colors are vibrant and they have softened just slightly. Reduce the heat to low and stir in the remaining 2 tablespoons tamari, the brown sugar, the sweet chili sauce, the vinegar, and the lime juice. Cook to heat through. $\longrightarrow$

4 (4- to 6-ounce) skin-on halibut fillets

4 tablespoons tamari, divided

2 tablespoons white sesame seeds

1 cup very thinly sliced rhubarb (from 1 to 2 large stalks)

1 teaspoon granulated sugar

2 tablespoons high-heat oil, such as sunflower or refined peanut oil

3 cloves garlic, minced

4-inch knob fresh ginger, peeled and minced

3 green onions, thinly sliced (white and light-green parts only), plus more for garnish

½ medium red bell pepper, cut into strips

½ medium pasilla or poblano chili, seeded and cut into strips

(ingredients continued on next page)

Divide the halibut among four plates and drizzle the sauce over the top. Serve garnished with thinly sliced green onion.

> **WINE PAIRING:** Halibut and rosé are meant to be—ideally a wine with dry minerality and cool citrus notes to play off the spicy-sweet rhubarb sauce.

¼ **RECIPE: 190 CAL., 11G FAT (1.5G SAT.), 20MG CHOL., 1080MG SODIUM, 16G CARB., 2G FIBER, 10G SUGAR, 10G PROTEIN**

1 tablespoon packed light
   brown sugar
2 tablespoons sweet chili sauce
1 tablespoon rice vinegar
1 tablespoon freshly squeezed
   lime juice

GINGER: A UNIVERSAL MEDICINE

Floral and pungent, ginger is a warming food that provides support for our immune, circulatory, and digestive systems. Fresh ginger is best for flavor and somewhat better when it comes to its use as a health aid, but we also can reap the benefits of this popular spice from ground ginger, teas, and spicy ginger beers. Fresh ginger stores in the refrigerator for several weeks and can be kept for months in the freezer. Ginger's peel is edible, but the many perks come from inside this unique root, so peel or not as you prefer. Add ginger early in cooking to mellow out its flavors; add it later if you want more zing.

Fresh ginger is a useful home remedy for cold symptoms. It can help soothe chills and open up clogged sinuses, and it contains enzymes that help soothe an upset stomach. It also contains unique molecules such as gingerols and shogaols that provide its ability to relieve nausea resulting from pregnancy, motion sickness, and chemotherapy.

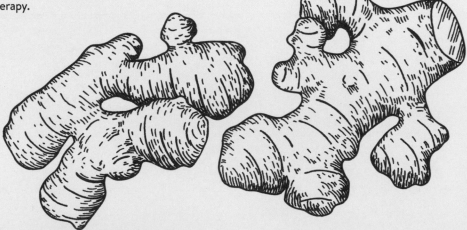

THIS DISH DIALS DOWN THE CHEESE component of classic enchiladas while upping the nutritional benefits by using black beans and brown rice. It's also fantastically kid friendly, and older kids can help with the enchilada rolling. Plain cooked rice freezes beautifully, so make a little extra (or pick up an extra container the next time you order takeout) and stash it in the freezer until you have a hankering for a pan of enchiladas. If you prefer, make this with extra-lean ground beef or ground dark turkey meat; they both have a little fat, but it's minimal.

BEEF AND BEAN ENCHILADAS

Makes 6 servings

Preheat the oven to 350 degrees F.

In a large skillet over medium-high heat, heat the oil. Add the onion and minced garlic and cook until soft, 4 to 5 minutes. Add the beef and cook until it is no longer pink, 8 to 10 minutes; drain it if you prefer. Stir in the chili powder, granulated garlic, cumin, and cayenne until the spices are evenly distributed. Add the beans, rice, and ½ cup of the enchilada sauce; simmer for 10 minutes, stirring occasionally. Remove the pan from the heat and fold in ¼ cup of the cilantro.

Pour in enough of the remaining enchilada sauce to coat the bottom of a 9-by-13-inch baking dish. Wrap the tortillas in aluminum foil and warm them in the oven until just pliable, 2 to 3 minutes.

To assemble the enchiladas, lay a tortilla on a flat surface and add ¼ to ½ cup of the beef filling as a line down the center. Roll it up and place seam side down in the prepared baking dish. Repeat until all the tortillas are used. (Any extra beef filling can be frozen for up to 3 months.) Cover the tortillas with the remaining enchilada sauce (you may not use all the sauce; it's up to personal preference, and you can freeze it for up to 3 months as well) and then sprinkle evenly with the Cotija and mozzarella.

Bake until the sauce is bubbly and the cheese is melted, 20 to 25 minutes. Top with the remaining ¼ cup cilantro.

2 teaspoons high-heat oil, such as sunflower or refined peanut oil

½ medium red onion, finely chopped

2 cloves garlic, minced

1 pound ground beef

1 teaspoon chili powder

½ teaspoon granulated garlic

½ teaspoon ground cumin

Pinch of cayenne pepper, or to taste

1 (15-ounce) can black or kidney beans, rinsed and drained

1 cup cooked brown rice

2 (15-ounce) cans red enchilada sauce, divided

½ cup chopped fresh cilantro, divided

12 (8-inch) corn or flour tortillas

2 ounces (½ cup) crumbled Cotija cheese

2 ounces (½ cup) shredded mozzarella or Mexican-blend cheese

BEER PAIRING: An American-style lager or pale ale will be just the ticket here—clean, refreshing, great with tortillas, and easy to drink.

⅙ RECIPE: 460 CAL., 21G FAT (7G SAT.), 65MG CHOL., 1050MG SODIUM, 41G CARB., 5G FIBER, 3G SUGAR, 25G PROTEIN

THIS UNUSUAL COMBINATION OF SEASONINGS pulls from many cultures. At its simplest, this chicken needs nothing more than a green salad on the side and a dollop of Greek yogurt for dipping (swirl some hot sauce into the yogurt if you like). You can also shred the meat and turn it into tortas or burritos, topped with beans, salsa, and slices of avocado. Or chop it into bite-size pieces and add it to your next bowl of ramen or udon. Leftovers will keep for three days in the refrigerator, or make a big batch and freeze half of it for later use; the grilled thighs can be frozen with no loss of quality for two months.

SPICY CHICKEN THIGHS PCC Deli Favorite

Makes 4 servings

In a small bowl, mix the paprika, curry, marjoram, sage, oregano, cayenne, tamari, and sesame oil. If you prefer very spicy chicken, add more cayenne to taste. Rub the marinade onto the chicken thighs, put the coated chicken pieces in a bowl, and cover.

Let the chicken rest in the refrigerator for at least 30 minutes or up to 4 hours.

Preheat the grill to medium (350 degrees F). Lightly oil the grates. Remove the chicken thighs from their marinade and grill until they are cooked through (the internal temperature taken with an instant-read thermometer should be 165 degrees F), 7 to 10 minutes per side, depending on the thickness of the chicken. It should be firm to the touch and juices should run clear. Garnish the chicken with the parsley before serving.

> **WINE PAIRING:** To pull together all the flavors of this marinade—not to mention the smoky char from the grill— go with a Washington State riesling. If you'd prefer a red, look for a not-too-tannic barbera from Italy.

2 teaspoons sweet
  smoked paprika
1¾ teaspoons curry powder
½ teaspoon dried marjoram
¼ teaspoon dried sage
¼ teaspoon dried oregano
¼ teaspoon cayenne pepper,
  plus more as needed
1 tablespoon tamari
1 tablespoon toasted sesame oil
1 pound boneless, skinless
  chicken thighs
High-heat oil, such as sunflower
  or refined peanut, for grilling
Chopped fresh Italian parsley,
  for garnish (optional)

¼ RECIPE: 210 CAL., 12G FAT (2G SAT.), 105MG CHOL., 360MG SODIUM, 1G CARB., 1G FIBER, 0G SUGAR, 23G PROTEIN

MARINADES

Marinades add flavor to grilled meats and vegetables and help to seal in juices. They contain acidic ingredients such as wine, vinegar, yogurt, or tomatoes, which help tenderize tougher cuts of meat and keep them moist. When you understand how the process works, it's easy to veer off from formal recipes to use condiments and spices that you have on hand. The basic ratio of oil to acid is simple to remember—just one to one.

When marinating meats, avoid using aluminum containers, which can produce off-flavors. Any glass or plastic container will get the job done beautifully.

1 START WITH OIL

Olive oil is a great choice for many dishes. If whatever you're marinating will be cooked over very high heat, either on the stove or on the grill, opt for an oil that can withstand higher temperatures, like canola, safflower, peanut, or sunflower oil. Whichever your choose, the oil will help reduce the amount of moisture lost during the cooking process and, depending on your other ingredients, add to the flavor that's being absorbed during marination. Some oils, like toasted sesame or walnut, are very flavorful and should be used as a seasoning, not a base.

2 ACIDIFY

Acids help soften and tenderize meats while adding their specific flavor too. Any vinegar will do, whether it's rice, red or white wine, champagne, balsamic, apple cider, or coconut. Wine also does the trick, as does fresh citrus juice, plain yogurt, or buttermilk. Beer can be used too—dark beer does wonderful things for beef and lamb.

3 BUILD SOME FLAVOR

Several cloves of garlic are almost always a good idea; they can be minced or just smashed with the flat of a large knife. Fresh parsley or celery leaves and fresh or dried thyme are solid choices too, regardless of whether you're marinating vegetables or proteins. Basil, tarragon, and fennel fronds lighten things up with their mild notes of sweet licorice flavor.

4 CHILL

For food safety, always marinate your food in the refrigerator. Remember to turn it occasionally so it's evenly coated; bags are easy to flip. The amount of time needed varies according to how large the pieces of food are in addition to what they are. With pork, beef, and lamb, tougher cuts need at least 8 hours to tenderize; 24 to 48 hours is also fine. With more tender steaks and chops or chicken pieces, 1 hour is a good minimum but overnight is also OK. Seafood needs much less time or it can get quite mushy. Just 30 minutes is the goal for most seafood, but whole sides of salmon can marinate for 1 hour.

- Seafood: 20 minutes to 1 hour
- Vegetables: 30 minutes to 3 hours
- Chicken, pork or lamb chops, or steaks: 1 to 24 hours
- "Low and slow" lamb, pork, or beef roasts: 8 to 48 hours

5 SALT

Ideally, the salt doesn't go in with the rest of the marinade ingredients. Seasoning with salt immediately before or after cooking will allow meat to retain its juices and brown properly when cooked. Remove the meat or vegetables from the marinade—don't pat them dry, but they shouldn't be completely dripping wet, either. Bring them closer to room temperature while the grill, oven, or burner preheats, then salt them only once as the very last step before cooking. Tamari is the sole exception—while salty, it doesn't seem to affect browning.

FLAVOR COMBINATIONS TO TRY

- Basic marinade: extra-virgin olive oil, red wine vinegar, Dijon mustard, garlic
- Italian marinade: extra-virgin olive oil, balsamic vinegar, lemon zest and juice, garlic, fresh parsley
- Mexican marinade: peanut oil, apple cider vinegar, lime zest and juice, garlic, ground cumin, ground coriander, ground chipotle, fresh cilantro
- Japanese marinade: peanut oil, mirin, tamari, toasted sesame oil, brown sugar, garlic, fresh ginger
- Jordanian marinade: extra-virgin olive oil, plain yogurt, lemon zest and juice, garlic, brown sugar, ground cumin, smoked paprika, fresh rosemary

MARINATED, GRILLED WITH A GORGEOUS sear, cooked medium rare, and sliced thin: the American classic known as London broil adapts nicely to tweaks of its classic seasoning and can be served in an endless variety of ways. Leftover slices are excellent cold, with or without a side of Grilled Corn Salad with Goat Cheese (page 51).

SESAME-GINGER LONDON BROIL

Makes 6 servings

In a small bowl, mix together ¼ cup of the tamari, the sugar, the oil, the ginger, the garlic, and the *gochujang*. Put the steak in a baking dish, combine with the marinade, and cover. Refrigerate for 4 to 24 hours.

Remove the steak from the marinade and allow it to come to room temperature for at least 45 minutes before cooking. In a small ramekin or bowl, mix together the butter and remaining 2 tablespoons tamari.

To grill the steak, preheat the grill to medium-high (375 degrees F). Grill the steak for 3 minutes, then rotate 45 degrees and grill for 2 to 3 minutes. Baste the steak with the butter mixture while grilling. Flip the steak with tongs and repeat the process, until medium rare, 10 to 12 minutes total (the internal temperature taken with an instant-read thermometer should be 125 degrees F).

To broil the steak, place an oven rack 4 inches from the broiling element and preheat the broiler to high. Broil the steak until it's medium rare, about 5 minutes per side. Baste the steak with the butter mixture while broiling.

Let it rest for 10 minutes before slicing against the grain. Sprinkle with the sesame seeds and green onions.

¼ cup plus 2 tablespoons tamari, divided

2 tablespoons packed light brown sugar

1 tablespoon toasted sesame oil

2-inch knob fresh ginger, peeled and minced

2 cloves garlic, minced

1 to 2 teaspoons *gochujang* chili bean paste (optional)

1½ pounds top round London broil

2 tablespoons unsalted butter, softened

2 teaspoons white sesame seeds, for garnish

2 green onions, thinly sliced (green and light-green parts only), for garnish

> **MAKE IT A MEAL:** Serve with Kale and Quinoa Salad with Lemon-Garlic Dressing (page 70) and you have a filling, protein-packed meal.

¼ RECIPE: 300 CAL., 18G FAT (7G SAT.), 100MG CHOL., 730MG SODIUM, 2G CARB., 0G FIBER, 0G SUGAR, 32G PROTEIN

SIDE DISHES

WHAT'S TURKEY WITHOUT THE STUFFING? What's a cookout without the pasta salad? For lots of us, calling a dish a "side" bears no relationship to its importance on the plate. Sides are where the magic happens, where whatever the protein du jour might be connects with carbs and braised greens and roasted vegetables and becomes a meal to remember. Cooks tend to stress more over the entrée, while the sides are where the creativity blooms. Don't shy away from trying a new-to-you ingredient like kohlrabi or harissa—you might discover something so great it ends up in the regular rotation.

While plenty of the basic side-dish ingredients haven't changed over the decades, they've shifted a bit. Vegetables are more likely to be fresh, not canned or frozen. Cooking methods have changed too, so most recipes can adapt to being served at a variety of temperatures. You might even find a dish that frees you from needing to claim some of the host's oven space to warm your Thanksgiving side.

But sides aren't just for big events; they're part of weeknight dinners too. To assist in a bit of meal planning for those nights, our suggestions to Make It a Meal pair these sides with the perfect entrée. (They're equally suited to nights when you're picking up a rotisserie chicken; half-homemade dinners are as much a part of modern life as the internet.)

Many of them reheat beautifully, keeping their textures and layered flavor after a day or two in the refrigerator. If you're really lucky, you can bring some leftovers of your favorite to the office the next day and live the dream of an entire meal from side dishes.

THE CREAMY BEANS AND CRUNCHY hazelnuts add body to the heap of barely-cooked asparagus and give this quick springtime dish the sort of elegance that is simple, not fussy. When it comes to choosing the beans, cannellini beans are the largest, with a silky texture that has a little more firmness to it than the creamy, medium-size great northern or small, soft navy bean. Any white bean will work, but red, black, and speckled beans have stronger flavors that will compete with the asparagus.

ASPARAGUS WITH WHITE BEANS AND HAZELNUTS

Makes 4 servings

In a large, heavy sauté pan over medium heat, heat the oil until the surface begins to shimmer. Add the asparagus and hazelnuts and sauté for 4 to 6 minutes, until the asparagus is crisp-tender and bright jade green. Add the garlic and cook, stirring, for 1 minute more.

Toss in the white beans, chopped basil, and salt and pepper to taste and heat through. Add the lemon juice and drizzle with oil. Garnish with the Parmesan and whole basil leaves. Serve warm.

> **MAKE IT A MEAL:** For a quick but elegant springtime dinner, serve with Seared Scallops with Arugula Pesto (page 152).

¼ RECIPE: 380 CAL., 30G FAT (3G SAT.), 0MG CHOL., 190MG SODIUM, 23G CARB., 9G FIBER, 4G SUGAR, 11G PROTEIN

3 tablespoons extra-virgin olive oil, plus more for drizzling

About 20 thin asparagus spears (about 1 pound), tough ends removed and cut into 2-inch pieces

1 cup chopped raw hazelnuts

3 cloves garlic, minced

1 (15-ounce) can white beans, rinsed and drained

½ cup coarsely chopped fresh basil, plus a handful of whole leaves for garnish

Kosher salt and freshly ground black pepper

Freshly squeezed juice of ½ medium lemon

Shredded Parmesan cheese, for garnish

BOTH EDAMAME AND CHICKPEAS HAVE a pleasant bite to them, and the mildly grassy flavor of the former rests nicely on top of the latter's nuttiness. Toss a few fresh, crisp vegetables into the mix and the result is just the right midpoint between a substantial side and a summery salad. Unless you dislike cilantro, use it rather than the parsley; it's a natural companion to the cumin and coriander in the sauce.

EDAMAME AND CHICKPEAS

with Tahini Dressing

Makes 4 servings

In a large bowl, whisk together the tahini, yogurt, lemon juice, water, garlic, cumin, and coriander until smooth. Add a little more water if necessary to form a creamy dressing. Season to taste with salt and pepper.

Add the edamame, chickpeas, cucumber, carrot, and cilantro to the dressing and fold the ingredients gently together. Cover and let sit for 30 minutes to allow flavors to meld. Serve immediately, or refrigerate. If you serve the dish later, the texture will be better if you bring it closer to room temperature before serving.

> **MAKE IT A MEAL:** For a weeknight dinner, serve alongside Pomegranate Molasses Grilled Chicken (page 98).
>
> For a spring feast, serve with Fresh Fava Bean Hummus (page 188), Roasted Leg of Lamb Stuffed with Herbs and Garlic (page 104), Summertime Fritters (page 132), and Cherry-Balsamic Upside-Down Cake (page 241).

¼ RECIPE: 340 CAL., 15G FAT (1.5G SAT.), 0MG CHOL., 210MG SODIUM, 30G CARB., 8G FIBER, 5G SUGAR, 20G PROTEIN

¼ cup tahini

2 tablespoons plain yogurt

2 tablespoons freshly squeezed lemon juice

¼ cup water, plus more as needed

1 clove garlic, minced

½ teaspoon ground cumin

¼ teaspoon ground coriander

Kosher salt and freshly ground black pepper

1½ cups shelled edamame (fresh and cooked, or frozen and thawed)

1 (15-ounce) can chickpeas, rinsed and drained

½ medium English cucumber, finely chopped

½ cup peeled and shredded carrots (from 1 large carrot)

¼ cup chopped fresh cilantro or Italian parsley

IT'S PAST TIME FOR KOHLRABI'S place as the superstar of the vegetable world. It is a relation to kale, broccoli, and brussels sprouts; its Sri Lankan name translates to "turnip cabbage," and that's exactly what it offers—the sweet density of the root vegetable with the nutritional benefits of the kale family. White or green are the most common colors, but it's also available in purple, which is the prettiest option when you want it for a slaw; roasted here, the more subtle colors are a better choice. If your kohlrabi has the leaves still attached, you can save them to replace some of the kale in Hearty Greens Caesar (page 72) or braise them as you would collards. This preparation tosses it with the more familiar cauliflower in a quick sauce that combines the nutty flavor of tahini with plenty of bright lemon.

ROASTED CAULIFLOWER AND KOHLRABI

with Lemon-Tahini Sauce

Makes 8 servings

Preheat the oven to 450 degrees F. Put two rimmed baking sheets in the oven for 4 minutes to heat.

Meanwhile, in a large bowl, combine the cauliflower and kohlrabi. Add the oil and toss to coat; season generously to taste with salt and pepper. Very carefully, spread the vegetables on the hot baking sheets. Roast, shaking the pan once or twice to turn the vegetables, until they are tender and golden, 20 to 25 minutes. Let cool slightly while you mix the dressing.

In a small bowl, whisk together the tahini, water, lemon zest and juice, garlic, cumin, and sumac. Thin the sauce with additional water, if desired, and season to taste with salt and pepper. Fold in the parsley.

In a serving platter or bowl, toss the roasted vegetables and lemon-tahini sauce together. Just before serving, mix in the greens. Serve warm or at room temperature.

> **MAKE IT A MEAL:** For a flavorful and hearty vegan dinner, serve alongside Egyptian Red Lentil Soup (page 35).

⅛ RECIPE: 90 CAL., 6G FAT (1G SAT.), 0MG CHOL., 200MG SODIUM, 8G CARB., 4G FIBER, 3G SUGAR, 4G PROTEIN

1 large head cauliflower (about 1¾ pounds), cut into 1-inch florets

2 medium kohlrabi, trimmed, peeled, and cut into ¾-inch cubes

2 tablespoons high-heat oil, such as sunflower or refined peanut oil

Kosher salt and freshly ground black pepper

2 tablespoons tahini

2 tablespoons water, plus more as needed

1 teaspoon freshly grated lemon zest

2 tablespoons freshly squeezed lemon juice

1 clove garlic, minced

¼ teaspoon ground cumin

¼ teaspoon ground sumac (optional)

2 tablespoons chopped fresh Italian parsley

2 ounces mixed baby greens

THESE SWEET RED TUBERS ARE a classic ingredient for the Thanksgiving table, so the pecans and dried cranberries are right at home. Nonetheless, the preparation is distinctly modern thanks to a sauce with honey and harissa. Harissa—a North African staple—is available in two different ways: a tangy hot sauce and a spice blend. Use the hot sauce here as a first choice, but if you can only find the dried spice mix, scale the amount back to one-half to one teaspoon.

PAN-ROASTED SWEET POTATOES

with Cranberries and Pecans

Makes about 10 servings

In a large cast-iron skillet over medium-high heat, heat 1 tablespoon of the oil. Add the onion, garlic, and thyme; cook until the onions are soft, 5 to 7 minutes. Add half the sweet potatoes and cook until golden and tender, stirring occasionally, about 20 minutes. Transfer the vegetables to a medium bowl. Add the remaining 1 tablespoon oil to the skillet and heat just until it shimmers. Cook the remaining sweet potatoes, stirring occasionally, for 20 minutes. Return the first batch of sweet potatoes to the skillet and season them to taste with salt and pepper. Reduce heat to low.

In a small bowl, whisk together the vinegar, orange juice, honey, and harissa. Toss with the cooked sweet potatoes and add the cranberries. Cook, stirring occasionally, until the sauce thickens, 5 to 10 minutes. Remove from the heat and stir in the pecans and parsley. Serve warm or at room temperature.

NOTE: This dish can be made up to 1 day ahead. Remove it from the refrigerator 1 hour before serving to bring it to room temperature.

> **MAKE IT A MEAL:** For a weeknight dinner, pair with Slow-Roasted Salmon (page 97).
>
> For a holiday menu, pair with Dry-Brined Roast Turkey (page 110), Northwest Celebration Stuffing (page 144), Hearty Greens Caesar (page 72), Sherried Leek and Chanterelle Gravy (page 141), and Salted Caramel Pumpkin Cheesecake (page 256).

2 tablespoons high-heat oil, such as sunflower or refined peanut oil, divided

½ medium yellow onion, thinly sliced

3 cloves garlic, minced

2 teaspoons chopped fresh thyme

3 pounds Red Garnet or Jewel sweet potatoes, peeled and cut into ½-inch cubes, divided

Kosher salt and freshly ground black pepper

3 tablespoons balsamic vinegar

3 tablespoons orange juice

1 tablespoon honey

1 to 3 teaspoons harissa sauce (optional)

½ cup dried cranberries

½ cup toasted chopped pecans

¼ cup chopped fresh Italian parsley

⅒ RECIPE: 210 CAL., 7G FAT (.5G SAT.), 0MG CHOL., 230MG SODIUM, 37G CARB., 5G FIBER, 13G SUGAR, 3G PROTEIN

FIVE TIPS FOR SMARTER HOLIDAY FEASTING

During the holidays it's easy to overindulge, given all the festive foods surrounding us at home, at work, and at parties. If you are worried you may be overdoing it and would like to better control the number of delicious calories you consume at your next holiday feast, here are our top-five tips for smart holiday feasting.

Use a smaller plate: Research proves that simply using a smaller plate will result in half as many calories being consumed. This also works for bowls and drinking glasses too. Want to force yourself to eat even less? Use a napkin rather than a plate—you won't pile up as much food on the napkin.

Use conservative serving sizes: Use smaller serving sizes at least for your first plate—you can always go back for seconds if you are still hungry. Also, don't feel like you have to try every single dish offered.

Don't skip breakfast: If you show up at the party starving, you will likely eat more food than if you already have something in your stomach. People think that skipping breakfast and/or lunch will save them more room for the feast. Most often this results in overdoing it at dinner and crashing soon afterward.

Drink water (or tea): Alcohol, cider, eggnog, fruit punch, and juice all have calories. Rotate a glass of water or hot tea in between each beverage to cut your liquid calories in half.

Bring something healthy: Chances are, other people will be watching what they eat at the feast too. Bring a plate of raw veggies, an appetizer salad, a light soup, sparkling water, a selection of hot teas, or a bowl of home-made popcorn.

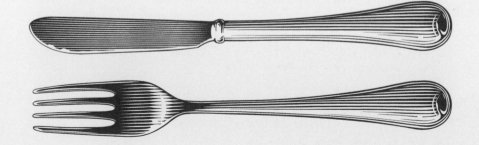

THE DRESSING WILL BE FAMILIAR, but this rich, warm side dish is in no way a true salad. Tossed on the warm sprouts, the dressing becomes a little like a cream sauce, only with much more tangy interest. If you want to play up its salad inspiration, sprinkle it with toasted bread crumbs right before serving— they provide something along the lines of croutons' crunch but stick to the not-quite-a-casserole feeling of this preparation.

ROASTED BRUSSELS SPROUTS CAESAR

Makes 6 to 8 servings

In a small bowl, combine the mayonnaise, mustard, lemon juice, anchovy paste, Worcestershire, garlic, and sugar. Slowly whisk in the oil until the dressing is emulsified. Stir in the Parmesan and season to taste with salt and pepper. Set the dressing aside.

Preheat the oven to 450 degrees F. Put a rimmed baking sheet in the oven for 4 minutes to heat.

In a medium bowl, toss the sprouts with oil, salt, and pepper to taste. Carefully transfer the sprouts to the hot baking sheet. Roast, shaking the pan occasionally, until the sprouts begin to brown, about 20 minutes.

In a serving dish, toss the hot sprouts with the dressing. Sprinkle with Parmesan. Serve warm or cold with lemon wedges.

> **MAKE IT A MEAL:** For a weeknight dinner, pair with Spice-Rubbed Grilled Pork Chops (page 93).
>
> For a holiday menu, pair with Grass-Fed Prime Rib with Fresh Herbs (page 107), Spiced Squash Salad with Lentils and Goat Cheese (page 58), Walnut-Beet Salad (page 68) and Flourless Chocolate Crinkles (page 244).

2 tablespoons mayonnaise

1 tablespoon Dijon mustard

1 tablespoon freshly squeezed lemon juice

1 teaspoon anchovy paste, or to taste

1 teaspoon Worcestershire sauce

3 cloves garlic, minced

Pinch of granulated sugar

¼ cup extra-virgin olive oil, plus more for roasting

¾ ounces (½ cup) shredded Parmesan cheese, plus more for serving

Kosher salt and freshly ground black pepper

3 pounds brussels sprouts, trimmed and halved

Lemon wedges, for serving

½ RECIPE: 220 CAL., 14G FAT (2.5G SAT.), 10MG CHOL., 440MG SODIUM, 19G CARB., 7G FIBER, 4G SUGAR, 9G PROTEIN

ANY LOVER OF LATKES WILL recognize the cooking style here, but potatoes have been replaced with summer squash and a few bright flecks of carrot. To grate them, use either a food processor's shredding blade or the largest holes on a manual grater—you want the pieces large enough to keep their texture.

If you want to make a big batch, the recipe can be doubled. Keep them warm in a 200-degree-F oven on a wire rack set on a baking sheet. Putting these crisp pancakes on the racks will prevent their bottoms from steaming and softening as they do when placed directly on the baking sheet.

SUMMERTIME FRITTERS

Makes 5 servings

In a colander, combine the zucchini, carrots, and salt. Put the colander in the sink and let sit for 15 minutes. Using a clean dish towel, squeeze out as much moisture from the zucchini and carrots as possible (this may be easier done in batches, depending on the size of your colander).

In a large bowl, combine the zucchini-carrot mixture, eggs, flour, Parmesan, onions, garlic, and pepper to taste; mix well with a broad spatula or wooden spoon.

In a large sauté pan over medium heat, heat a little oil. Scoop about ¼ cup batter into the pan and flatten into a pancake shape. Cook for 3 to 5 minutes per side, or until golden brown. Drain on paper towels. Repeat with the remaining batter, re-oiling the pan before cooking every other pancake.

Serve the fritters hot with a dollop of yogurt on top.

MAKE IT A MEAL: For a summery vegetarian dinner, serve alongside Emerald City Salad (page 61).

1½ pounds zucchini or other summer squash, coarsely grated

1 medium carrot, coarsely grated

1 teaspoon kosher salt

2 large eggs

¼ cup all-purpose flour

¾ ounce (¼ cup) shredded Parmesan cheese

2 green onions, thinly sliced (both white and green parts)

1 clove garlic, minced (optional)

Freshly ground black pepper

High-heat oil, such as sunflower or refined peanut oil, for cooking

Plain yogurt or sour cream, for serving (optional)

⅕ RECIPE: 120 CAL., 6G FAT (1.5G SAT.), 80MG CHOL., 500MG SODIUM, 11G CARB., 2G FIBER, 4G SUGAR, 6G PROTEIN

THE EXTRA STEP OF TOASTING the cumin seeds is entirely worth the brief time it takes and turns a simple panful of roasted carrots into something wonderful. Cumin's warm, earthy simplicity makes it a common spice around the world; combining it with orange accents the lemony aroma brought out by toasting it. For another orange-cumin combination, check out the Orange-Kümmel Cocktail (page 230).

ROASTED CUMIN CARROTS

Makes 4 servings

Preheat the oven to 425 degrees F.

In a small skillet over medium heat, toast the cumin seeds for 1 to 2 minutes, stirring until fragrant and slightly darker. Remove from the heat and cool to room temperature. In a spice mill or mortar, grind half the seeds to a fine powder. Combine the freshly ground powder with the whole seeds and set aside.

On a rimmed baking sheet, toss the carrots with the oil, orange juice, and salt and pepper to taste. Roast until golden brown and tender, stirring occasionally, 25 to 30 minutes. Remove from the oven and toss with the parsley and half of the cumin.

In a small bowl, combine the yogurt and remaining cumin; season to taste with salt.

Serve the warm carrots topped with cumin yogurt.

> **MAKE IT A MEAL:** For a quick weeknight dinner, serve with Spicy Chicken Thighs (page 117). The cumin yogurt is delicious alongside the chicken; you could even grill a few pitas and turn the chicken into sandwiches topped with more cumin yogurt.

¾ teaspoon cumin seeds

1 pound carrots, peeled and sliced ½-inch thick on the diagonal

1 tablespoon extra-virgin olive oil

2 teaspoons orange juice

Kosher salt and freshly ground black pepper

1 tablespoon chopped fresh Italian parsley

⅓ cup plain Greek yogurt

¼ RECIPE: 100 CAL., 4.5G FAT (1G SAT.), 0MG CHOL., 240MG SODIUM, 12G CARB., 3G FIBER, 7G SUGAR, 4G PROTEIN

SOFT, MEATY, AND TANGY, THIS Sicilian dish is meant to balance the sweetness of roasted vegetables and a pinch of sugar with bright vinegar; this version adds capers and olives, but some use raisins or pine nuts for contrast. If you have time to make it in advance, letting it sit overnight in the refrigerator lets its flavors mellow and meld. Along with being a side dish, it can be served as an appetizer alongside crostini; it's perfect this way (or really, any other way) as part of an end-of-summer outdoor dinner.

OVEN-ROASTED CAPONATA

Makes 6 to 8 servings

Preheat the oven to 425 degrees F. Line a rimmed baking sheet with parchment paper.

Put the eggplant, pepper, onion, and tomatoes on the prepared baking sheet, sprinkle with the salt, and drizzle with the oil. Using tongs, toss gently to coat everything with the salt and oil.

Bake for about 20 minutes, until parts of the vegetables are light golden. Stir the mixture gently and bake for 7 to 10 more minutes, until the color is beginning to deepen and you can see that more pieces of the vegetables are developing light-golden sections. Stir once more and bake for an additional 10 minutes, until all the vegetables are developing rich golden color and fairly soft.

Remove from the oven and sprinkle on the olives and capers. In a small bowl, combine the vinegar and sugar. Spoon this over the caponata and gently toss to combine. Cook for another 8 to 10 minutes, until it looks richly caramelized. Serve hot, cool, or at room temperature.

> **MAKE IT A MEAL:** Serve with Chicken Piccata Salad with Grilled Lemons (page 149) and a baguette.

1 large eggplant (about 1½ pounds), cut into 1-inch cubes
1 large red bell pepper, cut into 1-inch pieces
1 medium white onion, cut into 1-inch pieces
10 ounces plum or cherry tomatoes, halved
1 teaspoon kosher salt, plus more as needed
¼ cup extra-virgin olive oil
¾ cup pitted kalamata olives, chopped
¼ cup small capers, drained
3 tablespoons white wine vinegar
1 tablespoon granulated sugar

½ RECIPE: 150 CAL., 12G FAT (1G SAT.), 0MG CHOL., 620MG SODIUM, 12G CARB., 3G FIBER, 6G SUGAR, 2G PROTEIN

THIS IS A BEAUTIFUL BOWL of whole grains that will brighten up a late-winter night with its mix of fresh tangerine, sweet persimmon, and lemony pistachios. To stretch the season of this dish, substitute mandarin oranges in December or tangelos (the pomelo-tangerine hybrid) all the way into March. They will vary a bit in size but not enough to require adjustments to the recipe. If you like, you can cook the emmer farro ahead of time and freeze it for up to six months; it takes well to being cooked in a big batch and portioned for later use.

Make sure to use the slightly pointed, teardrop-shaped Hachiya persimmon here, rather than the flatter Fuyu, which has a different texture when fully ripe that makes it hard to slice.

EMMER FARRO WITH TANGERINES AND PERSIMMONS

Makes 4 to 6 servings

In a medium saucepan over medium-high heat, bring the farro and water to a boil. Reduce the heat to medium-low, cover the pan, and simmer until the farro is tender and pleasantly chewy, 50 to 60 minutes. Drain and set aside.

Meanwhile, zest and juice 1 tangerine; peel and segment the remaining 2 tangerines. Set aside.

In a small bowl, whisk together the tangerine zest and juice, vinegar, mustard, honey, and garlic. Slowly drizzle in the oil, whisking constantly until the dressing is emulsified. Season to taste with salt and pepper.

In a large bowl, gently toss together the farro, dressing, tangerine segments, persimmon, pistachios, endive, parsley, mint, and onions. Serve at room temperature.

> **MAKE IT A MEAL:** For a cozy winter's night in, serve with Butternut Squash–Apple Soup (page 34) and Vegan Gingersnaps (page 255).

1 cup **emmer farro**

5 cups water

3 medium tangerines

2 tablespoons champagne or white wine vinegar

1 tablespoon Dijon mustard

1 tablespoon honey

1 clove garlic, minced

¼ cup extra-virgin olive oil

Kosher salt and freshly ground black pepper

1 ripe Hachiya persimmon, peeled and diced (optional)

¼ cup shelled pistachios

1 medium head Belgian endive, cored and thinly sliced

2 tablespoons chopped fresh Italian parsley

1 tablespoon chopped fresh mint

3 green onions, thinly sliced (green parts only)

⅕ RECIPE: 320 CAL., 16G FAT (2G SAT.), 0MG CHOL., 240MG SODIUM, 42G CARB., 8G FIBER, 10G SUGAR, 8G PROTEIN

A SPECIFIC BRAND OF HOT peppers is called out here, but with good reason: Mama Lil's peppers are a regional classic that aren't quite like any other product—they're the sort of thing that Seattle expats have shipped to them by the case. They have been pickled and then oil cured, so they're sweet-hot, briny, and rich all in one intense little bite. If you can't find them, look for peppers that are both roasted and pickled. Whatever the brand, each jar is basically two separate ingredients: the peppers and the bright-red spicy oil they're packed in, which is tasty when brushed on bread before making a sandwich of cold cuts, drizzled on fresh mozzarella, or whisked in for a small part of the oil in a homemade vinaigrette.

SMOKED MOZZARELLA PASTA SALAD PCC Deli Favorite

Makes 6 servings

Bring a large pot of generously salted water to a boil and cook the fusilli according to the package instructions (usually 7 to 8 minutes), or until al dente. Drain, rinse, and let dry in a colander.

Quarter the pepper rings and set aside. Wash your hands thoroughly after handling the peppers to avoid accidentally getting any of the oil in your eyes.

In a blender or the work bowl of a food processor, pulse together the parsley, vinegar, mayonnaise, garlic, salt, and pepper until combined.

In a large bowl, toss the pasta with the peppers and dressing until the pasta is well coated; it will continue to absorb a little dressing, so it's fine if the pasta seems slightly overdressed at first. Sprinkle on the mozzarella and Parmesan and fold a few times with a broad spatula to mix. Serve cold.

> **MAKE IT A MEAL:** For a summer cookout, serve alongside grilled Italian sausages and Hearty Greens Caesar (page 72).

¼ teaspoon kosher salt, plus more as needed
8 ounces fusilli noodles
2 tablespoons drained Mama Lil's Original pickled peppers
2 tablespoons fresh Italian parsley leaves
1½ tablespoons white balsamic vinegar
¼ cup mayonnaise
1 clove garlic, minced
½ teaspoon freshly ground black pepper, or to taste
4 ounces (about 1 cup) shredded smoked mozzarella cheese
½ ounce (about 3 tablespoons) shredded Parmesan cheese

⅙ RECIPE: 280 CAL., 12G FAT (3G SAT.), 20MG CHOL., 350MG SODIUM, 31G CARB., 0G FIBER, 3G SUGAR, 9G PROTEIN

THIS GRAVY RECIPE IS ONE to keep handy if your family includes vegans or vegetarians, but the chanterelles make it so luxurious that it will also delight any gastronomes lucky enough to taste it. It's vegan, with deep flavor thanks to umami-boosting ingredients like nutritional yeast and tamari; it suits both vegetarian entrées and beef rib roast very well indeed. If chanterelles are not readily available, you may substitute cremini mushrooms.

SHERRIED LEEK AND CHANTERELLE GRAVY

Makes 8 servings

In a large, heavy pot over medium heat, heat the oil. Add the leeks and chanterelles and cook for 10 to 20 minutes, stirring occasionally, until the leeks are very soft and melted and the mushrooms are soft and deep golden. Pour in the vegetable broth and stir.

Add the sherry, tamari, pepper, flour, and yeast and stir until the mushrooms are coated and the liquid is bubbling, then pour in the boiling water and stir to blend. Reduce the heat to low and simmer for 3 to 7 minutes, until the gravy has thickened. If a smoother gravy is preferred, puree with an immersion blender or in small batches in a countertop blender. Serve immediately.

2 TABLESPOONS: 90 CAL., 4G FAT (.5G SAT.), 0MG CHOL., 550MG SODIUM, 10G CARB., 1G FIBER, 2G SUGAR, 3G PROTEIN

- 2 tablespoons extra-virgin olive oil
- 2 medium leeks (white and 3 inches of green parts only), washed thoroughly and thinly sliced
- 1½ cups very thinly sliced chanterelle mushrooms
- 2 cups vegetable broth
- ½ cup golden sherry or dry white wine
- ¼ cup tamari
- ½ teaspoon freshly ground black pepper
- ⅓ cup toasted all-purpose flour (see below)
- 2 tablespoons nutritional yeast
- 1 cup boiling water

TAKE TIME FOR TOASTED FLOUR

Cooking many foods to the point of caramelization adds a layer of nutty sweetness to whatever the flavor may be. Flours take well to this treatment, and toasting flour is fast and easy. Spread 3 cups of flour on a rimmed baking sheet (line it with parchment or a silicone baking mat, or not, as you prefer). Bake for about 6 minutes at 350 degrees F until it's taken on noticeable color but isn't truly dark brown; cool it completely before using. You can store it just as you would untoasted flour—in an airtight container in the pantry or stashed in the refrigerator or freezer. Use in gravy or chocolate chip cookies, and see how the flavor shines.

STUFFING

Perhaps obviously, stuffing used to be cooked stuffed inside a roast. In the South, the word "dressing" became the norm, and it was frequently cooked separately and served alongside the roast. Today, cooking on the side has become the best practice for food safety, but the name "stuffing" seems here to stay.

Knowing how the process works gives you complete freedom to work around any allergies to corn, wheat, gluten, nuts, or shellfish (all common in popular recipes), and it lets you make creative use of what you may already have in the pantry. For that matter, stuffing is so beloved that making a small batch to serve alongside a rotisserie chicken can provide serious comfort.

Cooking with the pan covered or uncovered makes a big difference in texture—from dry and crispy to soft and juicy. A double boiler is a good alternative if you want to go with a softer style or are attempting to safely replicate the cooked-in-the-bird method for very rich, moist stuffing; this also works well if you've got a recipe that binds the stuffing together with eggs.

1 BUILD THE BASE

The sky's the limit: start with a bread of your choice (crusts on!), cornbread, or cooked grains like quinoa or wild rice. You can blend them in all kinds of delicious ways for great texture, flavor, and nutrition. Use a bit of rye or sourdough bread for tanginess, cooked spelt berries for chewy sweetness, or fluffy baguettes for simplicity. Even couscous can be a fun addition. Chestnuts are so sweet and starchy they belong here rather than as a crunchy accent.

2 DRESS IT UP

Sweetness comes from fruit—you can use dried fruits like cherries, apples, prunes, or apricots, or dense, fresh fall fruits like apples, pears, or parboiled quince. On the savory side, roasted and finely chopped mushrooms, wild or cultivated, add moisture and umami, while sausage (cooked and crumbled fresh, or sliced cured) is one of the most flavorful ingredients you can choose. Smoked oysters are a classic stuffing component with strongly divided fans and opponents.

3 SLOSH IT AROUND

Where bread pudding relies on milk and eggs as binders, stuffing needs more savory liquids. Chicken or turkey broth is the obvious option—it complements the main course, adds tons of flavor, and supplies fat that will help make the bread crispy. Vegetable or mushroom broth is an equally flavorful choice. Hard cider, dark beer, or dry sherry make a noticeable difference to the final dish. Or lighten things up and use half water with any of these ideas. Finally, a few custard-style stuffings have an egg or two along with the liquid.

4 CHOOSE THE AROMATICS

Sage and thyme are the two classic herbs, but they're only a starting point. Fennel bulb or fronds, celery (if you don't like the texture, use celery leaves or diced celeriac), and caramelized onions are all excellent choices. A bit of orange zest can add fruit flavor without texture and is wonderful with toasted nut stuffings. Be generous with the salt and pepper too.

5 MAKE IT CRUNCHY AND CRISPY

If you have a favorite nut or seed, there's a way to make it work in stuffing. In general, nuts and seeds are better in crisp stuffing rather than the soft, custardy kinds. From pecans to pine nuts and pepitas, they can all work. Remember that salted nuts can add a lot of sodium to the final dish, so you may need to adjust with low-sodium broth or scale back on the added salt. Bake it, covered, until hot throughout, then bake uncovered until the top is crispy.

FLAVOR COMBINATIONS TO TRY

- Cornbread, cured Spanish chorizo, apples, fresh parsley
- Wild rice, dried currants, pecans, dark beer, orange zest
- Rye bread, caramelized onions, prunes, thyme
- Sourdough bread, dried apples, walnuts, dry cider, fresh sage
- Quinoa, chestnuts, pancetta, dried cranberries

THIS ISN'T A RECIPE THAT subscribes to the "less is more" style—it starts with bread but adds sausage, vegetables, apple, abundant fresh herbs, dried cranberries, and a handful of crunchy seeds and hazelnuts for good measure. Feel free to pare it back a bit if you prefer, skipping the seeds or dried cranberries in favor of a somewhat simpler dish. If your goal is a vegetarian stuffing, it's perfectly fine to skip the sausage or use a vegetarian sausage like Field Roast's Italian links. Swiss chard has white stems, so its color won't bleed into the rest of the dish; the color from red or rainbow chard stems will.

NORTHWEST CELEBRATION STUFFING

Makes 6 to 8 servings

Preheat the oven to 375 degrees F. Butter a 3-quart casserole dish or 9-by-13-inch baking dish and set aside.

Scatter the bread chunks on a rimmed baking sheet and bake until lightly toasted, 4 to 6 minutes. Set aside.

In a large sauté pan over medium heat, melt the butter and add the onion, celery, apple, sage, rosemary, and parsley. Cook for 5 to 7 minutes, until the onion becomes soft and translucent. Remove from the heat and cover.

In a large heatproof bowl, put the toasted bread chunks and chard. Add the hot onion-apple mixture, sausage, hazelnuts, sunflower seeds, pumpkin seeds, and cranberries and toss with tongs or two big spoons to mix the ingredients well. Add enough broth to moisten the mixture and season generously with salt and pepper.

Spoon the stuffing into the prepared casserole dish, cover with aluminum foil, and bake for 30 minutes, until heated through. Carefully remove the foil and bake for an additional 10 minutes, until the stuffing is sizzling and golden on top.

½ RECIPE: 430 CAL., 23G FAT (8G SAT.), 35MG CHOL., 710MG SODIUM, 42G CARB., 2G FIBER, 11G SUGAR, 17G PROTEIN

¼ cup unsalted butter, plus more for the pan

1 loaf day-old whole wheat bread, cut or torn into chunks

1 cup chopped yellow onion

1 cup chopped celery

1 large apple, peeled, cored, and chopped

1 tablespoon chopped fresh sage

1 tablespoon chopped fresh rosemary

¼ cup chopped fresh Italian parsley

1 cup chopped Swiss chard

8 ounces mild or hot fresh Italian sausage, crumbled and cooked

¼ cup chopped raw hazelnuts

2 tablespoons sunflower seeds

2 tablespoons pumpkin seeds

⅓ cup dried cranberries

¾ cup to 1 cup hot chicken or turkey broth

Kosher salt and freshly ground black pepper

EASY WEEK-NIGHT MEALS

AH, DINNER. Always necessary (over seven thousand will occur in twenty years), ideally simple enough to accomplish while multitasking with ever-changing family needs, hopefully both nutritious and tasty, and crafted in a way that doesn't destroy the monthly food budget: we demand a lot from our weeknight meals and award a few bonus points for leftovers that are well suited for workday lunches. That's a lot to expect at the end of the day, so it's no wonder that even if you truly love cooking, the endless stream of dinners can get a little discouraging.

The recipes here employ a broad mix of cooking techniques, from quick stir-frying to grilling to making casseroles to nothing more than whisking together a dressing while pasta cooks. Have leftover rice and a can of beans on hand? You're halfway there to family-favorite Burrito Bowls (page 156). Is it springtime and you're in love with fresh green vegetables? Head straight for Asparagus Ravioli Salad (page 165) or Linguine with Asparagus and Peas (page 162). Need a new idea for Meatless Monday? You need Egg Korma (page 172) in your life.

Every family has meals that end up part of the regular rotation. They're the fastest to assemble since the cooks don't need to refer to the printed recipe, and they're frequently featured in the best part of weeknight dinners: the memories. When we reminisce about childhood dinner traditions, when we talk about how no other version compares to what mom or dad made, when our grown kids ask us to pass along that family casserole recipe, we're talking about those greatest hits. Those keepers are worth searching for, and it's worth finding time for the occasional weeknight experiment. Weeknight dinners are worth the effort in the long run.

THIS CHICKEN DISH IS FANTASTICALLY flavorful, and with a base of grilled chicken breasts, it's quick to prepare. Then it's up to you—will you serve it plain, letting the capers and bits of grilled lemon shine? Or will you turn it into sandwiches (both crusty rolls and pita work nicely), perhaps with some baby greens for contrast?

CHICKEN PICCATA SALAD

with Grilled Lemons   PCC Deli Favorite

Makes 4 servings

Place the chicken breasts between two sheets of parchment paper. Pound them to an even 1-inch thickness with a mallet. Put the chicken in a broad, shallow bowl.

In a small bowl, combine the oil, lemon juice and zest, garlic, salt, and pepper. Pour half the dressing over the chicken, cover, and refrigerate for 30 minutes. Whisk 2 tablespoons of the Parmesan into the remaining dressing and refrigerate.

Preheat a grill to medium (350 degrees F). Lightly oil the grates. Using tongs, put the lemons on the grill and cook, without flipping, until deep grill marks appear, about 3 minutes. Leave the grill on. Cool the lemons to room temperature and finely chop half of them. Reserve the remaining lemon slices for garnish.

Lightly oil the grates again and use tongs to put the chicken on the grill. Cook until an instant-read thermometer inserted into the thickest part of the meat reads 155 degrees F, about 5 minutes per side. You can also make a small incision in the thickest part of the meat to make sure it's no longer pink. Cool the chicken until you can comfortably handle it and cut into bite-size cubes.

On a serving platter or in a large shallow bowl, combine the chicken with the finely chopped lemons, parsley, basil, capers, and green onion. Toss the remaining dressing with the chicken until everything is lightly coated. Garnish with the lemon slices and remaining 2 tablespoons Parmesan.

1¼ pounds boneless, skinless chicken breasts

¼ cup extra-virgin olive oil, plus more for grilling

¼ cup freshly squeezed lemon juice (from 1 medium lemon)

1 teaspoon freshly grated lemon zest

2 cloves garlic, minced

½ teaspoon kosher salt

½ teaspoon black pepper

¾ ounce (about 4 tablespoons) shredded Parmesan cheese, divided

½ medium lemon, very thinly sliced and seeded

2 tablespoons chopped fresh Italian parsley

2 tablespoons chopped fresh basil

2 tablespoons capers

2 tablespoons thinly sliced green onion (green parts only)

WINE PAIRING: Opt for a fresh, bright pinot grigio with lemony aromas and flavors to play up the grilled lemons in this dish.

¼ RECIPE: 340 CAL., 22G FAT (4G SAT.), 85MG CHOL., 500MG SODIUM, 5G CARB., 1G FIBER, 1G SUGAR, 31G PROTEIN

SPELT BERRIES HAVE A MILDLY sweet, nutty flavor and pleasantly chewy texture that create a sturdy base for tofu and crisp vegetables. As with other whole grains, it can be an excellent time-saver to cook a big pot of them and package smaller portions for later use. They'll cook fastest if soaked in cool water overnight. During both soaking and cooking, they will swell considerably—one cup raw spelt berries becomes about two and a half cups cooked.

SPICY TOFU AND SPELT PCC Deli Favorite

Makes 6 servings

In a medium saucepan over high heat, bring the water to a rolling boil. Add the spelt, stir vigorously, cover, and reduce the heat to low. Simmer for about 1 hour, until the grains are pleasantly chewy; if the grains were soaked overnight, they will cook in 40 to 45 minutes. Drain any excess water from the spelt, rinse, and cool to room temperature.

In a small bowl, combine the tamari, ginger, garlic, mirin, cayenne, sesame oil, and olive oil and mix until the sauce is blended.

Preheat the oven to 325 degrees F. Cut the tofu into 1-inch cubes and put on a rimmed baking sheet. Pour the sauce over the tofu and bake for 15 minutes. Stir gently and bake for another 15 minutes, or until the tofu is a rich shade of brown. Cool slightly, then put in a serving bowl.

Add the spelt, bell pepper, green onions, cabbage, carrot, and parsley; gently toss to combine. Serve warm, at room temperature, or cold.

> **BEER PAIRING:** To bring together the spicy tofu and nutty whole grains, look for a cream ale or blonde ale, both of which are typically smooth, malty beers that keep their bitter and hoppy notes in the background.

> **MAKE IT A MEAL:** Play up the sesame-tamari-mirin flavor combination with Cara Cara and Blood Orange Salad with Sweet Chili–Sesame Vinaigrette (page 87).

5 cups water

2 cups spelt berries

½ cup tamari

1 teaspoon minced peeled fresh ginger

1 teaspoon minced garlic

2 tablespoons mirin

½ teaspoon cayenne pepper

½ cup toasted sesame oil

½ cup extra-virgin olive oil

1¼ pounds extra-firm tofu

½ medium red bell pepper, very thinly sliced

3 to 4 green onions (both green and white parts), thinly sliced

½ cup finely shredded red cabbage

1 medium carrot, peeled and shredded

¼ cup coarsely chopped fresh Italian parsley

⅙ RECIPE: 620 CAL., 43G FAT (5G SAT.), 0MG CHOL., 830MG SODIUM, 51G CARB., 6G FIBER, 6G SUGAR, 16G PROTEIN

SCALLOPS ARE BOUNTIFUL IN PROTEIN, vitamin B12, omega-3 fats, and other nutrients such as magnesium and potassium that help us maintain normal blood pressure. They're also one of the quickest proteins to prepare, cooking in less than five minutes. Because they are perishable, it's best to either buy them the same day you'll cook them or buy frozen scallops—they lose nothing in quality and need about thirty minutes to thaw, all the time you need to prepare the pesto and relax with a glass of wine. A creamy risotto would be the ideal side dish.

SEARED SCALLOPS WITH ARUGULA PESTO

Makes 4 servings

In the work bowl of a food processor, combine the arugula, pine nuts, garlic, lemon juice, and Parmesan; pulse about eight times, until everything is chopped. With the machine running, drizzle in the olive oil until smooth. Season to taste with salt and pepper; set aside.

Rinse the scallops, pat them dry with paper towels, and season them generously with salt and pepper. In a cast-iron or stainless-steel sauté pan over high heat, heat the high-heat oil and butter until it shimmers, then place the scallops in the pan so they're not touching. Don't touch them again until you are ready to flip.

Sear the scallops until a golden crust forms, 1½ to 3 minutes on the first side. Gently flip them over and cook for an additional 30 to 90 seconds. They should have a golden crust on each side while their centers remain slightly translucent; the scallops will continue to cook a little once removed from the heat. Spread the pesto on a plate, top with the scallops, sprinkle with additional pine nuts, and serve immediately.

NOTE: Extra pesto can be refrigerated for up to 1 week or frozen for up to 1 month. Toss it with pasta, spread it on sandwiches, or serve it with roast chicken or any white fish.

4 cups baby arugula
  (about 4 ounces)
3 tablespoons toasted pine
  nuts, plus more for garnish
1 clove garlic
1 tablespoon freshly squeezed
  lemon juice
½ ounce (about 3 tablespoons)
  grated Parmesan cheese
¼ cup extra-virgin olive oil
Kosher salt and freshly ground
  black pepper
1 pound scallops
1 tablespoon high-heat oil,
  such as sunflower or refined
  peanut oil
1 tablespoon unsalted butter

WINE PAIRING:
Grassy, herbal sauvignon blanc is a great choice with assertive green vegetables, and that includes the arugula pesto here.

¼ RECIPE: 330 CAL., 26G FAT (5G SAT.), 40MG CHOL., 670MG SODIUM, 6G CARB., 1G FIBER, 1G SUGAR, 16G PROTEIN

SUCCULENT, WELL-SPICED PORK AND SWEET red grapes—this is a dish to come back to. You can serve the combination with nothing more than some garlicky greens, or use it to top polenta, gnocchi, or mashed potatoes. If you plan to take leftovers to work for lunch, they'll reheat more evenly if you slice the extra sausage links into thin rounds. Otherwise, the grapes will boil before the sausage is hot all the way through.

ITALIAN SAUSAGES WITH ROASTED GRAPES

Makes 4 servings

Preheat the oven to 450 degrees F.

In a large cast-iron or ovenproof skillet over medium-high heat, add the oil and sausage, and fry until browned on all sides, turning occasionally, about 5 minutes. Add the broth, thyme, grapes, and shallots and transfer to the oven.

Roast, turning the grapes and sausages halfway through the cooking time, until the grapes start to caramelize and the sausages are cooked through and begin to burst, 12 to 15 minutes.

Divide the sausages among four bowls, arranging the grapes alongside. Return the skillet to high heat and add the wine, scraping the browned bits from the bottom of the skillet. Drizzle this pan sauce over the sausages and sprinkle with the parsley before serving.

¼ RECIPE: 370 CAL., 22G FAT (5G SAT.), 75MG CHOL., 670MG SODIUM, 20G CARB., 1G FIBER, 15G SUGAR, 20G PROTEIN

1 tablespoon extra-virgin olive oil
1 pound fresh hot or sweet Italian sausage links
⅓ cup chicken broth
½ teaspoon dried thyme
1 pound seedless red grapes, stemmed
¼ cup chopped shallots
⅓ cup dry red wine
Fresh Italian parsley leaves, for garnish

> **WINE PAIRING:** A juicy Italian red with a hint of earthiness is just the thing with sweet roasted grapes and spicy sausage. Go fizzy with a lambrusco or keep it simple with a Chianti.

SKIP THE TORTILLA WRAPPER AND sit down with a hearty vegetarian bowl that includes the most nutritious parts of your favorite burrito. If you're not a fan of cilantro, try substituting Italian parsley for it in this recipe; mixing the lime juice, fresh herbs, and enough salt into the rice is an important step that functions almost like dressing a salad, giving the seasoned beans a contrasting base layer. Make sure to taste the rice on its own; if it seems flat, add another few shakes of salt.

BURRITO BOWLS

Makes 4 servings

In a medium bowl, put the cooked rice and use a wooden spoon or broad spatula to fold in the cilantro and lime juice. Season to taste with salt. Divide the rice among four bowls and set aside.

In a sauté pan over medium-high heat, heat the oil just until it shimmers. Add the onion, bell pepper, and garlic, and cook until the vegetables have softened, about 8 minutes. Add the beans, cumin, oregano, and paprika; heat through and stir well to mix the aromatics into the beans.

Top the rice bowls with scoops of the seasoned beans, along with avocado, lettuce, tomatoes, and sour cream. Sprinkle with additional cilantro.

> **BEER PAIRING:** Play up the bright flavors of these bowls with a Seattle-style IPA made with Citra hops. Some of these are so citrusy it's like they've dropped an invisible lime wedge into your pint glass.

¼ RECIPE: 280 CAL., 8G FAT (1G SAT.), 0MG CHOL., 170MG SODIUM, 45G CARB., 10G FIBER, 2G SUGAR, 9G PROTEIN

2 cups cooked brown rice

¼ cup chopped fresh cilantro, plus more for garnish

Freshly squeezed juice of 1 medium lime

Kosher salt

2 teaspoons high-heat oil, such as sunflower or refined peanut oil

½ medium white onion, chopped

1 medium red or yellow bell pepper, chopped

2 cloves garlic, minced

1 (15-ounce) can black beans, rinsed and drained

1 teaspoon ground cumin

1 teaspoon dried oregano

½ teaspoon sweet paprika

1 medium avocado, sliced

1 cup shredded romaine lettuce

Chopped tomatoes, for serving

Sour cream, for serving

IF YOU'VE NOT COOKED WITH celeriac before, this is a great place to discover just how it can shine—it offers the same peppery flavor as celery with a texture that's smooth and dense, like a turnip. While celery tends to dissolve into mush when it's cooked in soups, celeriac holds its shape but softens to a tender bite.

CHICKEN POTPIE WITH DILL BUTTERMILK BISCUITS

Makes 8 servings

Preheat the oven to 425 degrees F.

In a Dutch oven over medium heat, melt 4 tablespoons of the butter. Add the onion and garlic; cook until the onions are soft, about 7 minutes. Stir in ¼ cup of the flour to form a loose paste. Slowly whisk in the broth and milk; season to taste with salt and pepper. Bring to a boil. Reduce the heat to low and simmer until slightly thickened, 5 to 7 minutes.

Stir in the chicken, carrots, celeriac, peas, and 1 tablespoon of the dill and simmer for 20 minutes, stirring occasionally.

Meanwhile, prepare the biscuits by mixing together the remaining 2 cups flour, the baking soda, the baking powder, the sugar, a generous pinch of salt, and the remaining 2 tablespoons dill in a bowl.

Add the remaining 4 tablespoons butter and the Neufchâtel and combine with a pastry blender or your fingertips until mixture is crumbly and no piece is larger than an English pea. Stir in the buttermilk and gently mix with a large fork or your hands to form a dough.

Roll the dough out into a circle that will fit inside the Dutch oven; height will vary somewhat according to the size of the pot, but it should be between ½ and 1 inch thick. With a very sharp knife, cut the circle of dough into triangles (as if you were slicing a pie) and place them on top of the hot potpie filling. Bake until the biscuits are golden brown and the filling is bubbly around the edges, 15 to 20 minutes.

⅛ RECIPE: 390 CAL., 18G FAT (10G SAT.), 65MG CHOL., 690MG SODIUM, 41G CARB., 3G FIBER, 8G SUGAR, 18G PROTEIN

8 tablespoons (1 stick) unsalted butter, divided

1 medium yellow onion, finely chopped

2 cloves garlic, minced

2¼ cups all-purpose flour, divided

2 cups chicken broth

2 cups whole milk

Kosher salt and freshly ground black pepper

2 medium boneless, skinless chicken breasts (about 14 ounces), cooked and shredded

1 cup peeled and chopped carrots (from about 1 large carrot)

1 cup peeled and chopped celeriac (from about 1 medium celeriac)

1 cup frozen peas, thawed

3 tablespoons chopped fresh dill, divided

2 teaspoons baking soda

½ teaspoon baking powder

1 teaspoon granulated sugar

4 ounces cold Neufchâtel (low-fat cream cheese)

1 cup cultured buttermilk

WINE PAIRING: A glass of creamy (not oaky) chardonnay will be every bit as comforting as the chicken potpie itself.

INSTEAD OF SPENDING A LOT of time hand-rolling enchiladas, try this grain-based casserole for the same great flavor with much less fuss. While quinoa has plenty of protein already, you could add some shredded roast chicken to the mixture if you like. It's a great make-ahead dish to stash in the freezer, and the quinoa will hold its texture perfectly if baked straight from the freezer (see note).

QUINOA ENCHILADA BAKE

Makes 6 servings

Preheat the oven to 375 degrees F.

In a medium saucepan over high heat, bring the water and a generous pinch of salt to a boil; add the quinoa and return the pot to a boil. Stir, cover, and reduce the heat to medium-low. Simmer until the quinoa is tender but still chewy, about 15 minutes. Fluff with a fork and let cool slightly.

In a large bowl, combine the quinoa, enchilada sauce, chilies, beans, corn, chili powder, cumin, coriander, and cilantro; season to taste with salt and pepper. Stir in half of the cheese.

Spread the mixture in a 2-quart baking dish and top with remaining cheese.

Wrap the casserole in aluminum foil and bake, covered, for about 30 minutes. Remove the foil and bake until the cheese is bubbly and beginning to lightly brown, another 5 to 10 minutes. Serve with the avocado, tomato, and sour cream.

NOTE: Don't bake the dish if you are freezing it for future use. Allow the mixture to cool in the baking dish. Wrap the dish in foil, label, and freeze. To bake, preheat the oven to 375 degrees F. Do not thaw the casserole. Bake, covered, for about 50 minutes. Remove the foil and bake until the cheese is bubbly, about 10 additional minutes. Serve with the avocado, tomato, and sour cream.

2 cups water or vegetable broth
Kosher salt
1 cup quinoa, rinsed and drained
1½ cups green enchilada sauce
1 (4-ounce) can chopped green chilies, drained
1 cup black beans, drained and rinsed
1 cup corn kernels (canned and drained, or frozen and thawed)
1 teaspoon chili powder
½ teaspoon ground cumin
½ teaspoon ground coriander
¼ cup chopped fresh cilantro or Italian parsley
Freshly ground black pepper
6 ounces (1½ cups) shredded Mexican-blend cheese, divided
1 medium avocado, diced, for serving
1 medium tomato, diced, for serving
Sour cream, for serving (optional)

BEER PAIRING: Nutty beers play up the nutty side of quinoa, not its bitterness. Try a dark lager, brown ale, or bock for a casual week-night combo.

⅙ RECIPE: 430 CAL., 17G FAT (6G SAT.), 25MG CHOL., 940MG SODIUM, 53G CARB., 5G FIBER, 9G SUGAR, 19G PROTEIN

QUINOA BASICS

Each tiny grain of quinoa has a thin coating of chemical compounds called saponins. Many plants produce them as a natural insect repellent, and their mild bitterness can be noticeable to some eaters. The herb soapwort has the most concentrated source of them so far identified, and as the name implies, it's a great natural cleanser, complete with foaming bubbles. Saponins tend to get a bad rap, however, as a possible culprit for digestibility problems and related inflammation.

If you have digestive issues or your palate is sensitive to bitterness, rinsing quinoa isn't a bad idea. It's not absolutely necessary, though, and if you have a recipe that calls for toasting quinoa, it's best to skip (drying quinoa after washing takes quite a while and more than one dish towel!). Many packaged brands of quinoa tout that they are prewashed, but this process is actually more of a dry exfoliation.

Red, black, and white quinoa are similar nutritionally, and they're all a high-fiber, gluten-free seed that offers a complete protein with all nine amino acids. Manganese, copper, folate, zinc, and phosphorus are all present in high quantities. These nutritional advantages make sense when you learn that quinoa isn't a grain at all—it's related to chard, beets, and spinach. Even if flavor-wise it's not your favorite, there are great reasons to work it into your diet in moderation. But remember that brown rice, emmer farro, spelt berries, rolled oats, and cornmeal all have their unique qualities, as well as delicious flavors; be sure to enjoy the varieties just as you do for fruits and vegetables.

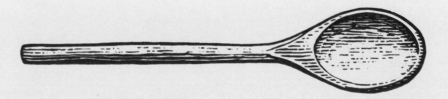

RATHER THAN A DINNER OF pasta with a few vegetables, this is a dinner of vegetables with just enough linguine to make it feel like a complete meal. The goat cheese softens and becomes a thin coating of rich-tasting, slightly tangy sauce. Don't worry about having the precise amount or type of each of the six vegetables; if you have spinach but no arugula, or snap peas but no English peas, the dish will turn out well: electric-green vegetables that deserve a "comfort food" label.

LINGUINE WITH ASPARAGUS AND PEAS

Makes 4 servings

Bring a large pot of salted water to a boil and cook the linguine according to the package directions, until just barely al dente. Err on the side of undercooked since it is going to be folded into the hot sauce and continue to cook. Drain, but don't rinse.

In a medium, heavy-bottomed sauté pan over medium heat, heat the oil. Add the leeks, garlic, asparagus, and peas. Sauté for about 2 minutes, until all the vegetables are bright green. Toss in the arugula, spinach, basil, cheese, and bacon, mixing well to wilt the leaves and melt the cheese. Season to taste with salt and pepper.

Fold the hot pasta into the creamy vegetables and drizzle with a little additional oil. Toss to combine and serve immediately. Garnish with the Parmesan.

WINE PAIRING: With all these crisp green vegetables and the tangy goat cheese, opt for a minerally sauvignon blanc.

¼ RECIPE: 360 CAL., 14G FAT (5G SAT.), 10MG CHOL., 290MG SODIUM, 47G CARB., 2G FIBER, 4G SUGAR, 14G PROTEIN

Kosher salt

8 ounces fresh linguine, or 4 ounces dried

2 tablespoons extra-virgin olive oil, plus more for drizzling

½ cup thinly sliced leeks (white and pale-green parts only), washed thoroughly

3 cloves garlic, minced

4 to 6 medium asparagus spears, tough ends removed and thinly sliced on the diagonal

½ cup sugar snap peas, halved on the diagonal

½ cup snow peas, halved on the diagonal

¼ cup shelled English peas (optional)

1½ cups baby arugula (about 1½ ounces)

1½ cups baby spinach (about 1½ ounces)

½ cup coarsely chopped fresh basil

4 ounces (about ½ cup) soft fresh goat cheese

¼ cup cooked and chopped bacon (optional)

Freshly ground black pepper

Shaved Parmesan cheese, for garnish

MOST LITERALLY AND SIMPLY, THIS is a pasta salad, but that name is entirely too limiting. The ravioli are fat and filled with creamy ricotta; the fresh lemony vinaigrette is enriched with sun-dried tomatoes and Parmesan cheese; sweet red peppers and sliced asparagus keep the flavor profile focused on the salad rather than the pasta; a handful of toasted almonds is just the right crunchy garnish. Served either at room temperature or chilled, it's perfect for dinner at home with a glass of white wine, but it's also a winner when brought as a side dish to a summer cookout.

ASPARAGUS RAVIOLI SALAD PCC Deli Favorite

Makes 4 servings

Bring a large pot of water to a boil and cook the ravioli according to the package directions (typically for 6 minutes). Drain and rinse well until cool. In a serving bowl or on a platter, toss the ravioli with 1 tablespoon of the oil, cover loosely, and set aside at room temperature or in the refrigerator.

In a large, shallow saucepan over high heat, bring several cups of salted water to a boil. Using tongs, put the asparagus in the pan and blanch it for 3 minutes, until it is vibrant green and still snappy-crisp. Drain and cool to the point where you can comfortably handle it, then slice the stalks thinly on the diagonal.

In a large bowl, combine the remaining ⅓ cup oil, the lemon juice, the tomatoes, the garlic, and the pepper and blend with a whisk for about 20 seconds. Pour the dressing over the ravioli. Add the asparagus, onions, bell pepper, and Parmesan, and toss gently to dress all the ingredients. Garnish with the almonds. Serve at room temperature, or cover and chill in the refrigerator for 1 hour before serving.

> **CIDER PAIRING:** Perry is the name for traditional pear cider made entirely from pears, while labels reading "pear cider" may well be describing a drink made of apples with pear flavoring added. A dry, aromatic perry is what you want here.

1 pound fresh cheese ravioli

⅓ cup plus 1 tablespoon extra-virgin olive oil, divided

1 bunch medium asparagus spears, tough ends trimmed

¼ cup freshly squeezed lemon juice (from 1 large lemon)

½ cup chopped sun-dried tomatoes

1 teaspoon minced garlic

¾ teaspoon freshly ground black pepper, or to taste

4 green onions, thinly sliced (both green and white parts)

1 small red bell pepper, julienned

1¾ ounces (½ cup) grated Parmesan cheese

⅓ cup slivered almonds, toasted

¼ RECIPE: 700 CAL., 43G FAT (9G SAT.), 70MG CHOL., 880MG SODIUM, 60G CARB., 3G FIBER, 8G SUGAR, 22G PROTEIN

WE'VE BORROWED A LOW COUNTRY classic to make use of small, sweet shrimp from US coastlines. Be generous with the pepper when preparing the grits—the goal is to have snappy bits of cracked peppercorns that cut through the rich saltiness of the cheese.

If you can't find andouille, smoky-sweet kielbasa (either turkey or pork) is a reasonable substitute but lacks some of the heat. If you make the swap, you might want to add a sprinkle of red pepper flakes to the shrimp right before you take the pan off the heat.

SHRIMP AND GRITS

Makes 4 servings

In a medium saucepan over medium-high heat, bring the broth to a boil. Whisk in the grits and reduce the heat to low. Cook, stirring often, until the grits are creamy, 20 to 30 minutes. Stir in the cheeses and cream, then season to taste with salt and pepper; cover and set aside, off the heat.

In a large skillet over medium heat, heat the oil just until it shimmers. Add the chopped sausage and cook until its edges are crispy, about 7 minutes. Increase the heat to medium-high and add the shrimp. Cook, turning only once with tongs, until they are bright pink and cooked through, about 3 minutes. Add the garlic, stir gently, and cook for 1 minute. Stir in the lemon juice and scrape the bottom of the pan to release any browned bits.

Divide the grits among four bowls and top with the sausage, shrimp, and pan sauce. Sprinkle with the onions and drizzle with hot sauce.

> BEER PAIRING: The right beer here is crisp and hoppy, but not strongly so. Northwest-style IPAs will likely have some citrus overtones to accentuate the sweetness of the shrimp, but a simpler pale ale can work wonderfully, too.

4 cups chicken broth

1 cup medium-grind grits (yellow or white)

2 ounces (½ cup) shredded cheddar cheese

2 ounces (½ cup) shredded Parmesan cheese

3 tablespoons heavy cream

Kosher salt and freshly ground black pepper

2 teaspoons extra-virgin olive oil

1 cup chopped andouille sausage

1 pound (26 to 30) large shrimp, peeled and deveined

3 cloves garlic, minced

1 tablespoon freshly squeezed lemon juice

¼ cup thinly sliced green onions (green and light-green parts only), for serving

Hot sauce, for serving (optional)

¼ RECIPE: 480 CAL., 23G FAT (10G SAT.), 210MG CHOL., 1430MG SODIUM, 33G CARB., 2G FIBER, 1G SUGAR, 34G PROTEIN

THE WAY THICK, VELVETY WINTER squash coats pasta with a sauce that seems much richer than it ought to be is nearly magical. Perhaps it's the rich orange color, or perhaps it's the crispy strips of pancetta as garnish, but this dish is enough to make the fettuccine noodles seem downright dull. While the sweetness of kabocha is delicious in this recipe, feel free to substitute an equal amount of fresh or canned butternut squash. If you start with canned squash puree (you will need three cups [twenty-four ounces]), rather than making your own, dinner comes together in no time.

CREAMY WINTER SQUASH FETTUCCINE

Makes 4 servings

Preheat the oven to 400 degrees F. Lightly oil a baking sheet.

Cut around the stem of the squash and discard the stem. Cut the squash in half and scoop out all the seeds. Place the halves cut side down on the baking sheet. Bake until tender, about 50 minutes for butternut squash or up to 65 minutes for kabocha. Let cool until you can safely handle it, then scoop out the flesh and puree in a food processor until smooth. You need 3 cups puree for this recipe; any extra may be frozen for later use.

In a large skillet over medium heat, heat the oil just until it shimmers. Add the pancetta and cook until crisp, about 3 minutes. Using a slotted spoon, remove the pancetta and set aside. In the same skillet over medium heat, cook the onion for about 10 minutes, until very soft and pale gold. Stir in the garlic, thyme, and pepper flakes. Add the squash puree and heat through, stirring gently; season to taste with salt and pepper. Keep warm over low heat.

Bring a large pot of salted water to a boil and cook the pasta according to the package directions, until al dente. Drain, then toss the pasta in the warm squash mixture. Add enough milk to create a sauce and heat through. $\longrightarrow$

2 tablespoons extra-virgin olive oil, plus more for the pan

1 medium kabocha or butternut squash (2 to 3 pounds)

4 slices pancetta, chopped (optional)

1 cup finely chopped white onion

3 cloves garlic, minced

2 teaspoons chopped fresh thyme

Pinch of red pepper flakes (optional)

Kosher salt and freshly ground black pepper

12 ounces fettuccine noodles

½ cup whole milk, or as needed

2 ounces (½ cup) grated fontina, divided

Stir in half the fontina and taste; adjust the seasoning as needed. Divide the pasta among four plates and sprinkle with the pancetta and the remaining cheese. Serve immediately.

> **CIDER PAIRING:** You'll want a long, tart finish to contrast with the smooth squash and crisp, fatty pancetta. Look for apple varieties Golden Russet or Gravenstein, used either as a blend or as a single varietal.

¼ **RECIPE: 590 CAL., 14G FAT (4.5G SAT.), 20MG CHOL., 300MG SODIUM, 100G CARB., 12G FIBER, 12G SUGAR, 19G PROTEIN**

GREAT REASONS TO EAT WINTER SQUASH

Winter squashes, in general, are far more nutritious than summer varieties, such as zucchini or pattypan. With their signature orange flesh and dense textures, winter squashes are an excellent source of heart-healthy vitamin A and a good source of both vitamin C and fiber. Their hard shells make them durable (you can store them in a cool, dark place for about 6 weeks), and they need only a quick scrub if you're roasting them whole.

When it comes to cooking, their textures, much like potatoes, fall into two classes: rich, grainy, and somewhat dry, or smooth and buttery. When you are using them in a pureed form, the types are fairly interchangeable, but when it comes to roasting them whole or in big wedges, the differences are more noticeable. In general, the dry squash varieties include acorn, buttercup, blue, hubbard, kabocha, kuri, and pumpkins. Smoother, more buttery types include butternut, delicata, and sweet dumpling.

THE APPLE SALSA TAKES A very simple dish and turns it into something fresh and quite kid friendly—they won't even notice you're taking leftover rotisserie chicken and turning it into dinner. Sweet, crunchy apples like Fuji or Gala are winners here, and if you have a bit of fresh chili pepper around and appreciate the heat, it can be a nice addition for adult palates. Medium cheddar or a mix of medium and sharp will melt down into smoothness; more aged cheeses can get grainy as they melt.

CHICKEN QUESADILLAS WITH APPLE SALSA

Makes 2 servings

In a small bowl, combine the apple, lemon juice, honey, onion, and salt. Set aside.

In a large skillet over medium heat, melt a little butter. Put 1 tortilla in the hot pan and sprinkle it evenly with chicken, cheese, and spinach. Put the remaining tortilla on top.

Cook until the cheese just begins to melt and the bottom of the tortilla is golden, 2 to 3 minutes. Using a broad metal or plastic spatula, carefully flip the quesadilla over and cook until the cheese is completely melted and the tortilla is golden, another 2 to 3 minutes.

Remove the quesadilla from the pan and allow to cool for 2 minutes. Cut into wedges and serve with the apple salsa.

> **CIDER PAIRING:** Quesadillas call for something as simple as they are themselves. Look for a great Washington or Oregon craft cider in a can; something slightly sweet with big apple flavor will work best with the spinach and apples.

1 medium apple, cored and chopped

1 tablespoon freshly squeezed lemon or lime juice

1 teaspoon honey

1 tablespoon finely chopped red onion

Kosher salt

Unsalted butter, for the pan

2 medium flour tortillas

½ cup cooked and shredded chicken or turkey

2 ounces (½ cup) shredded cheddar cheese

Handful of baby spinach

½ **RECIPE: 350 CAL., 14G FAT (7G SAT.), 50MG CHOL., 560MG SODIUM, 40G CARB., 3G FIBER, 13G SUGAR, 17G PROTEIN**

IT'S FOOLISH TO DESCRIBE A curry dating back to the sixteenth century as modern, but that's how this dish feels—although perhaps "timeless" is a better way to describe a spiced yogurt sauce served with hard-boiled eggs. Korma is a rich curry, not a spicy one.

If you haven't already learned the lesson, you'll discover that eggs are as welcome on the dinner table as they are at breakfast, and keeping a few hard-boiled eggs in the refrigerator means you always have one to add to a salad, or slice, salt, and serve as a side dish.

EGG KORMA

Makes 4 servings

In a large saucepan over medium-high heat, heat the oil. Add the cumin seeds and onion and cook, stirring, until the onions turn soft and golden, about 7 minutes. Add the garlic, ginger, cloves, cinnamon, cardamom, turmeric, and coriander; cook for 2 minutes, stirring constantly.

Add the tomatoes and water; reduce the heat to medium-low. Simmer, stirring often, until the sauce thickens slightly, 6 to 8 minutes. Stir in the yogurt and season to taste with salt and pepper.

Remove the eggshells from the cooked eggs and slit each down the middle without cutting it completely in half (about three-quarters of the way; this will keep the yolks in place while you finish the sauce). Gently put the eggs in the sauce, adding a little bit of water if the sauce is too thick (the sauce should look like a thick gravy). Cover and simmer for 5 minutes. Garnish with the cilantro and serve hot with naan or rice.

NOTE: To hard-boil eggs, put eggs in a saucepan, cover with cold water, and bring to a full boil over high heat. Cover and remove from the heat; let sit for 10 minutes. Transfer the eggs to a bowl of ice water and let cool at least 1 minute.

WINE PAIRING: Korma is a curry that's more rich than it is spicy, making it a little easier to pair than you might think. A dry sparkling rosé or spicy sangiovese will cut through the eggs and thick sauce in all the right ways.

2 tablespoons high-heat oil, such as sunflower or refined peanut oil

½ teaspoon cumin seeds

1 medium white onion, finely chopped

1 teaspoon minced garlic

1-inch knob fresh ginger, peeled and minced

⅛ teaspoon ground cloves

¼ teaspoon ground cinnamon

¼ teaspoon ground cardamom

½ teaspoon ground turmeric

½ teaspoon ground coriander

1 (15-ounce) can fire-roasted crushed tomatoes, drained

½ cup hot water, plus more as needed

1 cup plain yogurt (preferably not nonfat)

Kosher salt and freshly ground black pepper

8 eggs, hard-boiled (see note)

Fresh chopped cilantro, for garnish

Naan or cooked basmati rice, for serving (optional)

¼ RECIPE: 290 CAL., 18G FAT (4.5G SAT.), 375MG CHOL., 340MG SODIUM, 13G CARB., 2G FIBER, 9G SUGAR, 17G PROTEIN

WITH THE HEAT OF FRESH chili heightened with lime juice, this beef salad is sublimely refreshing on hot days and a welcome pick-me-up in the cooler months. It keeps for several days in the refrigerator, making for an excellent lunch of leftovers, and you can serve it with anything from a bowl of steamed jasmine rice to a pile of crunchy romaine leaves for lettuce wraps. With vermicelli noodles, shredded lettuce, a sprinkle of fresh basil and mint, and a bit of tamari or fish sauce as dressing, you have the makings for a flavorful noodle bowl. Or just eat it plain and enjoy the spicy protein.

When trimming the beef, you might find it easier if the meat is partially frozen—about twenty minutes in the freezer is typically long enough to firm it up.

THAI STEAK SALAD PCC Deli Favorite

Makes 6 servings

Preheat the oven to 325 degrees F.

Using a very sharp knife, trim any silver skin (the silvery-white connective tissue) and fat completely away from the beef, and slice the trimmed meat into 2 inch thick pieces, going with the grain. All pieces should be about the same size so they cook at the same rate.

Lightly oil the beef and sprinkle with the salt and pepper. In a large skillet over medium-high heat, sear the pieces on both sides until a caramelized brown crust forms, about 3 minutes per side. Transfer the browned meat to a rimmed baking sheet and roast in the oven, 15 to 20 minutes, until the internal temperature taken with an instant-read thermometer reaches 130 degrees F. The pieces should be medium rare, with noticeable red to pink centers. Cool completely.

Slice the jalapeño in half. Set half aside with the seeds intact (to use in the dressing), and remove the seeds from the other half. Thinly slice the seeded half and set it aside for garnish.

In a blender or the work bowl of a food processor, combine two-thirds of the cilantro, the unseeded jalapeño half, the garlic, the sugar, the lime zest, and the red pepper flakes and pulse about twenty times, until the mixture is a thick, slightly chunky paste. Drizzle in the tamari, lime juice, and oil; blend until smooth. →

1¾ pounds beef top round steak

½ cup extra-virgin olive oil, plus more for the beef

¾ teaspoon kosher salt

1 teaspoon freshly ground black pepper

1 small jalapeño pepper

⅓ cup chopped fresh cilantro, divided

1 tablespoon minced garlic

½ cup granulated sugar

1 tablespoon freshly grated lime zest

¾ teaspoon red pepper flakes

⅓ cup tamari

⅓ cup freshly squeezed lime juice (from about 2 limes)

2 green onions, thinly sliced (both green and white parts)

Slice the cooled meat across the grain very thinly, 2 to 3 inches long by ½ to ¾ inch wide. In a serving dish, toss the meat in the dressing. Garnish with the thinly sliced jalapeño, onions, and remaining cilantro. Let the salad marinate in the refrigerator for at least 30 minutes before serving. Drain any excess liquid and serve chilled.

> **MAKE IT A MEAL:** Shredded Seasonal Vegetables with Lime-Peanut Dressing (Som Tum) (page 82) is a natural pairing with a similar flavor profile but a base of shredded green papaya or other crunchy vegetables.

¼ RECIPE: 440 CAL., 24G FAT (4.5G SAT.), 85MG CHOL., 710MG SODIUM, 20G CARB., 0G FIBER, 16G SUGAR, 36G PROTEIN

MAKING NUTRITION DELICIOUS

Our first experiences with food as children impact our taste preferences throughout life. Strong flavors like garlic, cumin, and vanilla are detectable to the fetus in the mother's womb and even in breast milk, and researchers have confirmed that early exposures make kids more likely to enjoy these flavors when they're young. Early flavor experiences are so important in developing healthy eating habits throughout life that parents are advised to keep offering vegetables to children, even if kids say they don't like them. This has been seen during numerous attempts to get students to choose fresh vegetables when they are available at school—many won't even try them until they have been offered three times.

There is also a hypothesis that we love sweet, rich, and salty foods because of an evolutionary instinct that teaches us to crave foods high in fat, sugar, and salt. You can teach yourself to triumph over these tendencies by making gradual changes: your taste preferences will adapt as you add new foods into your diet.

Try these suggestions:

- Cook grains in broth or with a little wine for additional flavor.
- Lightly steam or blanch your dark-green veggies before adding them to soups and stir-fries. The cooking water will absorb the bitterness.
- Don't rely on salt. A well-balanced dish contains all five standard flavors: sweet, salty, sour, bitter, and umami.
- Try new ways of preparing disliked foods. Roasted brussels sprouts are very different from boiled.
- Look for new produce to try. Two out of three kids like red chard—maybe you will too.

STIR-FRY

It's far too easy to accidentally steam a meal that you intend to stir-fry. If the pan is hot enough and the ingredients aren't overly crowded, the vegetables will stay crisp and colorful. It's a technique worth mastering, because it's easily adaptable for whatever condiments, vegetables, and proteins you happen to have on hand, and it's one of the quickest ways to cook.

1   PREPARE ALL OF THE INGREDIENTS

If you don't start by prepping the entire list of ingredients and assembling any required sauces, vinegars, or cooking liquids close at hand, your stir-fry can get into trouble almost instantly. Every stage of the process cooks quickly and demands your full attention, so there's no time (or extra hands) to slice vegetables or fetch the tamari. Go through the recipe and double-check everything before beginning.

2   HEAT THE PAN

With other styles of cooking, heating the pan isn't such a key step. If you have a wok and a high-powered burner, now's the time to use them both. A well-seasoned wok on a regular burner is the second choice, followed by a very large saucepan or skillet. It's important that the pan is large so the vegetables don't simply cook in their own steam. Turn on the stovetop fan, heat the pan on high heat, add a high-heat oil, and let the oil heat until it shimmers obviously. Don't add any more ingredients until you can tell both the pan and the oil are very hot.

3   COOK THE AROMATICS

These are all members of the allium family—onions, shallots, green onions, garlic, and the like—as well as fresh ginger and chilies, usually very thinly sliced. It's a quick process, and the key to not burning them is tossing them constantly and paying close attention so as soon as they've taken on noticeable color, you're adding additional ingredients that will slightly reduce the temperature and keep them from scorching. It should take just 30 seconds. If the garlic is beyond toasty brown, chances are you've burned it, and it's best to cool down the pan, wipe it out, and start over.

4   COOK THE MEAT AND VEGETABLES

Thin slices and uniform sizing are critical to cooking your chosen proteins and vegetables. Again, rapid and nearly continual tossing of the ingredients is the way to go; you'll hear plenty of accompanying sizzle. If things are hot enough—if you have a powerful burner and a well-seasoned cast-iron or carbon-steel wok—you may even achieve *wok hei*, Cantonese for "breath of a wok," which refers to stir-frying's unique combination of lively, crisp ingredients and smoky, charred undertones. This stage of cooking takes anywhere from 90 seconds to 4 minutes.

5   SEASON WITH SAUCE

Just like the French stir in a bit of butter or a splash of vinegar to finish a sauce, your stir-fry will benefit from seasonings like tamari, black vinegar, mirin, toasted sesame oil, oyster sauce, or any number of styles of chili sauce. If you'll be using more than one sauce—and generally this is the most impactful way to season—you can stir them together in a small dish and add them all at once just before pulling the pan off the heat.

FLAVOR COMBINATIONS TO TRY

- Thin-sliced pork, red bell peppers, cashews, fresh ginger, red pepper flakes, tamari
- Tofu, white onions, green beans, garlic, fresh ginger, toasted sesame oil, rice vinegar
- Flank steak, fresh tomatoes, shallots, fresh ginger, toasted sesame oil
- Shrimp, white onions, snow peas, fish sauce, rice vinegar
- White or dark chicken meat, green bell peppers, shredded cabbage, green onions, tamari, teriyaki sauce

THIS QUICK DISH COMBINES STIR-FRYING with a brief steam to finish cooking, a method that gives all the intense flavor of a pure stir-fry while keeping the beans crisp. Cooking goes so quickly that it's important to have all the ingredients prepped and easily within reach before you add the oil to the pan. The obvious accompaniment is steamed rice, but cooled slightly and tucked into a crusty roll with a drizzle of sriracha sauce, the dish makes a mighty good hot sandwich too.

GARLICKY GREEN BEANS AND SHRIMP

Makes 4 servings

In a wok or large lidded skillet over high heat, heat the oil. Once the oil is shimmering hot, add the onion and cook, stirring constantly, for about 1 minute, until the edges are seared and the slices have slightly softened. Add the garlic, ginger, beans, and shrimp and stir-fry for about 90 seconds, until the beans are bright green, crisp on the ends, and still somewhat raw in the middle. Carefully pour in the broth, being cautious of the steam. Cover the pan and steam until the beans are tender and shrimp are just cooked through, about 3 minutes.

Uncover the pan and add the oyster sauce, red pepper flakes, and sesame seeds. Cook until it is heated through and most of the liquid has evaporated, about 3 more minutes. Serve immediately.

> **BEER PAIRING:** Your favorite IPA will suit this dish perfectly, either a Northwest style with citrusy overtones or something more generally bright and hoppy.

¼ RECIPE: 190 CAL., 8G FAT (2G SAT.), 145MG CHOL., 650MG SODIUM, 11G CARB., 3G FIBER, 4G SUGAR, 18G PROTEIN

2 tablespoons high-heat oil, such as sunflower or refined peanut oil

½ small red onion, thinly sliced

4 cloves garlic, chopped

1-inch knob fresh ginger, peeled and minced

1 pound green beans, trimmed into 2-inch pieces

1 pound (26 to 30) shrimp, peeled and deveined

2 tablespoons chicken or vegetable broth

2 tablespoons oyster sauce

½ teaspoon red pepper flakes (optional)

Black sesame seeds, for garnish

SNACKS & APPS

WE ARE FIRMLY ON TEAM "SNACKS ARE GOOD FOR YOU." Sure, those snacks shouldn't be soda and cookies, and they shouldn't be supersized any more than any other meal, but the world is full of delicious things that qualify as both seminutritious and seriously snackable. (Looking at you, Spicy Peanut Popcorn, page 207. Yes, carrot sticks, also looking at you, as long as Fresh Fava Bean Hummus, page 188, is involved.) If a few bites keep you from overeating at dinner or getting outrageously hangry at the last office meeting of the day, so much the better. Snacks are also a low-pressure way to experiment with unfamiliar ingredients or combinations. Mango and Avocado Fresh Rolls (page 198) take two popular ingredients and combine them in an unexpected way, while Roasted Red Pepper and Walnut Spread (Muhammara) (page 189) will forever destroy any lingering beliefs you might hold about vegan dishes not being flavorful.

While it's harder for home cooks to compete with professional chefs in the realm of appetizers, more formal apps don't have to be completely fussy or time consuming. In most of these cases, a food processor will definitely speed up the process, and it's always easier to put out several spreads family style than to take the time to assemble individual bites to pass around the room. Or turn to lentils—not for the expected soup, but for a sophisticate pâté (Lentil and Walnut Pâté, page 204) that is just the impressive sort of starter that can glam up your next Oscars party. And yes, we just used the words "glam" and "lentils" in the same sentence; they really do deserve to be together.

GRILLING JUICY, PEAK-SEASON STONE FRUIT gives it a subtle smoky aroma, caramelizes sugars, and concentrates flavors. Plums and pluots are essentially interchangeable; this is an easy recipe to experiment with different varieties and discover a new favorite. Pick fruit that is a day or two short of perfectly ripe; the extra firmness helps during the grilling process and the bit of lost sugar is more than made up for by the caramelized, concentrated flavors. Try serving this versatile salsa with grilled meats or over whole grains.

GRILLED PLUM AND NECTARINE SALSA

Makes about 2½ cups

Preheat the grill to high (400 degrees F). Put the chilies on the grill and cook, using tongs to turn them occasionally, until they are charred over a good portion of their skin. Leave the grill on. Put the chilies in a paper bag and let rest for 10 minutes. Scrape off the blackened skin, remove the stems and seeds, and chop finely.

Brush the cut sides of the fruit with a little oil and place cut side down on the grill. Cook until they have nice grill marks, 3 to 4 minutes, and use tongs to turn them over. Cook for another 1 to 2 minutes, until light marks appear. Don't overcook the fruit—you want it to still have a nice firmness for the salsa. Let the halves cool until you can comfortably handle them.

Dice the fruit into ½-inch pieces. In a small bowl, combine the fruit and chilies. Sprinkle with the onion, cilantro, and salt and mix gently. Season to taste with the lime juice, sugar, hot sauce, and more salt. Cover and chill in the refrigerator for at least 1 hour or for up to 2 days.

2 small (or 1 large) pasilla chilies

2 medium nectarines, halved and pitted

2 medium plums, halved and pitted

High-heat oil, such as sunflower or refined peanut oil, for brushing

¼ cup thinly sliced green onion (both green and white parts)

¼ cup chopped fresh cilantro

¾ teaspoon kosher salt, plus more as needed

1 to 2 tablespoons freshly squeezed lime juice

1 teaspoon granulated sugar, or to taste (optional)

5 to 6 dashes hot sauce, or to taste (optional)

¼ CUP: 50 CAL., 1.5G FAT (0G SAT.), 0MG CHOL., 290MG SODIUM, 10G CARB., 2G FIBER, 6G SUGAR, 1G PROTEIN

PLUM CRAZY

Plums are closely related to nectarines, peaches, almonds, and apricots. The hybrids known as pluots, apriums, and plumcots are all the result of farmers crossbreeding plums and apricots for fruit that has flavor components of both parents, frequently with pretty speckled skin. Along with their fiber, copper, and vitamin K content, they are all a very good source of vitamin C and antioxidants.

There are two major categories of plums, Japanese and European, and throughout the summer and fall you may spot dozens of different varieties available. As a general rule, European types are small and dense, with less juice. Usually freestone (the pits easily pull free), they have dark-blue or purple skin and yellow flesh. The Japanese varietals can have skin that is any shade of red, with soft, juicy yellow, orange, or red flesh. They tend to be clingstones (the pits are very clingy) and come in a big range of sizes. Yellow- and green-skinned plums can be both European or Japanese; they are generally extraordinarily sweet and soft, which makes shipping them long distances difficult. There are so many different shades that it's almost possible to eat an entire rainbow of plums and pluots.

PURPLE SKIN, YELLOW FRUIT
Plums: Italian and Early Italian, Stanley, Valor, Santa Rosa, Ozark Premier
Pluots: King Kong

RED SKIN, YELLOW FRUIT
Plums: Fortune, Hiromi Red
Pluots: Tropical Plumana, Marvel, Tropical Sunrise, Flavor Pop, Fall Fiesta

RED SKIN, RED FRUIT
Plums: Redheart, Duarte
Pluots: Jubilee, Summer Punch, Dapple Jack, Supernova, Flavor Flav

YELLOW-GREEN SKIN, YELLOW-GREEN FRUIT
Plums: greengage, Shiro, mirabelle, Kelsey
Pluots: Golden Treat, Emerald Beaut, Harvest Gold

TOWARD THE END OF SUMMER, this is a pretty way to feature all those gorgeous shapes and colors of cherry and grape tomatoes. When it's not the season for local tomatoes, this recipe does an excellent job of boosting the sweetness and flavor of out-of-season fruit (much like Roasted Rhubarb and Strawberries, page 253). They're wonderful as part of a cheese plate, particularly alongside fresh goat's milk or sheep's milk cheese, or they can be a simple snack with nothing more than crackers. If you like, add a few sprigs of thyme or a generous amount of cracked black pepper to the pan before roasting; the added flavor is subtle but brings a pleasantly savory undertone to the sweet tomatoes.

ROASTED CHERRY TOMATOES

Makes about 3 cups

Preheat the oven to 325 degrees F. Line a rimmed baking sheet with parchment paper.

In a large bowl, toss the tomatoes, oil, and vinegar and sprinkle generously with salt. Spread them out on the prepared baking sheet and roast for 1 to 1½ hours, until they are soft and caramelized. Let cool for about 10 minutes, then use a silicone spatula or wooden spoon to scrape the tomatoes and their juices off the parchment and into a ramekin. Serve warm or at room temperature.

1 quart (1¼ pounds, or about 55) cherry tomatoes, stems removed
1 tablespoon extra-virgin olive oil
1 teaspoon balsamic vinegar
Kosher salt

¼ CUP: 40 CAL., 2.5G FAT (0G SAT.), 0MG CHOL., 160MG SODIUM, 4G CARB., 1G FIBER, 3G SUGAR, 1G PROTEIN

FRESH FAVA BEANS MAKE A brief appearance at the very end of spring; because of the two-step shelling process, preparing them takes a bit of extra effort, but their creamy texture and mild vegetal flavor makes them worth it. This hummus is light and clean tasting, just right for serving with seasonal crudités like radishes, snap peas, and young carrots.

FRESH FAVA BEAN HUMMUS

Makes about 2 cups

Shuck the fava beans from their pods; you should have about 1½ cups of beans. In a small saucepan over high heat, bring about 3 cups of salted water to a boil and cook the beans for 5 to 6 minutes, until the inside of the bean is tender. Cool for 10 to 15 minutes, until you can comfortably handle them. Pop the soft inner flesh out of their skins and into a small bowl.

In the work bowl of a food processor, combine the fava beans, chickpeas, garlic, tahini, salt, and lemon juice. Pulse a few times, until the beans are chopped into coarse chunks and the flavorings are well mixed. With the motor running, slowly add the oil and puree to a smooth paste. If it seems a little dry, add more oil. Adjust the seasoning to your taste with more salt or lemon juice.

¼ CUP: 170 CAL., 10G FAT (1.5G SAT.), 0MG CHOL., 330MG SODIUM, 15G CARB., 4G FIBER, 1G SUGAR, 7G PROTEIN

1 pound fava bean pods

1 teaspoon kosher salt, or to taste, plus more as needed

1 (15-ounce) can chickpeas, drained

2 cloves garlic, minced

2 tablespoons tahini

3 tablespoons freshly squeezed lemon juice, plus more as needed

¼ cup extra-virgin olive oil, plus more as needed

APERITIF PAIRING: A crisp prosecco or sparkling rosé suits the snack and the season when fresh fava beans are available.

THIS DIP IS A CLASSIC meal accompaniment in Syria, Turkey, and throughout the Levant. The next time you plan to put out a tray of hummus and olives, put out a bowl of this alongside; it's vegan friendly, offers good nutrition, and has a gorgeous color—and the flavor is hard to beat.

Serve *muhammara* at room temperature with pita wedges or chips. Like *tzatziki* and salsa, *muhammara* is seen both as an appetizer and as a sauce to be served alongside the main course (and just like *tzatziki*, it's great with kebabs). Instead of roasting your own pepper, you can substitute an eight-ounce jar of roasted red peppers, drained and rinsed.

ROASTED RED PEPPER AND WALNUT SPREAD

(Muhammara)

Makes about 1½ cups

Place an oven rack 8 inches from the broiling element and preheat the broiler to high. On a baking sheet, place the whole red pepper on its side. Broil the pepper for 16 to 20 minutes, using tongs to rotate it every 4 to 5 minutes, until the skin is charred and black on all sides. Remove from the oven and use tongs to put it either in a paper bag (close the bag tightly) or under a bowl on the counter; steam for 15 minutes. Halve the pepper lengthwise, lay it flat, and remove the stem and seeds. Gently use your fingers to strip away most or all of the blackened skin.

In a blender or the work bowl of a food processor, coarsely chop the pepper with a few pulses. Add the bread crumbs, walnuts, vinegar, cumin, cayenne, and salt and pulse until the mixture forms a thick, fairly smooth puree. With the motor running, add the oil in a slow stream, blending until incorporated.

1 large red bell pepper
½ cup coarse fresh bread crumbs
½ cup walnuts, toasted and coarsely chopped
1½ teaspoons red wine vinegar
¼ teaspoon ground cumin
Pinch of cayenne pepper
Pinch of kosher salt
2 tablespoons extra-virgin olive oil

¼ CUP: 150 CAL., 12G FAT (1.5G SAT.), 0MG CHOL., 360MG SODIUM, 9G CARB., 1G FIBER, 2G SUGAR, 3G PROTEIN

TUCKED INTO A CELLOPHANE BAG and tied with a ribbon, these make an excellent homemade gift for the holidays, a generally sweet time of year when savory snacks can earn extra appreciation. Note that they can be baked up to two weeks before you plan to serve them, so you can have plenty of time to make multiple batches and get them wrapped.

When you're ready to serve them, their grainy cornmeal crunch is a lovely companion for creamy fresh goat cheese, but they offer so much flavor they can hold their own served alongside nothing but cocktails.

CORNMEAL, PARMESAN, AND THYME CRACKERS

Makes 50 to 60 small crackers

In the work bowl of a food processor (or a medium bowl), combine the cornmeal, flour, water, Parmesan, butter, 1 teaspoon of the salt, and pepper. Blend until the mixture forms a ball (or you can mix by hand with a pastry blender or your fingers). Remove the dough from the processor and wrap completely in plastic wrap. Let rest for 30 minutes.

Preheat the oven to 400 degrees F. Line a rimmed baking sheet with parchment paper.

Divide the dough into 4 portions, covering the pieces you are not working with in plastic wrap.

Lightly dust a work surface with flour and roll out one piece of dough to ⅛ inch thick. Sprinkle the surface with one-quarter of the thyme and ¼ teaspoon of the salt. Gently roll the dough two or three more times to embed the toppings. Cut the crackers to your desired shape and size. Try using a chef's knife, wavy-edge pastry cutter, pizza cutter, or cookie cutters. Repeat with remaining balls of dough.

Put the crackers fairly close together (just so they don't actually touch) on the prepared baking sheet. Depending on the shape of your crackers, you may need to line a second baking sheet to bake all the crackers at once. Bake until the edges turn golden and crisp, 15 to 18 minutes. Cool completely; store in an airtight container at room temperature for up to 2 weeks.

1 cup medium-grind cornmeal

1 cup all-purpose flour, plus more for dusting

¾ cup warm water

¾ ounce (¼ cup) shredded Parmesan cheese

3 tablespoons unsalted butter, at room temperature

2 teaspoons kosher salt, divided

Freshly ground black pepper

1 teaspoon fresh thyme or ½ teaspoon dried thyme, divided

5 CRACKERS: 130 CAL., 4.5G FAT (2.5G SAT.), 10MG CHOL., 420MG SODIUM, 19G CARB., 1G FIBER, 0G SUGAR, 3G PROTEIN

EQUAL PARTS PRETTY AND DELICIOUS, this bright-green spread is extra creamy thanks to the soft goat cheese, and the crisp slices of radish on top are the most cheerful way to gild the lily. If you want to make the batch of avocado spread ahead of time, or have leftovers, place a square of plastic wrap directly on top of it to reduce the browning that will occur as the avocado oxidizes.

AVOCADO TOAST WITH GOAT CHEESE AND RADISHES

Makes 4 servings

In a small bowl with a fork, or in the work bowl of a food processor, blend together the avocado, cheese, and lemon zest and juice until fairly smooth; leave as many small chunks of avocado as you prefer. Fold in the chives and parsley, and season to taste with salt and pepper.

Spread the mixture on the bread slices and top with radish and onion slices. Cut the bread in half on the diagonal. Serve immediately.

¼ RECIPE: 270 CAL., 12G FAT (5G SAT.), 15MG CHOL., 300MG SODIUM, 31G CARB., 2G FIBER, 7G SUGAR, 13G PROTEIN

½ medium avocado, peeled and pitted

4 ounces (about ½ cup) soft fresh goat cheese

1 teaspoon freshly grated lemon zest

1 teaspoon freshly squeezed lemon juice

1 teaspoon chopped fresh chives

1 teaspoon chopped fresh Italian parsley

Kosher salt and freshly ground black pepper

4 slices multigrain bread, toasted

4 to 6 medium radishes, thinly sliced

¼ medium red onion, thinly sliced

THE BEAUTIFUL BUTTER FRUIT

Whether you prefer the accuracy of their global names of alligator pear or butter fruit, it's very easy to love avocados. At their peak in early summer, avocados pack more potassium than bananas, more folate than kale, and more fiber than prunes. They're loaded with healthy monounsaturated fats that boost blood flow to help the brain function optimally and also help the body absorb nutrients. Their popularity feels like a deeply nutritious win: these days, Americans eat 7 pounds of avocado per person each year, up from about one pound a few decades ago.

Avocados continue ripening once they've been picked. If you want to hasten ripening at home, tuck them into a paper bag, which will trap the ethylene gas they emit naturally. Hurry it along even further by adding a ripe banana to the bag.

FANS OF SOFT, CHEWY ENERGY bars can use this recipe to make their own version of what our stores bake each day. If someone in your family has a peanut allergy, substitute a different nut or seed butter for the peanut butter and your favorite nut for the peanuts. For most people, salted nuts will provide the best balance of flavor to the sweet date paste, honey, and vanilla.

NUT AND HONEY CLUSTERS PCC Bakery Favorite

Makes about 45 clusters

Preheat the oven to 325 degrees F. Line two baking sheets with parchment paper.

In a small bowl, combine the water and dates. Soak for 20 to 30 minutes, until the water has been partially absorbed and the dates are soft. Transfer the dates to a blender and blend to a paste on low speed. Set aside.

In the work bowl of a food processor, combine the peanuts and 1½ cups of the rolled oats. Pulse for about 45 seconds, until the peanuts and oats are coarsely chopped and resemble small pebbles.

In the bowl of a stand mixer fitted with the paddle attachment, combine the date paste, peanut butter, honey, and vanilla on medium speed, until thick and fairly smooth (you might see a few small pieces of date). Add the chopped peanut mixture, the remaining 1½ cups oats, and the salt and mix on low speed until combined in a thick dough. Scrape down the sides of the bowl once or twice to make sure the dry ingredients are completely blended into the peanut butter mixture. The dough will be thick and sticky.

Scoop the dough by the tablespoon onto the prepared baking sheets, placing them about 2 inches apart. Bake for 12 to 14 minutes, until they're a uniformly deep-golden color and no longer shiny; they will still be fairly soft to the touch. Cool on the baking sheets for 10 minutes, then transfer to wire racks and cool completely. Store in an airtight container at room temperature for up to 4 days.

½ cup hot water

1 cup pitted and chopped dates (from 9 ounces whole dates)

1 cup peanuts

3 cups rolled oats, divided

1¼ cups creamy peanut butter

¾ cup honey

1 tablespoon vanilla extract

½ teaspoon kosher salt

NOTE: For a special at-home treat, drizzle a little melted chocolate on top of each cluster once it has completely cooled.

1 CLUSTER: 110 CAL., 6G FAT (1G SAT.), 0MG CHOL., 55MG SODIUM, 14G CARB., 1G FIBER, 7G SUGAR, 3G PROTEIN

THESE ROLLS ARE KID FRIENDLY enough for a summertime snack and interesting enough to serve as an appetizer when friends come over for dinner. Older kids can even help with the assembly—rolling them isn't difficult at all, once you have a sense of precisely the right amount of filling your wrapper will hold.

   The dipping sauce isn't absolutely necessary, but it's quick to whisk together, and the combination of sweetness and tangy fresh lime adds just the right notes to the filling.

MANGO AND AVOCADO FRESH ROLLS

Makes 6 rolls

In a small bowl or ramekin, whisk together the tamari, lime juice, mirin, and sugar to make the dipping sauce. Cover and set aside at room temperature.

In a shallow bowl, soak the rice vermicelli in hot water until they are soft and pliable, 15 to 20 minutes. Drain and set the noodles aside.

Fill a large, shallow bowl with warm (not hot) water. Soak one spring roll wrapper in water until it's pliable, 5 to 15 seconds. Put the wrapper on a clean, dry surface.

Place small amounts of the vermicelli, avocado, mango, cucumber, carrot, and tofu on the lower third of the wrapper, leaving a 1-inch border. Top the mixture with 2 basil and 2 mint leaves.

Bring the bottom edge of the wrapper up and over the filling and start to snugly roll it up. Tuck in the sides like a burrito and continue rolling until completely wrapped. Cover the finished roll with a damp towel and repeat the process with the remaining ingredients.

Cut the rolls in half on the diagonal and serve with the dipping sauce.

3 tablespoons tamari
2 tablespoons freshly squeezed lime juice
2 teaspoons mirin
2 teaspoons packed light brown sugar
2 ounces vermicelli rice noodles
6 brown or white rice paper spring roll wrappers
1 medium avocado, peeled, pitted, and sliced
1 small mango, peeled, pitted, and sliced
¼ medium English cucumber, thinly sliced
½ medium carrot, peeled and shredded
6 ounces extra-firm tofu, sliced (optional)
12 fresh basil leaves
12 fresh mint leaves

1 ROLL: 230 CAL., 6G FAT (1G SAT.), 5MG CHOL., 710MG SODIUM, 41G CARB., 3G FIBER, 10G SUGAR, 6G PROTEIN

FRESH GOAT CHEESE IS AT its finest when rhubarb is at its peak from early April to the end of June—the cheeses made then are created with the richest milk a goat gives in a year. If you want to skip the assembly yourself, it's perfectly fine to set out a platter of crostini and goat cheese along with a bowl of the jam, and let guests decide on their own ideal ratio. If you want a different use for the jam, try serving it alongside grilled pork skewers for a modern take on England's time-less pork and rhubarb stew.

CROSTINI WITH GOAT CHEESE AND RHUBARB-THYME JAM

Makes 30 crostini

In a small saucepan over medium-high heat, combine the rhubarb, ginger, cinnamon, thyme, black pepper, cayenne, shallots, salt, vinegar, sugar, and syrup. Bring to a boil, stirring occasionally, then reduce the heat to medium-low. Simmer, stirring often, for about 30 minutes, until it has thickened to a jam-like consistency. Cool to room tem-perature and remove the cinnamon stick.

Preheat a broiler. Brush the baguette rounds lightly on one side with oil and put on a rimmed baking sheet. Broil until lightly browned, 2 to 4 minutes. Spread them with a little cheese and top with a leaf of arugula and a dollop of the rhubarb-thyme jam.

> **APERITIF PAIRING:** A young, well-chilled white like Sancerre or grüner veltliner will have the minerality and the fresh stone-fruit flavors to suit this combination of goat cheese and savory rhubarb.

1 CROSTINI: 180 CAL., 3G FAT (.5G SAT.), 0MG CHOL., 350MG SODIUM, 34G CARB., 0G FIBER, 5G SUGAR, 6G PROTEIN

3 cups chopped rhubarb (from 2 medium stalks)

3-inch knob fresh ginger, peeled and grated

1 (3-inch) cinnamon stick

1 tablespoon chopped fresh thyme

10 grinds of fresh black pepper

Pinch of cayenne pepper

2 tablespoons diced shallots

½ teaspoon kosher salt

⅓ cup apple cider vinegar

½ cup packed light brown sugar

2 tablespoons maple syrup

1 baguette, sliced into rounds

Extra-virgin olive oil, for brushing

4 ounces (about ½ cup) soft fresh goat cheese

1 cup baby arugula (about 1 ounce)

THIS SPREAD COMES TOGETHER QUICKLY, particularly if you use sun-dried tomatoes that don't need rehydrating (see Choosing Sun-Dried Tomatoes, below). Keep things simple and serve it with pita chips or a sliced baguette, or upgrade and use it as a filling for stuffed mushrooms (see note).

FETA AND SUN-DRIED TOMATO SPREAD PCC Deli Favorite

Makes about 2 cups

If using traditional sun-dried tomatoes, rehydrate them in a glass bowl of hot water for about 30 minutes. Press out the excess liquid.

In the work bowl of a food processor, combine the tomatoes, feta, milk, onion, oregano, garlic, and pepper. Pulse until the seasonings are evenly blended, about 45 seconds. Add small chunks of the cream cheese and continue pulsing until smooth. Use immediately, or refrigerate overnight for flavors to blend.

NOTE: To stuff mushrooms, choose about 24 small button mushrooms, remove their stems, and pack the caps full to the brim with the spread (you'll likely have leftover spread). Put them on a rimmed baking sheet and bake at 300 degrees F for about 20 minutes, until the caps are soft and the filling is heated through. Let them cool for at least 5 minutes before digging in.

3 tablespoons diced sun-dried tomatoes

1 tablespoon hot water (if needed for tomatoes)

8 ounces (about 1½ cups) crumbled feta cheese

1 tablespoon milk

1 green onion, chopped (both green and white parts)

1 teaspoon dried oregano

½ teaspoon minced garlic

½ teaspoon freshly ground black pepper

8 ounces cream cheese (not nonfat), at room temperature

¼ CUP: 140 CAL., 11G FAT (7G SAT.), 40MG CHOL., 370MG SODIUM, 5G CARB., 0G FIBER, 3G SUGAR, 7G PROTEIN

CHOOSING SUN-DRIED TOMATOES

There are three different types of sun-dried tomatoes. Oil-packed sun-dried are ready to use right out of the jar. They're the most expensive, but the oil that they're packed in has great flavor, so it's like buying two ingredients. Plain sun-dried last the longest and are the least expensive. They need to soak in hot water to rehydrate before using. The newest option is known as soft-dried. You can skip the rehydrating step; they're soft, plump, and chewy without being tough.

IT BOILS DOWN TO JUST how greedy you are, or more nicely, how much you like sharing: these nuts make a lovely gift wrapped in a small cellophane bag, or a fantastically nutritious and flavorful snack just for yourself to enjoy over the course of a few weeks. Starting with raw nuts lets you determine exactly how much salt you want to add, while the maple syrup offers a sweet, earthy base for the spices to cling to. The house will smell fantastic as these bake; make sure to keep an eye on them as they approach the final cooking time—they can scorch. To avoid this, it's best to set the timer for the lesser amount of time until you know for sure just how your oven will treat them.

SPICY HERB-ROASTED NUTS

Makes 5 cups

Preheat the oven to 325 degrees F.

In a large bowl, stir together the syrup and oil. Add the cayenne, oregano, sage, thyme, rosemary, marjoram, and salt and blend. Add the nuts, tossing with a broad silicone spatula or wooden spoon to coat them evenly. Spread the coated nuts in a single layer on a rimmed baking sheet.

Bake for 35 to 50 minutes, stirring every 10 to 15 minutes to break up the clumps, until all the moisture is absorbed and the nuts are fragrant and nicely toasted. Cool completely. Store for 3 days in an airtight container at room temperature or up to 1 month in the refrigerator or freezer.

¼ CUP: 240 CAL., 20G FAT (2G SAT.), 0MG CHOL., 120MG SODIUM, 11G CARB., 3G FIBER, 6G SUGAR, 5G PROTEIN

½ cup maple syrup

3 tablespoons extra-virgin olive oil

¼ teaspoon cayenne pepper (for spicier nuts, use up to ½ teaspoon)

½ teaspoon dried oregano

½ teaspoon dried sage

½ teaspoon dried thyme

½ teaspoon dried rosemary

½ teaspoon dried marjoram

1 to 1½ teaspoons kosher salt

1½ cups raw almonds

1½ cups raw walnuts or raw unsalted cashews

1 cup raw hazelnuts

1 cup raw pecans

THE TRICK TO MAKING A meatless pâté that even ravenous meat eaters will enjoy is to use ingredients with plenty of umami, the palate-satisfying richness found in foods with lots of glutamic acid. In this recipe, the tamari, balsamic vinegar, lentils, walnuts, and mushrooms all chime in on the umami note. For a meatless *assiette de charcuterie*, serve this with cold pickled onions, roasted red peppers, dense brown bread, and a stout mustard. It's equally delicious spread on a sandwich or scooped up with crackers.

LENTIL AND WALNUT PÂTÉ

Makes 6 appetizer servings

Preheat the oven to 425 degrees F.

In a large bowl, whisk the oil, vinegar, and tamari until combined. Add the mushrooms, garlic, and onion and toss with a wooden spoon or broad spatula until the dressing evenly coats the mushrooms. Spread the mixture on a rimmed baking sheet and bake for 10 to 15 minutes, until the mushrooms are soft and the garlic and onions are dark brown.

In a medium saucepan over medium-high heat, bring the water, bay leaf, salt, pepper, and lentils to a boil. Cook the lentils, covered, until very soft, about 35 minutes. Drain any extra liquid if necessary and discard the bay leaf.

In the work bowl of a food processor, pulse the roasted mushroom-onion mixture until it is a rough puree. Add the lentils and walnuts and blend until completely smooth, scraping down the bowl occasionally as needed.

Scrape the puree into one 12-ounce ramekin or several smaller ramekins. Wrap well and refrigerate for at least 8 hours before serving with the parsley.

3 tablespoons mild-tasting olive oil

2 tablespoons balsamic vinegar

1½ teaspoons tamari

8 ounces button or cremini mushrooms, quartered

3 cloves garlic, peeled

1 small yellow onion, roughly chopped

2 cups water

1 bay leaf

1 tablespoon kosher salt

1 teaspoon freshly ground black pepper

½ cup brown lentils, rinsed

1 cup walnut pieces, toasted

Fresh thyme leaves or chopped Italian parsley, for garnish

¼ CUP: 170 CAL., 14G FAT (1.5G SAT.), 0MG CHOL., 700MG SODIUM, 10G CARB., 3G FIBER, 2G SUGAR, 5G PROTEIN

THIS SPREAD IS A BIT like turning your favorite winter side dish into a year-round snack. It's also got things in common with hummus (more so if you use tahini in place of nut butter), but with an overall more kid-friendly flavor, including plenty of wholesome sweetness from its main ingredient. It's important to use red, not beige, sweet potatoes here; the latter just don't have a strong enough flavor, aside from being too easy to visually confuse people expecting it to taste like chickpea hummus. Serve with pita or pita chips, or with a spread of crudités.

ROASTED SWEET POTATO DIP

Makes about 2 cups

Preheat the oven to 375 degrees F. Lightly oil a rimmed baking sheet. In a medium bowl, toss the sweet potatoes with the oil, salt, and pepper. Roast for about 40 minutes, stirring once or twice, until the sweet potatoes are soft and caramelized in a few places but not uniformly deep brown. Cool to room temperature.

In the work bowl of a food processor, pulse together the sweet potatoes, pecan butter, garlic, paprika, coriander, cumin, and lemon zest and juice until the mixture is fairly smooth. With the machine running, add water as necessary for a smooth and creamy consistency. Season to taste with more salt and pepper. Sprinkle with the sesame seeds and serve at room temperature.

¼ CUP: 90 CAL., 6G FAT (.5G SAT.), 0MG CHOL., 130MG SODIUM, 12G CARB., 2G FIBER, 1G SUGAR, 1G PROTEIN

1 tablespoon high-heat oil, such as sunflower or refined peanut oil, plus more for the pan

2 small Red Garnet or Jewel sweet potatoes, peeled and diced (about 3 cups)

½ teaspoon kosher salt, plus more as needed

¼ teaspoon freshly ground black pepper, plus more as needed

3 tablespoons creamy pecan butter or other creamy nut butter

1 clove garlic, smashed

½ teaspoon smoked paprika

¼ teaspoon ground coriander

¼ teaspoon ground cumin

½ teaspoon freshly grated lemon zest

1 tablespoon freshly squeezed lemon juice

½ cup water, or as needed

Toasted white sesame seeds, for garnish

MOVIE NIGHT AT HOME JUST got an upgrade, and it's sweet, spicy, and salty all at once. As far as nutritional pros and cons, popcorn itself is high in fiber and low in calories, and offers a surprising range of antioxidants. Popping it in coconut oil and coating it in peanut butter adds some healthy fats and a bit of protein, but sweetening it is purely for the sake of happy taste buds.

Almond or pecan butter makes a great substitute for the peanut butter, but make sure it's unsalted or you'll need to reduce the suggested amount of salt by about one-third.

SPICY PEANUT POPCORN

Makes 2 servings

In a 3-quart saucepan over medium-high heat, melt the coconut oil. When the oil is shimmering but not smoking, add the popcorn kernels and shake to evenly distribute. Cover, leaving a small crack for steam to escape. As the popcorn starts popping, shake the pan vigorously to distribute the kernels evenly. When the popping slows to a few seconds between pops, remove the pan from the heat. Pour the popcorn into a large bowl.

In a small saucepan, combine the honey and sugar. Bring to a simmer over medium-low heat and cook for 2 minutes. Remove from the heat and add the peanut butter, hot sauce, salt, and garlic. Stir the sauce vigorously until smooth and well combined. Pour the peanut butter sauce over the popcorn and mix gently with a wooden spoon or silicone spatula until evenly coated. Stir in the peanuts. Let cool 10 minutes before serving.

1 tablespoon coconut oil

⅓ cup popcorn kernels

2 tablespoons honey

1 tablespoon granulated sugar

2 tablespoons unsalted creamy peanut butter

1 to 2 teaspoons sriracha sauce, or to taste

1 teaspoon kosher salt, or to taste

½ teaspoon granulated garlic

Roasted salted peanuts (optional)

½ **RECIPE: 370 CAL., 16G FAT (7G SAT.), 0MG CHOL., 1,1000MG SODIUM, 53G CARB., 6G FIBER, 25G SUGAR, 8G PROTEIN**

ENERGY BARS

Do-it-yourself energy bars are less expensive than the prepared kind, and understanding how they come together lets you easily work around household allergies and dietary preferences. And an easy no-bake method makes it easy to involve kids from preschool ages on up.

1 BE FLAKY

Start with a rolled grain of some sort—rolled oats are the standard choice, but rolled spelt, emmer, rye, triticale, rice, barley, wheat, or a multigrain hot-cereal blend will all work nicely. Of these choices, oats and rice are the only two that are gluten-free, while the multigrain hot cereal offers the broadest mix of nutrients. You can also choose two contrasting grains like rice and rye for balanced nutrition and flavor.

2 GO NUTS

Using sliced or slivered nuts won't offer much in the way of textural difference with the rolled grains, so the final bars will have a much more delicate crispy crunch that is appealing to eat but a little more fragile when it comes to packing. If you have a favorite trail mix, that's an easy place to start, and with this no-bake recipe, it's fine if that mix includes chocolate chips or bits of dried fruit. Don't skip the seedy side of things—pumpkin seeds, shelled sunflower seeds, and toasted sesame seeds all add good flavor and texture.

3 SWEETEN THE DEAL

Liquid forms of sugar do two important things: help everything stick together and make the bars more palatable. Using all maple syrup is tasty (and vegan), while honey allows you to select a variety that brings rich spice or delicate floral notes to the finished bars. Don't overlook sweeteners like barley malt syrup, date syrup, brown rice syrup, or coconut nectar. You can also use a small amount of molasses blended in with a milder syrup if you like its flavor.

4 BRING IT ALL TOGETHER

Nut or seed butter is key in no-bake bars to help form a solid base—the mortar between the other ingredients. Choose whatever you like, with or without chocolate. These days, such butters are available in flavors like pecan and pistachio as well as classics like peanut or chocolate-hazelnut. Tahini or sunflower butter is also wonderful, particularly if you've added sesame seeds or sunflower seeds to the mix.

5 WRAP 'EM UP

Once the mixture is pressed firmly and evenly in its pan, it simply needs time to set up. If you're making the bars on a particularly hot day, cooling them in the refrigerator will help things along. Once they're cut, each one should be wrapped up so it doesn't dry out. Wax paper, parchment paper, and plastic wrap all work nicely; aluminum foil tends to stick. If it's particularly humid, you can stash the wrapped bars inside an airtight container to keep their textures at their best.

FLAVOR COMBINATIONS TO TRY

- Rolled oats, sliced almonds, shredded coconut, chocolate chips, honey, almond butter
- Rolled spelt, pecans, dried apples, maple syrup, pecan butter
- Rolled rice, pistachios, dried cherries, honey, tahini
- Rolled rye, walnuts, raisins, maple syrup, cashew butter
- Rolled oats, almonds, dates, date syrup, almond butter

EASY TO CARRY ALONG IN a pocket on hikes or bring in a stack to soccer games, these bars are packed with nuts and whole grains to balance the quick hit of sugar provided by the honey and maple syrup. They're no-bake and simple enough to prepare that this makes a great recipe to get the kids involved in the kitchen—and if they help make them, they're more likely to eat them later.

HOMEMADE ENERGY BARS

Makes 18 (2-inch) bars

Lightly oil an 11-by-7-inch baking dish or a 9-inch square baking dish. Set aside.

In a medium bowl, combine the oats, trail mix, and salt. Set aside.

In a small saucepan over medium heat, combine the maple syrup and honey and bring to a low boil for 2 to 3 minutes. Reduce the heat to low and add the coconut oil and nut butter. Stir continuously until the mixture is smooth and evenly heated.

Stir the wet ingredients into the dry ingredients and use a wooden spoon or broad silicone spatula to combine until evenly mixed. Press the mixture evenly into the prepared pan. Cool completely, then flip upside down onto a cutting board and cut into 18 bars.

Wrap the bars in wax paper, parchment, or plastic wrap to keep from drying out.

NOTE: For a more robust flavor, put the oats on a baking sheet and toast them in the oven at 325 degrees F for about 15 minutes, until they are golden brown. Nuts and seeds can be toasted in the same way for 6 to 7 minutes. Do not toast trail mix with chocolate chips or dried fruit; things will get very messy indeed and can also burn.

2 tablespoons coconut oil, plus more for the pan
2 cups rolled oats (see note)
2 cups prepared trail mix (or nuts, seeds, and dried fruit of your choice)
½ teaspoon kosher salt
¼ cup maple syrup
¼ cup honey
1 cup nut or seed butter

1 BAR: 240 CAL., 15G FAT (3G SAT.), 0MG CHOL., 55MG SODIUM, 23G CARB., 3G FIBER, 7G SUGAR, 7G PROTEIN

DRINKS

GORGEOUS COLORS, FRESH INGREDIENTS, flavors from around the world, and a chance to play the friendly neighborhood mad scientist: mixing drinks is some of the most fun you can have in the kitchen. These beverages show off the enormous range of refreshments that lie between the necessary (and admittedly dull) plain water and supersized sodas, those fizzy contenders for the most contentious public-health problem of the century thus far. The recipes here rely heavily on the natural sweetness of spices and seasonal fruit and put the control of added sugars firmly in your own hands.

Fair Trade certification is an important detail when it comes to choosing your coffee, tea, and drinking chocolate. This program is separate from farming practices like organic certification or shade forestry management and focuses on making sure farmers in developing nations get better prices and improved terms of trade. For shoppers, certification provides a clear, meaningful way to fight poverty abroad. It's all we use at our coffee bars, and the labeled products aren't hard to find when you're stocking your personal pantry.

Explore these recipes to discover a party beverage that genuinely delights nondrinking friends and family, or unearth the coolest possible additions to your boozy weekend brunch. Trim a few bucks off the budget by making your own cold brew coffee or golden milk for daily use. Go healthy with a cultured buttermilk smoothie (Pineapple-Buttermilk Smoothie, page 222) or healthy-*ish* with a spicy Ginger-Cranberry Kombucha Mimosa (page 228). Drinks may not be the centerpiece of the menu, but they deserve to be as well-considered as the rest of your menu—and a truly great beverage can make all the difference in a meal.

IN THE PACIFIC NORTHWEST, COUNTERTOP brewing typically works well and prevents the coffee from absorbing any strong food flavors from the refrigerator. However, if the temperature of your kitchen is over 80 degrees F, we suggest brewing this in the fridge. If you'd like to experiment with naturally flavored cold brew, try adding a cardamom pod or a small piece of cinnamon stick or vanilla bean to the grounds before you add the water. To serve, remember that this is a concentrate. Dilute to your taste with ice, water, milk, or the milk alternative of your choice. A basic starting point for coffee and other liquid is one to one, but you may prefer it more diluted.

COLD BREW COFFEE

Makes about 2 quarts concentrate

In a half-gallon pitcher, put the coffee. Add half the water, stir gently, and let sit for several minutes until the grounds have absorbed some of the water. Add the remaining water and stir gently. Cover and let the coffee steep for 8 to 11 hours; after 10 hours, your concentrate will begin to get the bitter edge of traditional coffee.

Strain through a double layer of cheesecloth or a fine-mesh sieve. Put in a clean pitcher or jug and store in the refrigerator for up to 2 weeks.

11 to 14 ounces coarsely ground coffee
8 cups cold water

COFFEE CONTAINS CLOSE TO 0 CAL.

BASED ON ITS POPULARITY AROUND the world in warm climates, hibiscus may well be earth's most cooling beverage. It's primarily tart, with a subtle hint of earthiness and an absolutely beautiful fuchsia color, which you might recognize from that famous line of Zinger herbal teas or the Jamaica flavor of Mexican sodas. Names for it include rosella (Australia), *gumamela* (Philippines), *bissap* (Senegal), *agua de jamaica* (Mexico), *saril* (Panama), sorrel (the Caribbean), *karkadé* (Egypt and other Arabic-speaking North African countries), and *carcadè* (Italy).

To serve, dilute the concentrate to taste with water or sparkling water; two parts concentrate to one part water is a good starting point. To use this concentrate in an adult beverage, try a Trinidadian shandy by blending one part concentrate to two parts crisp pilsner. Or, for the prettiest possible margarita, combine four parts hibiscus concentrate with one part tequila, one part triple sec, one part water, and a squeeze of fresh lime juice.

HIBISCUS TEA CONCENTRATE

Makes about 2 quarts

In a half-gallon pitcher, combine the hibiscus flowers, cinnamon, and clove. Pour the hot water over the mixture and stir gently. Cover and let sit overnight at room temperature.

The next day, use a fine-mesh strainer or double layer of cheesecloth to remove the solids and sweeten the concentrate to taste with sugar. Pour into a clean pitcher or jug and store in the refrigerator for up to 3 weeks.

½ cup (1 ounce) dried hibiscus flowers
1 (2-inch) cinnamon stick
1 whole clove
2 quarts hot water
1 to 2 cups granulated sugar

3½ OUNCES CONCENTRATE: 60 CAL., 0G FAT (0G SAT.), 0MG CHOL., 0MG SODIUM, 16G CARB., 0G FIBER, 15G SUGAR, 0G PROTEIN

GLOBAL FLAVOR VARIATIONS FOR HIBISCUS TEA

- Add a split 2-inch piece of vanilla bean during steeping; serve garnished with fresh mint (Senegal).
- Add a splash of orange blossom water after steeping; garnish with fresh mint (Egypt).
- Add a 1-inch knob of fresh peeled gingerroot during steeping (Jamaica).
- Steep plain, with no spices (Mexico).
- Steep with no spices and add a 3-inch piece of fresh lemongrass (Philippines).

THE NATURAL SWEETNESS OF BLUEBERRIES turns fresh lemonade into something downright fancy—and their wide-ranging nutritional benefits are a very satisfying bonus. Frozen blueberries can fill in nicely here if fresh ones aren't in season. Thaw out what you need to make the blueberry-lemon syrup, but keep the ones you'll use as garnish frozen. The frozen berries function as ice cubes if you drop a few into the bottom of each glass.

SPARKLING BLUEBERRY LEMONADE

Makes 8 (6-ounce) servings

In a blender, combine the sugar, lemon juice, blueberries, and hot water. Blend on medium-low speed until smooth, about 45 seconds. If desired, press this mixture through a fine-mesh sieve to remove the seeds and any large pieces of berry pulp. Refrigerate for at least 1 hour or for up to 3 days.

Just before serving, in a half-gallon pitcher, combine the chilled blueberry-lemon juice, sparkling water, and ice. Serve in individual glasses garnished with blueberries.

1 cup granulated sugar, or to taste

1 cup freshly squeezed lemon juice (from 3 to 4 large lemons)

1 pint fresh or frozen blueberries, plus more for garnish

1 cup hot water

3 cups sparkling water

Ice, for serving

---

6 OUNCES: 100 CAL., 0G FAT (0G SAT.), 0MG CHOL., 10MG SODIUM, 26G CARB., 1G FIBER, 24G SUGAR, 0G PROTEIN

WHEN LIFE HANDS YOU LEMONS

To get the most juice from your lemons, start with lemons that feel noticeably heavy for their size, as these will contain the most juice. First, make sure they're at warm room temperature before juicing. If you keep your lemons in the refrigerator, or if your house is a little chilly, microwave them on high for 20 seconds so they're just slightly warm to the touch. Then roll them several times on the counter, firmly under your hand, to soften their fibers. Warm softened lemons can release more than 1 extra tablespoon on top of their expected ⅓ cup.

WHILE THERE ARE A HALF dozen mango varieties commercially available in the United States, there are two basic varieties that are easy to spot. One is larger with mottled patches of purple, red, yellow, and green (usually labeled Tommy Atkins, Kent, or Palmer); the other (sold as honey or Ataulfo) fits easily in your hand and is a fairly uniform shade of apricot. The latter variety averages about half the size of the more colorful type. With this in mind, it's easier to weigh your purchases for this recipe rather than grab a set number of mangoes.

It's best to use a thinner yogurt for this recipe—even plain kefir will work nicely—rather than Greek yogurt, which can make for a drink too thick to slurp through a straw. If all you have on hand is Greek, use three-quarters cup thinned with one-quarter cup water or milk.

MANGO LASSI

Makes 2 (8-ounce) servings

In a blender, combine the mango, honey, and cardamom. Blend on medium speed until you have a thick, smooth puree. Add the yogurt and milk and blend until the lassi is the consistency of a thin milkshake. Serve chilled over ice.

1¼ pounds mango, peeled and chopped (about 1½ cups)

1 tablespoon honey, or to taste

¼ teaspoon ground cardamom (optional)

1 cup plain yogurt

⅓ cup whole milk

Ice, for serving (optional)

8 OUNCES: 150 CAL., 2G FAT (1G SAT.), 5MG CHOL., 55MG SODIUM, 31G CARB., 2G FIBER, 28G SUGAR, 5G PROTEIN

IN PRAISE OF WHOLE-MILK DAIRY

Saturated fats may increase blood cholesterol levels, but this doesn't always contribute to heart disease. For example, coconut oil (rich in saturated fats) raises total cholesterol, but also raises good cholesterol (HDL) levels. Only elevated LDL cholesterol levels increase heart disease risk.

Milk fat isn't like coconut oil, but it does have its own unique mix of fats. You may have heard of two of these healthy fats, conjugated linoleic acid and omega-3 fatty acids, but there are other fats that are less commonly discussed, like vaccenic acid, rumenic acid, and trans-palmitoleic acid. Researchers have found that people with the highest levels of trans-palmitoleic acid (a "good" fat in whole milk) in their bodies have lower rates of obesity and diabetes, and that drinking whole milk increases the levels of this unique fat in our bodies.

IT'S HARD TO IMAGINE A more refreshing drink for days so hot that all you can do to cope is plunk your feet in the nearest body of water and doze. The lemongrass syrup can be made several days ahead of time, and you can experiment with flavor combinations for it other than lemongrass. To complement the sweetness of the melon, try substituting one tablespoon of chopped fresh mint, fennel bulb, or pineapple mint. Or offset honeydew's sugar with something a bit more savory, like one tablespoon of fresh cilantro, lemon thyme, or tarragon. Planning a party? This can be doubled or even tripled with success.

HONEYDEW-LEMONGRASS AGUA FRESCA

Makes about 4 (8-ounce) servings

In a small saucepan over low heat, combine ¼ cup of the water, the sugar, and the lemongrass; bring to a simmer and cook for 3 minutes. Remove from the heat, cover, and steep for 15 minutes. Remove the lemongrass.

In a blender or food processor, combine the honeydew, lime juice, and remaining 2 cups water and puree on medium speed until smooth. Strain through a medium-mesh strainer into a pitcher. Add lemongrass syrup to taste. Chill in the refrigerator for at least 1 hour, and serve over ice.

2¼ cups cold water, divided

¼ cup granulated sugar

1 stalk fresh lemongrass, lightly smashed

2 pounds honeydew melon, peeled, seeded, and chopped (about 3 cups)

2 tablespoons freshly squeezed lime juice

Ice, for serving

> **SPIRITS PAIRING:** A smooth, peppery añejo tequila or craft-distilled gin will add robust depth to the simplicity of the honeydew.

8 OUNCES: 130 CAL., 0G FAT (0G SAT.), 0MG CHOL., 45MG SODIUM, 34G CARB., 2G FIBER, 31G SUGAR, 1G PROTEIN

DRINKING CULTURED BUTTERMILK WAS POPULAR in the United States from the 1930s to 1960s, but it fell out of favor sharply as dairy fat became viewed with suspicion. Now that fermented foods are at the forefront of nutrition, it's time to bring buttermilk back to the refrigerator. It's a different product than traditional buttermilk, the thin but flavorful liquid that is left after making butter. Rich, tangy, cultured full-fat buttermilk is wonderful in smoothies, where it offers a compelling change from the more usual yogurt. If you like, substitute plain kefir or low-fat cultured buttermilk for a somewhat lighter, thinner consistency that might appeal more on a hot day.

PINEAPPLE-BUTTERMILK SMOOTHIE

Makes 1 (12-ounce) serving

In a blender, combine the banana, pineapple, yogurt, buttermilk, and honey and blend on medium-low speed until smooth. Add additional honey to taste. Serve immediately.

1 very ripe frozen banana, cut into chunks
½ cup fresh pineapple chunks
½ cup plain yogurt
1 cup cultured full-fat buttermilk
1 teaspoon honey, or to taste

1 SMOOTHIE: 200 CAL., 2.5G FAT (1.5G SAT.), 10MG CHOL., 330MG SODIUM, 38G CARB., 3G FIBER, 29G SUGAR, 9G PROTEIN

CULTURE CLUB

Fermented foods like cultured buttermilk are popular because of the health benefits of probiotic bacteria, but fermentation enhances the nutritional profile of milk beyond its probiotic benefits. Fermentation boosts milk's vitamin content (K, folate, B12, and biotin) and conjugated linoleic acid content, along with supporting gut health with unique prebiotics and probiotics.

Cultured dairy products, including buttermilk, yogurt, and cheese, taste less sweet and more tangy because of their reduced lactose (milk sugar) content. Many people with lactose intolerance can eat cultured dairy safely because most of the lactose is predigested by the "good bacteria" in these cultured foods.

This lower lactose level benefits everyone, not just those with lactose intolerance. Lactose is broken down in our digestive tract and becomes galactose, a potentially proinflammatory sugar. The reduced lactose content of fermented dairy could result in less milk-induced inflammation and might also explain why researchers are finding different health impacts from the consumption of fermented dairy versus nonfermented dairy.

THICK, CREAMY, AND COMFORTING, *CHAMPURRADO* is a warming treat on cold days, but it demands a few minutes of near-constant whisking to prevent little clumps from forming. If you use a very dark chocolate and skip the spices, the result is much like Italian hot chocolate and suits being served alongside shortbread or biscotti. A milder, milkier mug of *champurrado*, particularly one made with the spices, goes nicely with breakfasts of all kinds, including Chilaquiles (page 22).

MEXICAN HOT CHOCOLATE

(Champurrado)

Makes 2 (about 5-ounce) servings

In a small saucepan over medium heat, whisk together the sugar, cornstarch, and water until the mixture is thick and smooth. Whisk in the milk and cook, whisking frequently, until it just boils, between 1 and 2 minutes. Sprinkle on the chocolate, cinnamon, and cayenne and whisk until the chocolate has melted, less than 1 minute. Divide between two mugs and serve hot.

NOTE: Mexican chocolate is stone ground and can be fairly sweet. Its coarseness makes it easy to grate and melt. Taza is a brand that is Direct Trade and offers a range of 50 to 85 percent cocoa solids; some of their tablets have additional flavorings.

2 teaspoons packed dark brown sugar

2 tablespoons cornstarch or masa harina

¾ cup hot water

1¼ cups whole milk

3 ounces (about 5 tablespoons) grated semisweet chocolate

¼ teaspoon ground cinnamon (optional)

Pinch of cayenne pepper (optional)

5 OUNCES: 360 CAL., 18G FAT (11G SAT.), 15MG CHOL., 70MG SODIUM, 25G CARB., 0G FIBER, 15G SUGAR, 8G PROTEIN

A POT OF THIS WARMING on the stove is pretty effective aromatherapy to combat a chilly, gray afternoon. If you're hosting a pumpkin-carving party or other fall festivity, this spicy cider goes perfectly with Finnish Buttermilk Cake (page 247) or Vegan Gingersnaps (page 255), and you can double or triple the batch of cider as long as you have a pot big enough to contain it. For a more delicate flavor, start with fresh pear cider rather than apple.

ZESTY FALL CIDER

Makes 6 (8-ounce) servings

In a deep 3-quart pot over medium heat, combine the cider, cinnamon, cloves, cardamom, and ginger. Simmer for 15 minutes. Strain out the spices through a medium-mesh strainer and return the strained cider to a pot over low heat or a slow cooker set to a low temperature. Stir in the water. Serve warm.

1 quart fresh apple cider

3 (4-inch) cinnamon sticks

6 whole cloves

2 cardamom pods

1-inch knob fresh ginger, peeled and thinly sliced

2 cups water

> SPIRITS PAIRING: A smooth barrel-aged rum is just the ticket. Be sure to choose one that isn't already spiced; that's unnecessary with the fresh ginger and whole spices that are in the cider. Something with warm caramelly notes is a better choice.

---

8 OUNCES: 80 CAL., 0G FAT (0G SAT.), 0MG CHOL., 20MG SODIUM, 20G CARB., 0G FIBER, 17G SUGAR, 0G PROTEIN

IF YOU'RE ALREADY A FAN of chai or other spiced teas, making the leap to warm milk spiced with turmeric and ginger is an easy one. You can find fresh turmeric roots in produce departments from approximately January through early summer. Stock up when you see them and freeze them whole, so you can grate what you need throughout the year; there's no need to bother peeling them whether you're using them fresh or frozen. Remember that fresh turmeric stains fingers as well as plastic or wood surfaces, so gloves aren't a bad idea.

If you like unsweetened chai, taste this before adding any honey; most people will want at least a bit of sweetener, though.

GOLDEN MILK

Makes 2 (10-ounce) servings

In a small saucepan over medium-low heat, combine the milk and water. Stir in the turmeric and ginger, then add the cinnamon, fennel, cardamom, and pepper to taste. Bring the mixture to a simmer and cook for about 10 minutes, reducing the heat as needed to prevent a full boil, until the flavors have melded and the milk has taken on an intense lemon-yellow color. Remove from the heat and strain out the spices. Sweeten to taste with the honey and divide between two mugs. Serve hot.

1½ cups whole milk or coconut milk beverage
1 cup water
1-inch piece turmeric root, grated (about 1 tablespoon)
1-inch piece fresh ginger, peeled and grated (about 1 teaspoon)
1 (3-inch) cinnamon stick
10 whole fennel seeds
5 green cardamom pods
Freshly ground black pepper
4 teaspoons honey, or to taste

10 OUNCES: 160 CAL., 6G FAT (3.5G SAT.), 20MG CHOL., 80MG SODIUM, 22G CARB., 1G FIBER, 19G SUGAR, 6G PROTEIN

GET TO KNOW TURMERIC

Fresh turmeric root adds a rich, bright, peppery flavor that puts the slightly muted mustard flavor of the dried spice to shame. Turmeric also contains curcumin, a nutrient whose potential health benefits have been the subject of thousands of medical studies, with most of the research focused on inflammatory disorders like arthritis, colitis, and gastritis (stomach ulcers). Further research is exploring the benefits of curcumin in autoimmune disorders, cancer, and Alzheimer's. It's important to know that curcumin is poorly absorbed and it stays in your system for only a couple hours. You can boost the health benefits of turmeric by consuming it with black pepper and some fats—a perfect combination for either golden milk or your favorite curry. Fats help promote greater absorption and black pepper keeps the curcumin in your system longer.

THIS TANGY, SPICY COCKTAIL IS the best possible introduction to kombucha for anyone who has decided they don't like it before they've ever had a sip. A dry sparkling wine, like prosecco or cava, is important to dilute the bigger flavors of the juice and kombucha; anything with noticeable sweetness will fight with them, rather than provide balance. With all of its heat and acidity, this mimosa is a great choice alongside buttery breakfast pastries, from croissants to coffee cake.

GINGER-CRANBERRY KOMBUCHA MIMOSA

Makes about 10 (6-ounce) servings

In a half-gallon pitcher, combine the cranberry juice and ginger, stirring to release as much juice from the ginger as possible. Gently add the kombucha and wine. Serve immediately in champagne glasses, garnished with fresh cranberries.

¾ cup cranberry juice, chilled

1-inch knob fresh ginger, peeled and smashed

2 (16-ounce) bottles ginger-flavored kombucha, chilled

1 (750-milliliter) bottle dry sparkling wine, chilled

Fresh cranberries, for garnish (optional)

---

6 OUNCES: 70 CAL., 0G FAT (0G SAT.), 0MG CHOL., 10MG SODIUM, 5G CARB., 0G FIBER, 3G SUGAR, 0G PROTEIN

WHEN IT COMES TO SPICING up tomato juice for a weekend morning wake-up call, why limit yourself to the classic rendition? Using Korean chili paste instead of Tabasco, fish sauce instead of Worcestershire, and the spicy, tangy brine from a jar of kimchi instead of dill pickle juice, this recipe hits the expected flavor notes but with just enough differences to spark a conversation. A clean, smooth vodka is an obvious choice, or lighten up on the alcohol by substituting your favorite IPA or lower-alcohol session ale and call it a Korean-inspired *michelada*. If you're hosting a weekend brunch for a long morning of football, it's a down-right sensible choice.

KIMCHI BLOODY MARY

Makes about 4 (8-ounce) servings

In a large pitcher, combine the lime juice, kimchi brine, *gochujang*, fish sauce, tamari, celery salt, and garlic. Slowly pour in the tomato juice, stirring continuously. Season to taste with salt and pepper. Chill in the refrigerator for at least 2 hours.

To serve, pour the tomato mixture over ice and add the desired amount of vodka. Garnish with your choice of cucumber slices, lime wedges, and mint sprigs.

---

8 OUNCES (WITHOUT ALCOHOL): 170 CAL., 0G FAT (0G SAT.), 0MG CHOL., 960MG SODIUM, 12G CARB., 0G FIBER, 6G SUGAR, 2G PROTEIN

3 tablespoons freshly squeezed lime juice

3 tablespoons kimchi brine

2 teaspoons *gochujang* chili bean paste, or to taste

1 teaspoon fish sauce

1 teaspoon tamari

½ teaspoon celery salt

¼ teaspoon granulated garlic

2 cups tomato juice

Kosher salt and freshly ground black pepper

Ice, for serving

Vodka, gin, or beer (about 1 to 2 ounces per glass), for serving

Cucumber slices, for garnish (optional)

Lime wedges, for garnish (optional)

Fresh mint sprigs, for garnish (optional)

KÜMMEL'S SAVORY SPICE FLAVORS TURN simple orange juice into something special. If you appreciate the flavor of kümmel straight, use the smaller amount of juice; if you want to mellow it out further (or didn't add the honey when making the liqueur), you might prefer the extra splash of sweet juice. Either way, the cumin-caraway flavors come through first, with the sweet fennel fading away into a long, slightly sweeter finish. Served on the rocks, this makes for an interesting aperitif.

ORANGE-KÜMMEL COCKTAIL

Makes 1 serving

In a cocktail shaker, shake together the ice, kümmel, orange juice, and bitters. Strain into a double old-fashioned glass with ice. Add the strip of lemon zest and top up the glass with the desired amount of mineral water.

Ice, for shaking and serving

1 ounce Cumin Cordial (Kümmel) (opposite page) or store-bought kümmel

1 to 1½ ounces orange juice

3 dashes aromatic bitters

1 wide strip fresh lemon zest

Mineral water or club soda, for finishing

---

1 COCKTAIL: 150 CAL., 0G FAT (0G SAT.), 0MG CHOL., 0MG SODIUM, 19G CARB., 0G FIBER, 18G SUGAR, 0G PROTEIN

CUMIN: AN INTERNATIONAL CLASSIC

Cumin is a key component in the cuisines of Mexico, India, and numerous Mediterranean countries. Its pungent flavor balances and connects myriad spices, which is why it's critical in blends like garam masala and chili powder.

It's useful to have ground cumin on hand to sprinkle into barbecue rubs or chili. The flavor of ground cumin is common in Mexican food. Whole cumin seed is frequently used in Indian and eastern Mediterranean cuisines and is great with vegetables like sweet potatoes and carrots. Briefly toasting the whole seed in a skillet over medium heat makes its flavor softer and earthier.

The seeds are a remarkable source of iron; just 2 teaspoons contain 16 percent of the daily value. While there isn't much research on it as a digestive aid, it's a not-uncommon home remedy for indigestion and reflux, in the form of hot tea. To make a cup of cumin tea, soak 1 teaspoon of seeds in very hot water for 3 minutes. Strain and give it a sip—some people add a bit of honey.

KÜMMEL IS A TRADITIONAL DUTCH liqueur that is flavored with a blend of caraway, cumin, and fennel; in the United States, it's typically found as a cocktail ingredient rather than sipped straight. It's not easy to find, but it's very easy to make, and you can turn 750 milliliters into a homemade gift for several friends by pouring it into small, pretty bottles. Its spicy, savory flavor is particularly delicious with orange juice or orange liqueurs; try it in the Orange-Kümmel Cocktail (opposite page).

Cumin Cordial (Kümmel)

Makes 1 (750-milliliter) bottle

Add the caraway, fennel, and cumin to the bottle of vodka, cover, and rotate the bottle gently to distribute the spices; they will sink as they take on liquid. Place the bottle in a dark cupboard, on its side if possible, and steep for 2 weeks, gently shaking the bottle to move the spices halfway through the steeping time. The vodka will take on a light golden-brown tint as it absorbs the oils in the spices.

With a fine-mesh strainer, strain out the spices and sweeten the spiced vodka with the honey.

Kümmel keeps refrigerated for up to 6 months.

2 teaspoons caraway seeds

1 teaspoon fennel seeds

1 teaspoon cumin seeds

1 (750-milliliter) bottle vodka

1 tablespoon mild honey (optional)

1½ OUNCES: 120 CAL., 0G FAT (0G SAT.), 0MG CHOL., 0MG SODIUM, 0G CARB., 0G FIBER, 0G SUGAR, 0G PROTEIN

SANGRIA

It got its start centuries ago as a spiced red-wine punch, so it's no surprise that after all that time sangria recipes come in any variety under the sun. It's a beautiful way to work your favorite seasonal fruits and herbs into your party punch, and it can also help you rescue less-than-great wine and stretch your budget to cover a festive beverage for a large crowd. Remember that it's meant to be refreshing and flavorful, not sugary sweet.

1 CHOOSE YOUR FRUIT

Starting with the fruit rather than with the wine lets you vary it to best suit the season's most delicious (and generally most inexpensive) produce. In winter, all varieties of citrus are fantastic (don't skip Cara Cara oranges and tangerines), and as we progress through the warmer months, it's time for cherries and berries, apricots, peaches, and nectarines, and late-season plums, followed by juicy melon. Next comes fall, when a mix of sweet and tart apples can be fantastic, and soft, sweet pears provide a wonderfully subtle surprise that you can brighten up for the holidays with a sprinkle of pome-granate seeds. Don't miss the tropical fruits as you spot them through the seasons, like star fruit, pineapple, and mango, which can be fantastic with white or sparkling wines.

2 CHOOSE YOUR WINE

While anything from a dry to a semisweet wine can work, any reds that are too tannic won't play very nicely with the fresh fruit. That said, red, rosé, white, and sparkling wines can all make fantastic sangria used individually, or you can blend a few bottles if you're trying to make do with what you have on hand. As a loose general rule, it's easier to blend red varietals with other reds or rosés, while whites and sparkling wines work well together or with the addition of a rosé. Whatever you use, have it well chilled before you begin. Leave the dessert wines out of the mix; their textures are too heavy and flavors too rich.

3   MARINATE THE FRUIT

The most common choices for marinating are either straightforward brandy or something with sweet orange flavor like Grand Marnier, triple sec, or curaçao. Soak the fruit in your chosen alcohol for one to twenty-four hours before drinking the sangria. If you use brandy, you may want to stir in some sugar as well, particularly if you're using mainly citrus or apples. For white or rosé sangria, the aperitif Lillet has enough sweetness and citrus flavor to make an appealing lower-alcohol substitute. If raspberries are included in your fruit selection, don't marinate them in advance; they're so fragile they tend to dissolve. Blackberries and sliced strawberries hold up just fine.

4   MAKE IT FIZZ

If it's a bubbly beverage, chances are someone has used it as a mixer to lighten up sangria; the choices run all the way from lemon-lime soda to seltzer water or a dry sparkling wine. Selection should be based both on personal preference for overall sweetness and on the best way to balance your other ingredients. If you're planning a sangria based on peaches and triple sec, lemon-lime soda will be far too sweet. Try a tart, fizzy lemonade or club soda to keep the sugar in check.

5   GARNISH FOR FLAVOR

If you want the sangria fruit forward, garnish each glass with additional wedges of your chosen fruit. To spice things up, stir in a few drops of your favorite hot sauce or garnish with a thin slice of jalapeño. A sprig of mint is lovely with stone fruits and white wine, while a leaf from a rose geranium is a nice touch if your sangria leans toward citrus flavors.

FLAVOR COMBINATIONS TO TRY

- Rosé, Lillet, or Cointreau; pink grapefruit juice; Cara Cara oranges; tangerines; fresh mint
- Viognier, apple or pear brandy, Bosc pears, honey, fresh ginger, cardamom
- Dry riesling, sweet vermouth, honeydew melon, pasilla chili
- Lambrusco, blackberry brandy, fresh blackberries, pineapple, pineapple sage
- Prosecco, limoncillo, fresh raspberries, lemons, fresh mint
- Rioja, brandy, Cointreau, pomegranate juice, oranges, limes, pomegranate seeds

THIS IS A WHITE-WINE SANGRIA that's perfect for midsummer evenings. If you plan to serve it in narrow glasses, it's best to trim the peel off the orange and cut it into chunks—it's not as pretty as thin wheels in each glass, but it's much more practical when it comes to pouring. The choice of yellow or white nectarines, or red or golden raspberries is purely aesthetic; the sangria will be lightly sweet and deeply flavorful whichever you choose.

SANGRIA BLANCA

Makes 4 (10-ounce) servings

In a half-gallon pitcher, gently stir together the nectarine and orange. Sprinkle on the sugar, then add the triple sec. Add half the wine and chill in the refrigerator for at least 1 hour or up to overnight. The more time it sits, the more the flavors will meld.

When you're ready to drink it, add the remaining wine, the raspberries, and the seltzer water. Serve poured over ice and garnish with the mint.

---

10 OUNCES: 260 CAL., 0G FAT (0G SAT.), 0MG CHOL., 15MG SODIUM, 44G CARB., 2G FIBER, 37G SUGAR, 1G PROTEIN

1 medium nectarine, halved, pitted, and thinly sliced

1 medium orange, thinly sliced and seeded

¼ cup granulated sugar, or to taste

½ cup triple sec or Lillet

1 (750-milliliter) bottle chilled white wine, divided

½ cup fresh raspberries

About 2 cups seltzer water

Ice, for serving

Fresh mint leaves, for garnish (optional)

DESSERTS

WHILE OUR STORES MIGHT BE MORE associated with salad than dessert, trust us: We're the first to get giddy when a local ice-cream company introduces a new flavor or when we get a chance to taste a new treat from our favorite chocolatier. We also love tinkering with classic desserts to make them a little more healthful, thanks to fresh fruit, whole grains, and healthy fats. If you haven't yet tried an Avocado Brownie, you've got a major new dessert discovery ahead of you.

We also know that those who have family members with food allergies turn to homemade baked goods to make safe treats for loved ones. Sometimes we all need a little extra sweetness in our lives, and that doesn't change just because you need to avoid nuts, gluten, eggs, or dairy. There are recipes here that will suit almost everyone, like Finnish Buttermilk Cake (page 247), Flourless Chocolate Crinkles (page 244), or Roasted Rhubarb and Strawberries (page 253).

For some people, baking is their favorite way to express themselves. With a bit of practice, it becomes soothing, not stressful—and seasonal ingredients like citrus, berries, and stone fruit can inspire endless creativity at home just as they do for chefs. If you lack such confidence, try a forgiving fruit crisp. You'll develop new skills more quickly than you'd ever guess. Dessert is a lot of different things, depending on who you ask—but we can agree that above all, it should tempt us all into lingering together at the table.

RICH, FUDGY BROWNIES RANK MIGHTY high on the list of popular chocolate treats, and they use the incredible natural richness of avocados plus a bit of coconut oil to replace the more typical butter. They're the sort of dessert that will create a stampede of recipe requests in your direction if you bring them to the office—after everyone finishes registering their disbelief at the secret ingredient. If you want a gluten-free version, substitute your preferred gluten-free flour mix for the all-purpose flour. These brownies don't freeze well (the texture gets mushy), but they will do fine in an airtight container at room temperature for up to three days.

AVOCADO BROWNIES

Makes 16 (2-inch) brownies

Preheat the oven to 350 degrees F. Line an 8-inch square baking dish with parchment paper.

In the top of a double boiler over barely simmering water, melt the chocolate. (If you don't have a double boiler, you can make one by setting a small, heatproof glass bowl on a saucepan that has a few inches of simmering water in it. The bottom of the bowl should not reach the bottom of the pan and should sit above the water, not in it.) Remove the chocolate from the heat. Stir in the oil until no streaks remain.

In a large bowl, whisk together the avocado and chocolate mixture until the ingredients are completely blended, about 1 minute. Whisk in the sugar until the mixture is smooth. Mix in the eggs, one at a time, until they are well combined and no streaks of yolk or white remain. Add the vanilla and stir to combine.

In a small bowl, combine the flour, cocoa powder, baking powder, and salt. Stir the dry ingredients into the avocado mixture until just combined—be careful not to overmix! Spread the batter in the prepared pan.

Bake until a toothpick inserted into the center comes out clean, 30 to 35 minutes. Cool completely on a wire rack before cutting the brownies into squares.

8 ounces (1⅓ cups) chopped semisweet or bittersweet chocolate

3 tablespoons coconut oil

2 very ripe large avocados, peeled, pitted, and mashed until creamy (about 1 cup)

¾ cup granulated sugar

2 large eggs

1 teaspoon vanilla extract

¾ cup all-purpose flour

¼ cup unsweetened cocoa powder, sifted

½ teaspoon baking powder

¼ teaspoon kosher salt

1 BROWNIE: 200 CAL., 11G FAT (6G SAT.), 25MG CHOL., 40MG SODIUM, 18G CARB., 2G FIBER, 11G SUGAR, 3G PROTEIN

SOMETHING ABOUT DESSERT COOKED IN a skillet seems summery, particularly when that dessert is topped with a pretty layer of sour cherries wrapped in rich caramel. Thanks to frozen sour cherries, you can have that summer effect the whole year and skip the tedious step of having to pit fresh sour cherries. Using a good-quality balsamic vinegar here is worth it, as you want that rich, tangy sweetness to come through cleanly in the caramel.

It's fine to use entirely all-purpose flour if you don't have any whole wheat pastry flour, but the small amount is a nice way to boost the fiber content of the cake without changing its flavor or texture.

CHERRY-BALSAMIC UPSIDE-DOWN CAKE

Makes 12 servings

Preheat the oven to 350 degrees F.

In a 10-inch cast-iron skillet over medium heat, melt 4 tablespoons of the butter. Add the brown sugar and cook, stirring occasionally, for about 2 minutes, until foamy. Stir in the vinegar and a pinch of salt; cook for 30 seconds. Remove from the heat, stir in the cherries, and arrange them in an even layer across the caramel.

In a small bowl, combine the flours, the baking powder, and the remaining ½ teaspoon salt. In a stand mixer fitted with the paddle attachment, or with an electric hand mixer, beat the remaining 8 tablespoons butter until fluffy, about 1 minute. Beat in 1 cup of the granulated sugar and mix for 3 minutes on medium speed, until it is pale and very fluffy. Beat in the egg yolks and vanilla until combined. Reduce the speed to low and add half the dry ingredients, then half the buttermilk; repeat with the remaining halves of each. Mix just until smooth. The batter will be very thick.

In a large, clean bowl, beat the egg whites on high with an electric mixer until frothy, about 1 minute. With the mixer running, slowly add the remaining 2 tablespoons sugar and beat until stiff peaks form, about 2 minutes. Using a spatula, fold about one-quarter of the egg whites into $\longrightarrow$

12 tablespoons (1½ sticks) unsalted butter, softened, divided

¾ cup packed dark brown sugar

1 teaspoon balsamic vinegar

½ teaspoon plus a pinch of kosher salt, divided

2 cups frozen sour cherries

1⅓ cups all-purpose flour

¼ cup whole wheat pastry flour

1½ teaspoons baking powder

1 cup plus 2 tablespoons granulated sugar, divided

4 large eggs, separated

1 teaspoon vanilla extract

⅔ cup cultured buttermilk

the batter to thin it out a bit, then gently fold in the remaining whites just until there are no visible white streaks. The batter will be airy and spreadable.

Pour the batter into the skillet over the fruit layer. Bake until the top is golden, about 1 hour; a toothpick inserted into the center should come out clean. Let the cake cool for 5 minutes. Loosen from the sides of the pan with a paring knife, then carefully invert onto a cake plate; you can gently arrange the fruit in place if some of it slides when you flip the cake. Serve warm or at room temperature.

---

1 SLICE: 340 CAL., 14G FAT (8G SAT.), 95MG CHOL., 150MG SODIUM, 50G CARB., 1G FIBER, 36G SUGAR, 5G PROTEIN

A CHERRY ON TOP

Cherries are one of the oldest known and most beloved cultivated fruits. Ancient Rome's famed gastronome General Lucullus brought a cultivar to Rome from what is now Turkey in 72 BC; many centuries later, Henry VIII demanded they be grown in England after tasting his first one in Flanders. That love has lasted all the way through to the Rainier cherry, hybridized at Washington State University in 1952.

Soft, tender, and easily damaged in spring's unpredictable storms, cherries are one of the earliest tree fruits of the year. Like all of summer's stone fruits, cherries are an impressive source of fiber, potassium, and vitamins A and C. Red cherries include more than a dozen unique beneficial nutrients and get their hue from powerful antioxidants such as anthocyanins and flavonols that block the production of inflammatory proteins. Their robust quantities of diverse antioxidants make them a standout among the most potent anti-inflammatory foods, potentially helping manage chronic inflammation. They're also one of the few food sources of melatonin, a natural hormone that helps regulate sleep.

THIS GLUTEN-FREE RIFF ON A holiday cookie classic is an ideal treat for chocolate lovers. They're rich, they melt in your mouth like your favorite flourless chocolate cake, and they bring out the pure flavor of the chocolate you've used (so use good chocolate!). For the deepest flavor that isn't bitter, somewhere between 60 and 72 percent cacao is a good choice. If you like, you can even use bars that have been flavored with chilies or coffee. Good-quality chocolate chips are also a fine option.

You can roll the crinkles in coarse sugar or granulated sugar if you prefer the sparkly look to the snowy effect of powdered sugar. Either way, they freeze well for up to one month. Defrost, covered, at room temperature.

FLOURLESS CHOCOLATE CRINKLES

Makes 2 dozen cookies

In the top of a double boiler over barely simmering water, melt the chocolate. (If you don't have a double boiler, you can make one by setting a small, heatproof glass bowl on a saucepan that has a few inches of simmering water in it. The bottom of the bowl should not reach the bottom of the pan and should sit above the water, not in it.) Remove the chocolate from the heat. Cut the butter into a few pieces and stir into the chocolate until no yellow streaks remain. Set the mixture aside at room temperature.

In a large bowl, use an electric mixer to beat the eggs on medium-high speed, gradually adding the granulated sugar until ribbons form when you lift up the beater and the mixture is thick and pale yellow, 5 to 10 minutes. With a spatula or wooden spoon, gently fold in the chocolate-butter mixture just until no streaks of yellow remain. Gently fold in the flour. Cover the bowl and refrigerate for at least 2 hours or overnight.

8 ounces (1⅓ cup) chopped bittersweet or semisweet chocolate
3 tablespoons unsalted butter, at room temperature
2 large eggs
⅓ cup granulated sugar
¾ cup almond flour
Powdered sugar, for rolling

THE DEAL WITH ALMOND MEAL

Almond flour is simply whole almonds that have been ground into a fairly fine powder. You'll sometimes see it labeled as almond meal or almond powder; whatever it's called, it has almost no recognizable almond flavor. This delicate gluten-free flour works especially well in baked goods such as muffins, cookies, cakes, and pancakes, adding both moisture and a fluffy, light texture. It's also useful if you want to reduce carbs and eat lower glycemic index foods while adding protein and antioxidants to your diet.

Preheat the oven to 325 degrees F. Line two baking sheets with parchment paper.

Scoop the dough into 1-tablespoon balls. Roll them in powdered sugar, place on the baking sheet about 2 inches apart, and immediately put in the oven. For a softer cookie, bake only until the edges are set and centers are no longer wet, 13 to 15 minutes; for a crunchier cookie, bake for 16 to 18 minutes. Let cool on the baking sheets for 5 minutes, then transfer to wire rack to cool completely.

---

1 COOKIE: 100 CAL., 7G FAT (3G SAT.), 20MG CHOL., 5MG SODIUM, 5G CARB., 0G FIBER, 4G SUGAR, 2G PROTEIN

IT'S THE BEST OF ALL worlds: an easy one-bowl cake that looks gorgeous and has a complex flavor thanks to fresh orange zest and plenty of cardamom. Once you pop it out of the Bundt pan, you'll see a shiny, dark golden-brown crust that gives the cake an appealing crunch; the generous amount of full-fat buttermilk makes the interior rich and tender. It's lovely with nothing more than a cup of coffee, but a spoonful of seasonal berries (or Roasted Rhubarb and Strawberries, page 253) makes for a fresh accessory. A bonus is its lack of eggs—it's a great recipe to have on hand when you're cooking for those who avoid them.

If you are using cardamom that you purchased ground, you might like to add an extra one-half to one teaspoon, as its flavor fades quite quickly after grinding.

FINNISH BUTTERMILK CAKE

Makes 8 to 10 servings

Preheat the oven to 350 degrees F. Lightly butter and flour a 9- or 10-cup (23-centimeter) Bundt pan.

Whisk together the flour, sugar, cardamom, orange zest, baking powder, baking soda, and salt. Make a well in the dry ingredients and slowly add the butter, followed by the buttermilk. Using a wooden spoon or silicone spatula, stir just until the batter is smooth, no more than 1 minute. Pour into the prepared pan and bake for 1 hour, until there is a shiny brown crust and a skewer inserted into the center comes out clean.

Cool for 15 minutes, then gently loosen the cake from the pan and invert onto a wire rack. Cool completely before slicing.

½ cup (1 stick) unsalted butter, melted and cooled, plus more for the pan

2½ cups all-purpose flour, plus more for the pan

1⅓ cups granulated sugar

2 teaspoons freshly ground cardamom

2 teaspoons freshly grated orange zest

1 teaspoon baking powder

1½ teaspoons baking soda

¼ teaspoon kosher salt

1½ cups buttermilk

1 SLICE: 350 CAL., 11G FAT (7G SAT.), 30MG CHOL., 340MG SODIUM, 58G CARB., 1G FIBER, 31G SUGAR, 5G PROTEIN

CARDAMOM KITCHEN CURRICULUM

Related to ginger and turmeric, cardamom is a frequent ingredient in herbal teas designed to aid digestion and soothe irritated throats. Its complex flavor, with notes of citrus, herbaceous pine, and warm spice, goes well with its cousins; you can try them all together in Golden Milk (page 227). White and green pods are the same thing (the white pods have been bleached). As a loose guideline, there are about a dozen seeds per pod, and thirteen pods will produce about 2 teaspoons of ground cardamom.

PERHAPS BEST KNOWN IN THIS country for the colorful role they play in some popular herbal tea blends, hibiscus flowers have a tart, fruity flavor with a faint touch of earthiness; they add a subtle interest to the taste of bright and simple lemon. Many stores that sell bulk teas will have them, as will groceries that feature South American or Caribbean packaged ingredients. They contribute an absolutely beautiful deep rose-pink color to the filling that makes these bars stand out at a bake sale or on a dessert table. If you want more hibiscus in your life (it's every bit as fun for photos as it is to eat), make a pitcher of Hibiscus Tea Concentrate (page 216).

HIBISCUS LEMON BARS

Makes 24 (2-inch) bars

Preheat the oven to 350 degrees F. Lightly butter a 9-by-13-inch baking dish.

In the work bowl of a food processor, combine 1½ cups of the flour, the powdered sugar, and ½ teaspoon of the salt. Coarsely chop the butter and drop the pieces on top of the dry ingredients. Pulse until the butter has been evenly blended into the flour mixture and looks like coarse cornmeal.

Pour the mixture into the prepared pan. Press it firmly with your fingers across the entire bottom of the pan and about ½ inch up the sides to form a crust.

Bake until light golden brown, about 20 minutes.

While the crust bakes, prepare the filling. In a small saucepan over medium heat, warm the lemon juice slightly. Sprinkle the hibiscus flowers on top of the juice, stir them gently, and remove from the heat. Let steep for 10 minutes, until the lemon juice is bright pink. Strain out the flowers and stir the lemon zest into the hibiscus-lemon juice.

In a medium bowl, whisk together the juice and eggs until the eggs have been completely incorporated, then whisk in the granulated sugar, remaining ¼ cup flour, and remaining pinch of salt. Pour the filling into the warm crust.

¾ cup (1½ sticks) unsalted butter, at room temperature, plus more for the pan
1¾ cups all-purpose flour, divided
⅔ cup powdered sugar, plus more for serving
½ teaspoon plus a pinch of kosher salt, divided
⅔ cup freshly squeezed lemon juice (from 2 large lemons)
¼ cup (½ ounce) dried hibiscus flowers
1 tablespoon freshly grated lemon zest
5 large eggs, beaten
1⅔ cups granulated sugar

Reduce the oven temperature to 325 degrees F. Bake for 25 to 30 minutes, until the filling is mostly set but not completely firm to the touch. Cool in the pan for at least 1 hour and then cut into bars.

Served chilled or at room temperature. Just before serving, sift powdered sugar on top, if you like. Bars will keep refrigerated for up to 1 week.

1 BAR: 170 CAL., 7G FAT (4G SAT.), 55MG CHOL., 65MG SODIUM, 25G CARB., 0G FIBER, 18G SUGAR, 2G PROTEIN

THESE HEARTY, CHEWY COOKIES ARE sturdy enough for school lunches or soccer games, with the oats and peanut butter providing a nutritious base of complex carbohydrates and protein that supply lasting energy to help balance the quick sugar rush.

For a special summertime dessert, turn them into ice-cream sandwiches. Cut the cookies in half and freeze the halves for at least one hour or overnight. Spread a half-inch layer of your preferred ice cream from edge to edge on one half and gently top it with another. Freeze on a baking sheet for several hours, until they are firm enough to pick up. You can keep them in the freezer for up to one week or enjoy them as soon as they've set.

FLOURLESS PEANUT BUTTER– OATMEAL COOKIES PCC Bakery Favorite

Makes about 16 large cookies

Preheat the oven to 325 degrees F. Line two baking sheets with parchment paper.

In the work bowl of a food processor, put 1½ cups of the oats. Pulse about five times to chop them coarsely. Add the remaining 1½ cups oats and set aside.

In the bowl of a stand mixer fitted with the paddle attachment, beat the butter on medium speed until smooth, about 30 seconds. Add in both of the sugars and beat for about 2 minutes, until the mixture is thick and fluffy. Blend in the peanut butter on low speed just until incorporated. Beat in the eggs, one at a time, until no streaks of yolk remain, about 30 seconds per egg, scraping down the sides of the bowl as needed. Stir in the vanilla, baking soda, and salt. Add the oats and blend on low speed until

3 cups rolled oats, divided (see note)

½ cup (1 stick) unsalted butter, at room temperature

¾ cup packed dark brown sugar

¾ cup granulated sugar

1¼ cups peanut butter (creamy or crunchy)

2 large eggs

1 teaspoon vanilla extract

1½ teaspoons baking soda

¾ teaspoon kosher salt

1¼ cups semisweet chocolate chips

OATS ARE AWESOME

Oats are one of the few food sources of beta-glucans, an unusual type of fiber (also found in mushrooms) with great potential to boost your immunity. Research shows that beta-glucans help your immune system respond more rapidly to infections, enhance your immune system's ability to eliminate bacteria, and may even reduce the risk of some types of cancer. Oats also are a good source of selenium, manganese, and zinc—three minerals that support your body's antioxidant and immune defenses.

the oats are completely coated with the wet ingredients; scrape down the sides of the bowl several times to make sure they are evenly distributed.

Using a wooden spoon or a spatula, fold in the chocolate chips. The dough will be thick and slightly sticky.

Shape into generous ¼-cup balls and place about 3 inches apart on the baking sheets. With slightly wet hands to prevent sticking, press to flatten the balls into pucks that measure about 2½ inches across and ¾ inch thick. Bake for 12 to 15 minutes, until light brown around the edges but still slightly soft in the middle. Cool completely on their baking sheets; the cookies will be fragile when hot but firm up as they cool. Store in an airtight container for up to 3 days.

The cookies may also be frozen for up to 1 month.

NOTE: If you'd like to skip the step of grinding half the oats in a food processor, try using half quick-cooking (not instant) oats; the results will be very similar.

---

1 COOKIE: 340 CAL., 19G FAT (7G SAT.), 30MG CHOL., 290MG SODIUM, 40G CARB., 3G FIBER, 26G SUGAR, 7G PROTEIN

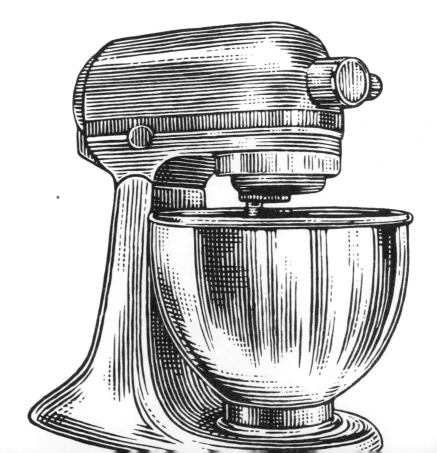

THIS TECHNIQUE IS A WONDERFUL way to dress up the flavor of peak-season berries or concentrate the sweetness of out-of-season berries or stone fruit. Strawberries, blackberries, peaches, and apricots are four fruits that shine with roasting; the result is delicious enough to eat on its own, but roasted fruit is a welcome ice-cream topping, shortcake accessory, or additional treat to garnish Finnish Buttermilk Cake (page 247). It's also appealingly low effort—just cut the lucky fruit into bite-size pieces and proceed with the remaining steps.

ROASTED RHUBARB AND STRAWBERRIES

Makes 4 to 6 servings

Preheat the oven to 350 degrees F.

In a medium bowl, combine the sugar, orange zest and juice, and salt, mixing with a spatula or wooden spoon to make a grainy paste. Add the strawberries and rhubarb and stir gently to coat with the sugar mixture.

Transfer to a rimmed baking sheet. Roast for 25 to 30 minutes, stirring once or twice, until the fruit is tender to the touch.

While they are still warm, transfer the berries, rhubarb, and all the juices to a bowl. Cool to room temperature and serve, or refrigerate for up to 5 days.

¼ cup granulated sugar

1 small orange or tangerine, freshly zested and juiced

¼ teaspoon kosher salt

1 pint fresh strawberries, hulled and halved

2¼ cups rhubarb (from 2 large stalks), thinly sliced

⅓ RECIPE: 70 CAL., 0G FAT (0G SAT.), 0MG CHOL., 100MG SODIUM, 17G CARB., 2G FIBER, 14G SUGAR, 1G PROTEIN

CHOOSING BETTER BERRIES

When it comes to choosing the best-tasting berries, let color be your guide. Strawberries don't ripen after picking, so any that show white or green around the stem or tip will stay that way. Berry varieties that are suitable for shipping have pale, sturdy cores that you can see when you slice them in half. Local berries, which don't need to hold up to long-distance shipping, will frequently be a mix of different varieties that have softer pure-red cores that are a signifier of a berry that is sweeter and muskier than the white-cored varieties. Whatever variety they may be, strawberries are an amazing source of vitamin C. Just 8 organic strawberries contain your entire daily requirement for this essential antioxidant.

ONE OF PCC'S MOST POPULAR cookies, this gingersnap can be chewy or crunchy, depending on how long it's baked. If you'd like to bake your own gingersnaps for the crust of the Salted Caramel Pumpkin Cheesecake (page 256), make sure to bake them up crunchy.

The egg replacer called for is made of a mixture of potato starch and tapioca starch. If you have a different egg replacer you prefer, you'll need the volume that matches two eggs' worth; it may change the texture of the final product.

VEGAN GINGERSNAPS PCC Bakery Favorite

Makes about 25 cookies

Preheat the oven to 350 degrees F. Line two baking sheets with parchment paper.

In a small bowl, mix together the egg replacer and water until smooth. Set aside.

In the bowl of a stand mixer fitted with the paddle attachment, or using a handheld electric mixer, combine the shortening, sugar, and molasses; beat on medium speed for 1 minute until everything is smooth and thoroughly blended. Add the egg-replacer mixture, ginger, cinnamon, lemon zest, baking soda, and salt and beat for 1 minute; the dough will be sticky and somewhat shiny. Add the flour in two batches, mixing on low speed just until no white streaks remain.

Roll the dough into balls about 2 inches in diameter and then roll the balls in sugar. Place 2 inches apart on the prepared baking sheets. Bake for 11 to 14 minutes, until the edges are set and the tops are cracked. It's OK if some of the dough in the cracks looks a little wet. If you prefer a completely crunchy gingersnap over a chewy one, bake for an additional 2 minutes.

Cool on the baking sheets for 5 minutes, then carefully transfer to wire racks to cool completely. The cookies will be fragile when warm but will firm up as they cool.

Store in an airtight container at room temperature for 2 days, or freeze for up to 1 month.

1 tablespoon Ener-G powdered egg replacer

¼ cup warm water

1 cup vegetable shortening, at room temperature

1¾ cups granulated sugar, plus more for rolling

½ cup molasses (not blackstrap)

1 tablespoon ground ginger

1½ teaspoons ground cinnamon

1 teaspoon freshly grated lemon zest

1¼ teaspoons baking soda

½ teaspoon kosher salt

3 cups all-purpose flour

1 COOKIE: 200 CAL., 8G FAT (2G SAT.), 0MG CHOL., 105MG SODIUM, 31G CARB., 1G FIBER, 19G SUGAR, 2G PROTEIN

IT'S EASY TO OVERBAKE CHEESECAKE, which can result in a deeply cracked surface and a dry texture. Remember that it's essentially a custard-based dessert, so it will still be a little loose in the center when it is done, while its edges will be firm. If it cracks, just send caramel sauce and gingersnap crumbs to the rescue! With a bit of artful drizzling and crumb patting, it will still be gorgeous. If you'd like to bake your own gingersnaps for the crust, try the Vegan Gingersnaps (page 255) and bake them for the longer amount of time so they will have the correct crunch.

SALTED CARAMEL PUMPKIN CHEESECAKE

Makes about 12 servings

In a medium bowl, stir together the gingersnaps and brown sugar; drizzle with the melted butter and toss to combine. Using your fingers, press into the bottom of a 9-inch springform pan and set aside.

Preheat the oven to 350 degrees F.

In the bowl of a stand mixer fitted with the paddle attachment, beat the cream cheese on medium speed until completely smooth, about 90 seconds. Beat in the eggs and egg yolk until they are incorporated and no yellow streaks remain, about 1 minute. On low speed, beat in the pumpkin puree, sugar, sour cream, flour, nutmeg, cloves, cinnamon, vanilla, and caramel sauce, scraping down the sides of the bowl with a spatula to make sure all the cream cheese is fully blended and no white streaks remain, about 2 minutes. Pour the filling onto the prepared crust. If you like, gently heat a little caramel sauce and drizzle a pattern over the top of the cheesecake.

Bake for about 1 hour, until the edges are firm and the center is just set; the temperature taken with an instant-read thermometer should be 155 degrees F in the middle. Turn the oven off and let the cheesecake rest in it with the door propped open for 20 minutes. Refrigerate for at least 4 hours or overnight before serving.

1 cup gingersnap crumbs (about 5 ounces)

2 tablespoons packed dark brown sugar

4 tablespoons unsalted butter, melted

24 ounces cream cheese, at room temperature

3 large eggs plus 1 egg yolk

1 (15-ounce) can pumpkin puree

1¼ cups granulated sugar

⅓ cup full-fat sour cream

2 tablespoons all-purpose flour

¼ teaspoon ground nutmeg

¼ teaspoon ground cloves

½ teaspoon ground cinnamon

1 tablespoon vanilla extract

¼ cup prepared caramel sauce, plus more for drizzling

DESSERT PAIRING: Look for an ice cider (for sweeter apple flavor) or barrel-aged pommeau for something like port made from apples.

1 SLICE: 360 CAL., 17G FAT (9G SAT.), 110MG CHOL., 280MG SODIUM, 45G CARB., 1G FIBER, 34G SUGAR, 8G PROTEIN

HAND PIES TAKE A LITTLE more fuss to assemble than one big pie, but there's a bonus to their small size on hot summer days: they need only twenty minutes to bake. The addition of fresh basil complements sweet fresh plums, but feel free to leave it out for a simpler flavor profile. Use whatever plum or pluot variety you enjoy the most, but a mixture that includes purple, red, and green or yellow plums will provide the most balanced flavor and texture.

Usually egg wash on pies is an optional step that makes the crust a little prettier, but in this case, it's also helping to firmly seal the edges, so don't skip it.

PLUM HAND PIES

Makes 8 (3-by-6-inch) pies

Preheat the oven to 400 degrees F. Line a baking sheet with parchment paper.

In a medium bowl, combine the plums, brown sugar, cornstarch, and lemon zest and juice; set aside. In a separate small bowl, mix together the cheese and basil.

On a lightly floured surface, roll out the pie crust until ⅛ inch thick. Using a 5- to 6-inch round cookie cutter, cut out as many rounds as you can. Reroll the dough scraps and cut out more rounds. You should end up with 8 rounds plus a few additional scraps.

Place 1 teaspoon of the cheese mixture in the center of each round. Top with a generous tablespoon of plum filling, making sure to leave a ½-inch border around the entire edge. In a small bowl, beat together the egg and water. Brush the border with the egg wash and fold the dough over to enclose the filling. Press the dough tightly closed with your fingers, then crimp the edges all the way around with a fork to seal.

Transfer the pies to the prepared baking sheet, brush the tops with more of the egg wash, and sprinkle with a little coarse sugar. Cut a small vent (between ½ inch and 1 inch long) in the top of each pie. Bake until the crusts are golden and the filling is bubbling from the vents, about 20 minutes. Cook in the pan for at least a few minutes before serving, or serve at room temperature.

1½ cups diced plums or pluots (4 to 5 medium plums or pluots)

3 tablespoons packed dark brown sugar

1 tablespoon cornstarch

1 teaspoon freshly grated lemon zest

1 teaspoon freshly squeezed lemon juice

3 ounces (about 3 tablespoons) soft fresh goat cheese, at room temperature

2 teaspoons chopped fresh basil (optional)

All-purpose flour, for dusting

1 prepared double pie crust

1 large egg

1 tablespoon water

Coarse sugar, for sprinkling (optional)

1 PIE: 150 CAL., 8G FAT (2.5G SAT.), 25MG CHOL., 130MG SODIUM, 18G CARB., 0G FIBER, 8G SUGAR, 3G PROTEIN

CRISPS & CRUMBLES

There's no easier way to turn fresh fruit into a baked dessert than adding a quick, crumbly topping to a dish of minimally sweetened wedges or heap of berries. Traditionally, a crisp topping involves oats or nuts mixed into the streusel, while a crumble has a streusel topping that's based on flour, but many people use the words interchangeably today. When it comes to choosing the flour for your streusel, know that in such a forgiving recipe you can just use your favorite, whether it's all-purpose, whole grain, or gluten-free.

1 PREPARE YOUR FRUIT

Almost any dessert-friendly fruit or combination of fruits can work as the base for your crisp or crumble, and that includes bananas. We'll even stretch this to include vegetables like rhubarb and mashed sweet potatoes. For a 9-inch round or 8-inch square pan, or a 9-inch cast-iron skillet, you want to start with 5 cups of prepared fruit. The preparation will change depending on the fruit: peel, pit, core, or stem as your selection demands. No need for precision knife work; just chop it up into pieces no larger than 2 inches. You can also use frozen fruit; if that's the case, thaw before baking, but retain all the juices.

2 THICKEN IT UP

Flour, cornstarch, and instant tapioca all have their fans, but tapioca flour is a more modern choice with a lot going for it. Allergies to it, unlike flour and cornstarch, are a rarity; you'll never end up with undissolved crunchy bits in your fruit as you can with instant tapioca. Thickener isn't absolutely required for apples or starchy ingredients like bananas or sweet potatoes, but everything else needs some. Cherry, rhubarb, and berry fillings are particularly juicy; 3 tablespoons of all-purpose or tapioca flour is a good amount. Peaches, mangoes, apricots, and pears can get away with just 1 tablespoon.

3 SWEETEN TO TASTE

With peak-season fruit, a little sugar goes a long way, and the best way to know how much is needed is to taste. Three tablespoons of sugar (white, brown, or coconut) is a reliable ballpark for the majority of fruit; sour cherries and tart rhubarb benefit from closer to ½ cup. Don't be afraid to play around with alternatives like honey or maple syrup, which can be substituted at a one-to-one ratio for sugar.

4 CHOOSE YOUR TOPPING

This is where you can decide between selecting ingredients that will perfectly pair with the fruit or that will simply clean out the pantry. For a crisp, you'll want ½ cup of crunchy toppings (chopped nuts, shredded coconut, rolled oats, or spelt flakes) and the same amount of some sort of granular sugar bound together with about ¼ cup each of your preferred flour and your favorite fat (butter or coconut oil are both terrific). A crumble is a sweeter, more delicate affair, with ¾ cup each of flour and sugar bound together with ¼ cup of fat; a pinch of cinnamon is a fine idea too.

5 BAKE TO BROWN AND BUBBLING

The winning temperature is 375 degrees F, and crisps and crumbles are baked in 30 to 40 minutes. The topping should take on a noticeably darker color— rich golden brown for crumbles or a deep toasted brown for a crisp. The filling will bubble around the edges, sometimes to a startling degree. To avoid potential overflow (and unplanned smoke-alarm tests), place the pan on a rimmed baking sheet to catch any escaping juices.

FLAVOR COMBINATIONS TO TRY

- Rhubarb, candied ginger, streusel
- Mangoes, coconut streusel
- Sour cherries, sprinkle of ground cloves and ground cinnamon, oat streusel
- Apricots, cardamom-almond streusel
- Nectarines, raspberries, oat streusel
- Mashed sweet potatoes, orange zest, gingersnap-pecan streusel
- Pears, cranberries, hazelnut streusel
- Bananas, rum, pecan topping

USING SUMMER'S JUICIEST FRUITS IN this style of dessert solves the problem of soggy-bottom crusts, and the brown sugar in both the topping and the filling is one of the all-time great flavor combinations with peaches. This crisp is also a terrific way to take advantage of the grainy texture of almond flour, as it adds body and extra crumbliness to the entire top. There's no need to peel either kind of fruit, but you can if you prefer.

PEACH OR NECTARINE CRISP

Makes 6 servings

Preheat the oven to 375 degrees F.

In a medium bowl, combine the peaches or nectarines with ⅓ cup of the sugar. Let the mixture sit for 15 to 20 minutes, or until the fruit releases its juice. Drain the fruit pieces from the juice, reserving just 2 tablespoons of the juice. (If you like, use the excess juice in lemonade or add a splash of it to seltzer water.) Toss the fruit with the lemon juice and cornstarch and drizzle on the reserved juice. Arrange the fruit in a shallow 9-inch baking dish or pie plate and set aside.

In a medium bowl, combine the remaining ⅓ cup sugar, the flour, oats, salt, and nutmeg. Rub in the butter with your fingertips until coarse crumbs form. Sprinkle the oat topping over the fruit mixture. Place the dish on a rimmed baking sheet to catch any drips while it bakes.

Bake for 40 to 45 minutes, until the topping is golden brown and the filling is bubbling around the edges. Let the crisp cool at least 15 minutes before serving; it can also be served at room temperature.

2 pounds peaches or nectarines (about 6 medium-size fruits), pitted and cut into 1-inch pieces

⅔ cup packed dark brown sugar, divided

2 teaspoons freshly squeezed lemon juice

1 tablespoon plus 1 teaspoon cornstarch

⅔ cup almond flour

⅔ cup rolled oats (not quick-cooking)

¼ teaspoon kosher salt

⅛ teaspoon freshly grated nutmeg

6 tablespoons (¾ stick) cold unsalted butter, cut into small pieces

---

1 SERVING: 340 CAL., 19G FAT (8G SAT.), 30MG CHOL., 110MG SODIUM, 42G CARB., 5G FIBER, 27G SUGAR, 6G PROTEIN

COOKING
BY THE
SEASONS

EATING SEASONALLY PUTS THE FRESHEST FLAVORS on your table. Sometimes we can't resist the temptation of raspberries in January, but adapting our diets to the seasons is a smart call across the board, from flavor quality to nutritional benefits to environmental impact. Chances are good that if you're eating freshly harvested produce, it's been grown locally. The less time your food spends on a boat or plane, the fresher it is and therefore the more nutrients it contains. You also support the local economy, improving the economic viability of agricultural communities within an hour or two of your kitchen. Seasonal eating encourages a diverse diet too, which means a wider range of nutrients.

Most of the recipes below are arranged by the prime months you can find their star ingredient in peak supply in Washington State. In the case of the holiday section, the recipes are based on what our delis feature (and our customers ask for); you'll also see a few dishes that could go in any season but have been assigned to a specific spot. It might be, as with Homemade Energy Bars (page 211), that they suit the season for reasons other than their ingredients (energy bars are great for busy summers). Or it might be, as with Lentil and White Bean Stew (page 38), that it's the cooking technique that suits the season.

SPRING

SUMMER

AUTUMN

WINTER

HOLIDAY

ACKNOWLEDGMENTS

THANK YOU TO Lynne Vea and Jackie Freeman, for their roles as PCC recipe developers over the years, as well as to their fellow PCC Cooks instructors Iole Aguero, Erin Coopey, Seppo Ed Farrey, Pranee Halvorsen, Ami Karnosh, Omid Roustaei, Becky Selengut, and Lesa Sullivan. Goldie Caughlan, Leika Suzumura, and Nancy Taylor also contributed recipes. Nutrition educators Nick Rose and Marilyn Walls contributed their expertise to many of the sidebars; Nick also made sure that our nutrition facts were complete and accurate. Trudy Bialic played, and continues to play, a vital role in shaping our approach to food policy, issues, and advocacy—including how it is presented here. Leon Bloom, Robin Cantor, Jeff Cox, and Noah Smith assisted on numerous details, from chasing down recipes and ingredients to advising on our pairings. The technical expertise of Chris Schults helped keep this project alive and provided a massive boost in getting things started.

Taste (2011 to 2017) lit the spark for this cookbook and, led by Lydia Cox and Sue Aho, continues to spark at-home cooks' creativity each season. The PCC merchandising team, past and present, has played the role of conscientious purveyors of food that has resulted in the deep, long-lasting relationships our co-op holds with countless local ranchers, farmers, and producers, including those mentioned in this book. Alicia Guy and the PCC Cooks team created an outlet where PCC Cooks instructors and students can express their culinary curiosity. Heather Snavely dusted off the co-op's cookbook proposal and recognized the potential in the pages. Thanks to Cate Hardy for her enthusiasm for this project.

The book would not have been possible without Jennifer and Henry Gordon, who opened our first deli at our View Ridge store in Seattle and inspired the passion for flavorful cooking from scratch that continues in our store kitchens today. Our co-op is better because of the dedication and culinary talent of countless PCC store staff over many years.

Many thanks for feedback, photos, smart suggestions, and occasional hilarity to testers and eaters Amy Broomhall, Laney Daughtry, Kaisa Dawson, the Deeken family, Jennifer Harris, Vanessa Lee, Jan Lightner, Tom Marshall, Angela Murray, and Marc Schermerhorn.

INDEX

Note: Page numbers in *italic* refer to photographs.

INDEX

279